DIRTY
WARS
AND
POLISHED
SILVER

DIRTY WARS

AND

POLISHED SILVER

**THE LIFE AND TIMES
OF A WAR CORRESPONDENT
TURNED AMBASSATRIX**

LYNDA SCHUSTER

MELVILLE HOUSE
BROOKLYN • LONDON

DIRTY WARS AND POLISHED SILVER

Copyright © 2017 by Lynda Schuster

First Melville House Printing: July 2017

Parts of this book appeared in slightly different form in the following publications: *Granta*, *The Christian Science Monitor*, and Thought Catalog. Some names and identifying details have been changed to protect the privacy of individuals.

Melville House Publishing   and   8 Blackstock Mews
            46 John Street   Islington
        Brooklyn, NY 11201   London N4 2BT

mhpbooks.com   facebook.com/mhpbooks   @melvillehouse

ISBN: 978-1-61219-634-3

Book design by Jo Anne Metsch

Library of Congress Cataloging-in-Publication Data
Names: Schuster, Lynda, author.
Title: Dirty wars and polished silver : the life and times of a war
    correspondent turned ambassatrix / Lynda Schuster.
Description: First edition. | Brooklyn : Melville House, 2017.
Identifiers: LCCN 2017006719 | ISBN 9781612196343 (hardback)
Subjects: LCSH: Schuster, Lynda. | War correspondents--United States--Biography. |
    Women war correspondents--United States--Biography. |
    Foreign correspondents--United States--Biography. | BISAC: BIOGRAPHY &
    AUTOBIOGRAPHY / Personal Memoirs. | BIOGRAPHY & AUTOBIOGRAPHY / Editors,
    Journalists, Publishers.
Classification: LCC PN4874.S3455 A3 2017 | DDC 070.4333092 [B] --dc23
LC record available at https://lccn.loc.gov/2017006719

Printed in the United States of America

10 9 8 7 6 5 4 3 2 1

For Noa, who changed everything

ALSO BY LYNDA SCHUSTER:

A Burning Hunger: One Family's Struggle Against Apartheid

One does not, in retrospect, record what one has experienced, but what time—with its increasing shifts in perspective, with one's own will to shape the chaos of half-buried experiences—has made of it. By and large, one records less how it actually was than how one became who one is.

JOACHIM FEST, Not I

Everything is copy.

NORA EPHRON, Heartburn

CONTENTS

DIRTY
WARS
AND
POLISHED
SILVER

ISRAEL, 1973

In search of adventure and not quite seventeen years old, I wash up
on a kibbutz in Israel's northern Galilee. As in most teenaged exis-
tential crises, I know precisely what I'm fleeing: a dreary Midwestern upbringing, my parents' messy divorce, the fear that I'm never
going to win a Nobel Prize. What I'm seeking instead is unclear.

The geography alone makes adolescent angst worthwhile. Beyond the settlement's eastern boundary, the terrain snakes steeply
down to the now not-so-mighty Jordan River, then up to the Golan
Heights, snaggle-toothed against a heat-hazed sky. Mount Hermon,
of biblical renown, looms moodily to the north. Damascus is just
over the horizon.

My roommate Selena, who's from Canada and has a cigarette permanently soldered to her bottom lip, doesn't like the place because she can't get decent coffee. The kibbutz's original settlers come mostly from Britain. Tea drinkers. Someone's always asking us around for a cup. That suits my other roomie, Sybil, a cheerless South African vegetarian, who grew up on a strong black brew, splash of milk, no sugar. She intends to live here for the rest of her life and has no use for anyone who doesn't try to fit in.

"Just suck it up," she says to Selena.

"Go fuck yourself," Selena says.

Sybil's jealous of the attention the kibbutz boys pay Selena. They come in a pack to our room, reeking of newly released male hormones and speaking Hebrew-accented English. Everyone knows the boys don't really respect volunteers like us; we're just spoiled suburban brats on a lark, in their estimation. They pop up on our side of the kibbutz for one-night stands or to wheedle a pair of the latest jeans that we foreigners bring from abroad. Selena dismisses them regally, flips her chestnut mane and lights another cigarette, blowing lazy blue-gray speech balloons across the room.

Sybil looks up from her book. "Aim it elsewhere, hey?"

I roll over and bury my head under my pillow, too tired to butt in, too tired even to shower off my bodysuit of dirt from toiling in the apple orchards. Slaving, is the way one of my co-pickers describes it. We're up at 4:30 every morning, stumbling through the cool-hot air to the dining hall to choke down tea and stale bread with strawberry jam. The roosters are just beginning their maniacal wake-up calls when we crowd onto a tractor-pulled cart, our orchard transportation. For hours we clamber up and down ladders in brain-boiling heat, squinty-eyed from the stinging perspiration, to get at the farthest reaches of the trees. *Just the way to find myself!* I think, doubled over from eating too much unwashed fruit.

But it beats chicken duty. I did that exactly one time. It started at midnight. The lights in the coop were turned off, as if this would keep the birds from noticing that they were being rounded up for deportation. As instructed, I blindly grabbed two handfuls of poultry by the legs and slipped-skated across the feces and feathers to the doorway, where someone shoved the shrieking birds into cages on a waiting truck. Then back inside the coop to grope another batch: the chickens crapping and pecking at my arms, me wondering whether staying home and going to my high school prom might not have been so bad after all. Hand them off to the cage people, shit-slide the length of the coop for more, relinquish them to their fate. Repeat until dawn.

After that, apple picking is pure pleasure.

Selena tries to get the work coordinator to assign her the cushy jobs, wiping off the tables in the dining room or folding underpants in the laundry. Sybil stomps off every day to the hangar-sized kitchen to peel potatoes, mutilate cabbages, and wrestle frozen chickens into submission. The other people in our group do likewise. We're a random sprinkling of pre- and post-college students and backpackers, mixed in among a British group from Manchester. The Brits seem relentlessly uninterested in doing anything. One of them, after spraying his room with shaving cream, is found wandering naked and babbling on the sizzling tarmac of a nearby airstrip. He's packed off to a local asylum, then shipped home to England.

Simcha, my Hebrew teacher, says the place is a magnet for misfits.

I suppose that includes me—but nice Jewish girls don't run away from home to join the circus. They go to a kibbutz. When I went to the Israeli embassy, the dark-eyed official looked at my passport and didn't seem to notice—or care—that I wasn't the required age of eighteen. The next opening on a kibbutz ulpan (a work/study program) will be here, he said, pointing to a small speck on a map. Upper Galilee, near the Golan Heights. Very beautiful.

I said, "I'll take it."

Like it was the last car left on the lot.

I feel almost immediately at home on the kibbutz. Maybe it's the sense of living in a perpetual overnight camp: the rows of squat little bungalows and rooms, the dining hall, swimming pool, laundry, clinic, SUV-sized mosquitoes. A self-contained miniature hamlet where, in the waning half-light of sunset, the sad-sweet singsong of the muezzin's call to evening prayer wafts across from a mosque in the Arab village on a nearby hill. Nothing says you're no longer in Middle America quite like a minaret.

Or maybe it's Simcha. After Hebrew class one day, she says, "Come around for tea tomorrow afternoon, if you're free. I'm one of the houses at the edge of the kibbutz, on the Golan Heights side. With the rosebushes out front."

When I arrive, she's writing the lesson for the next day's lecture, hunched over a table in the one room that serves for sitting, eating, and sleeping. "Kettle's in the kitchen," she says, without looking up. "Put it on, will you?" I squeeze into a space the size of an airplane lavatory. The kettle is electric and plugs into a wall socket. A miniature refrigerator nestles cutely under the counter, a two-burner hot plate sits atop. This being a communal settlement, people don't need to cook for themselves; they eat in the dining hall. The kitchen forces a typical Cold War–era choice: socialism, or having to stand sideways while sautéing.

Sim motions for me to sit while she finishes preparing the lesson. Her love of language snagged me from the first day of class. I never went to Hebrew school; my mother has no formal religious training and Dad's an agnostic. They sent my sisters and me to a secular Sunday school that treated Judaism as an exotic culture along the lines of, say, World Wide Wrestling or clogging. The sole concession to tradition was an annual program that featured a mezzo-soprano with a monumental bosom belting out songs about the holidays. Sim's unspooling of a language that works nothing like English—right-to-left, no less, and in a scribbly beautiful cursive— is sheer revelation.

"You know," she says, "women in the Bible were terribly bloody-minded." She's in her late thirties, slim, with a helmet of dense dark hair and a brash British accent. "Take Eve. She disobeyed God because she decided that knowledge mustn't be withheld from people."

I'm way out of my depth here. "Uh, wasn't she tempted by a serpent?"

"That's just one interpretation. Another is that she was brave. It's not an easy thing disobeying God in the Bible."

The kettle's whistle draws her to the kitchen. "You Americans don't take milk in your tea, do you?" she yells.

"I do. My father lives in London."

"Well now, that's different. Tell me about it."

That's all it takes for me to spill my guts about my teenaged search for meaning. Back then, someone just had to appear to lend a sympathetic ear and I'd bare the most intimate and unnecessary details of my soul before the poor person even had a chance to finish forming a question. Sim refills the teapot; twice I have to excuse myself to pee. As I'm leaving, finally, she says, "You can come for Saturday dinner, if you'd like."

Officially, I'm adopted by another couple. All the ulpan students are assigned to kibbutz members who look after their care and feeding on a Saturday night, the only time the dining room doesn't serve a proper meal. When I point this out, Sim says: *Oh, bugger that.* She has a history of taking in strays that interest her and folding them into her family of two young daughters, an ex-husband, a dog, a cat, various rodents and smallish reptiles—although it's more like I push my way in at knifepoint.

Yom Kippur, I awake to a khamsin. The suffocating wind that blows in from the Arabian desert shoots the temperature to over one hundred degrees and deposits a sandy veneer on everything. Even my teeth are crunchy with grit. Khamsin means "fifty" in Arabic: the number of days that the wind supposedly blows. It drives people to madness. Popular lore has it that during the Ottoman Empire, when Turkey ruled this part of the world, a man wouldn't be held responsible for killing his wife during a khamsin.

Those Ottoman women must have trembled at every breeze.

Sim says there's always a khamsin on Yom Kippur, just to add to the misery of fasting-to-atone-for-all-our-sins. I'm already knee-wobbly with hunger; the heat makes it hard to breathe. Selena, unfazed by the day's strictures, goes off in search of coffee. Sybil is spending the holiday with relatives. I sit in a chair in our room in front of a uselessly whirring little fan, then flop on the bed because it looks more comfortable, then change to another chair because it might be cooler. Trying to imagine frigid things such as igloos and glaciers, my mind instead conjures up sorbets and slushies. *Heretical slut,* I think, giving up and trudging to the main building.

The kibbutz is echo-quiet; no one works on Yom Kippur, the holiest day of the year. The little paths that crisscross the settlement, usually filled with people walking or riding bicycles or pushing carts stuffed with small, communally raised children, are deserted. Even the running radio chatter that seeps out from buildings with the hourly beeping time signal is silent. The Voice of Israel goes dead for the day.

There's air conditioning in the recreation room. A couple of my comrades from the ulpan sprawl on a sofa. In the distance, the Golan's usually craggy profile is barely visible behind the quivering mask of heat. Michael, my newly minted boyfriend from the British group, shuffles in: black curls and emerald cat-slitted eyes, topped with an antic sense of humor.

Michael says, "I was wondering where you got to."

"I'm trying not to think about food," I say.

He reaches across me to grab an outdated copy of *Time,* but never gets there—the air around us is suddenly exploding. "Bloody hell!" he says. "What was that?"

More eardrum-shredding detonations in rapid succession shake the ground. We're all standing now, staring stupidly out the picture window at smoke billowing from the Golan Heights. "Maybe an earthquake?" one of the other students suggests.

Michael says, "Don't be an idiot."

There's commotion outside; someone shouts at us to run to the bomb shelters. I have no idea where to go. We follow a kibbutz member to a clearing, my heart a little tom-tom in my chest, then down leaf-strewn steps to a door. He tugs on it. Locked.

Michael and I take off at a sprint for Simcha's house, dog-cringing at each explosion. She's standing in her garden with some neighbors.

I say, "What's happened?"

"We're under attack," she says. "The Syrians crossed the border and are bombing the Golan. The Egyptians crossed into Sinai."

"How do you know?"

"The Voice of Israel came back on the air. The chief rabbis said we're at war and that it's okay to break your fast now and not wait until sunset."

"What should we do?"

"Go back to your building."

We follow her advice, but no one in charge is around. Michael retrieves a radio·from his room; we hear the urgent codes being broadcast on the army channel that call up people to reserve duty. The attacks have taken the country completely by surprise. The kibbutz, too; the place is suddenly swarming with men half-dressed in military uniforms, guns slung over their shoulders, gear falling out of hastily packed duffel bags. This does not inspire confidence. *If I'm going to die,* I think, heading to the dining hall, *at least now I won't die hungry.*

A woman in charge of the kitchen is dishing out pieces of chicken left over from the previous night. Gnawing on a drumstick, I jog back to Simcha's. She's gone. Michael and I feel our way in the dark to the cliff beyond her house. I can make out a few other people. They're looking at pinpricks of light, tiny jewels in a miles-long necklace, twisting across the Golan Heights toward us. Tanks. Someone in the blackness asks, "Theirs or ours?"

"I don't know," comes the reply. "But we'd better go to the bomb shelters."

Lying on my back on a wooden bunk in a shelter deep underground, I watch the sleeve on my shirt fluttering, as if in a strong wind, from the concussion of the artillery above. The little kids in the shelter are crying. I'm up for hours, unable to sleep for the noise and fear and excitement—and because I'm looking out for spiders or other insects that may have taken up residence in my bunk since the last war. That's the adolescent mind for you: worrying about creepy-crawlers in the face of death and destruction.

Nights we hunker outside the shelters until it's time to sleep, listening to the static-swooshed reports of the BBC from London. The kibbutz is spotlit by a glaring harvest moon that makes a mockery of the blackout. A radio announcer informs us that Jordan might send troops to fight alongside its Arab brethren. *Those guys are just down the road from us,* I think, with a little thrill-seeking shiver. I sit spellbound, listening to the kibbutz members who are assigned to babysit us—veterans all of Israel's wars—as they debate the ramifications long into the shimmery night.

And go to bed dreaming of Henry Kissinger.

Daytime we pop up above ground for air—prairie dogs from our burrows—during lulls in the fighting. Pairs of Israeli Mirage jets shriek low over the Galilee and into the Golan, so low they make you want to hit the ground for cover. We learn to brace as they drop their load of bombs, then count the seconds until they screech back overhead to base. Several days into the war, when we're finally allowed back to our rooms to shower, we find a bunch of long-snouted howitzers have taken up residence on the football pitch below. Just as I'm sneaking down to get a peek at them, the commanding officer suddenly shouts, *"Aish!" (Fire!)*—and I'm nearly thrown to the ground from the explosions. Someone yells at me to get my sorry ass back to the bunker; the Syrians are going to answer the guns any minute now. I gallop to the shelter, sweating and dizzy with fear but thrilled, in a voyeuristic way, to be at the center of world events.

The thing about war—as long as you're not dying—is that it's oddly exhilarating. One minute you're an angst-ridden adolescent moping about your parents, your place in the world, the latest outcropping of pustules on your chin. The next thing you know, you're sucked into the vortex of geopolitics and a three-week-long conflict, listening with puffed-up importance to worldwide news on the radio about your own situation and spouting off about balance of forces. What could be better? Perhaps if I could foresee that this was a portent of my adult life to come, that war would dominate my existence both as a reporter and as a wife, I wouldn't be quite so enthusiastic.

But all that is in the future. For now, I'm convinced—with the certitude of any self-absorbed, seemingly immortal teenager—that this is what I've been seeking.

PART I

CHAPTER ONE

DETROIT, 1966

My yearning to live far, far away begins with a snot-green triangular stamp from Qatar.

Bev says, "Lynda, please can I have the green stamp? Please, please, please." It's so weird and wonderful-looking that she'll trade a favorite from her collection: the Polish one with galloping horses and POLSKA spelled out in bold letters, or the one from Romania that has a spaniel staring somberly off into the middle distance, as though recalling a tragic event in its life. She's even willing to give up the San Marino stamp with the periscope-necked dinosaur paddling freestyle through the water, schools of clueless fish blithely swimming nearby.

If Bev wanted anything else, I'd probably let her have it. She doesn't torture me with Indian burns on my arm, twisting the skin in opposite directions across the bone, the way Sandy, my older sister, does. Bev is nine years old, a year younger than I, and will do anything I say, mostly minor infractions such as coloring in our coloring books after Mom has put us to bed or spitting on the head of a passing teenaged boy when we're up in my favorite tree.

But I won't trade the green stamp to her. I got it from coupons off the backs of our *Archie* and *Betty and Veronica* comic books: one hundred stamps for twenty-five cents. We asked Mom for two quarters and taped them to the coupons and sent them off through the mail; a few weeks later, two fat yellow envelopes stuffed with stamps fell through the mail slot. Most of the stamps are from the Union of Soviet Socialist Republics or German Democratic Republic: drab little squares with laborers and machinists grimly trying to look happy in their workers' paradises. But in one of my piles, that stamp from Qatar appeared like a shining jewel.

I pasted it onto the "Q" page of my album, which is otherwise completely empty. I paste all my stamps into my album, licking little hinges that taste worse than the fluoride treatments the dentist gives us. The extras I keep in an old Antonio y Cleopatra cigar box that Bev and l like because of its risqué picture: a tunic-clad Antonio paying his respects to a reclining and *bare-breasted* Cleopatra. I pull out my album when Bev isn't in our bedroom and examine the Qatari stamp. The disembodied head of a goateed man, adorned in an Arab headdress, bobs atop a gushing oil well; he has an expression of mild astonishment, as though surprised to find himself in this situation amid palms, sand dunes, and squiggly Arabic calligraphy.

I go downstairs to where we keep the Encyclopedia Britannica to look up Qatar. There's the Arabian Peninsula, shaped like an elongated, sideways heart; Qatar sticks up in the middle, where the two lobes should meet. I say the capital aloud: Doha. And places nearby along the coast, many of which are about to disappear in a flurry of post-colonial nation building: Ras-al-Khaima, Sharjah, Umm al-Quwain. It's not so much the specifics of Middle Eastern culture that grab me, but the *otherness,* the anti-Detroitness. You'd be hard-pressed to find dromedaries strolling the streets of downtown.

Upstairs in my room, I look at the Qatari stamp one last time before carefully putting the album in my closet. Sandy, whose bedroom is next door, collects coins instead of stamps. Coins are stupid. They're ugly and heavy and you can't even spend them in this country. They don't make me dream of leaving Detroit the way the stamps do. Sandy says they're better, just because she likes to lord things over me.

Sandy is two-and-a-half years older, which makes her a preteen. A Preteen Queen. She subscribes to magazines that have articles about how to stop zits and attract boys. She carefully cuts out the pictures of her favorite bands, Herman's Hermits and the Beatles, and plasters her door and walls with them. She plays their records on her little black-and-white phonograph when Bev and I are trying to sleep at night. She listens to WKNR ("Keener 13, Detroit's Top 40 Radio Station!"), or CKLW, from across the Detroit River in Canada, on her transistor radio.

Sandy says, "Bev, who do you love?"

All three of us are in the back seat of our black Plymouth. Dad is driving us down the Lodge Freeway to Olympia Stadium. We're going to a matinee concert with the Beatles.

"What do you mean?" Bev asks.

Sandy says, "I mean, which Beatle do you love?"

"I dunno."

"Love Paul, because I love Paul."

"Okay."

"At the concert, you have to shout, 'I love you, Paul!'"

"Okay."

Sandy says the same thing to me, but I don't answer. First of all, I don't like her to boss me around. Second, I'm not all that happy about going to this concert. I don't even like the Beatles that much. It's a muggy August day. We don't have air conditioning, so the windows are rolled down and my hair is whipping around my head. The backs of my thighs stick to the black-and-gray plastic seat covers. They make a little ripping sound when I lift them up: first the left, *rrrrip*, then the right, *rrrrip*. Sandy is bouncing in place, her head almost touching the overhead light. This is the biggest day of her life.

The traffic backs up on Grand River Avenue and stops. It takes forever for Dad to get to the front of Olympia, a big reddish brick building where the Detroit Red Wings hockey team plays. He says, "Be sure to hold hands and stick together." About a million kids are trying to press through the arena's doors. Bev hangs onto my arm so tightly her nails dig into my skin; Sandy's got my other arm. She's looking at our tickets and pulling us along. I can barely breathe, there are so many people. She somehow finds the entrance ramp; an usher escorts us to our chairs on the stadium floor. Around us, rows of seats rise almost to the ceiling.

A bunch of groups I don't know perform first: the Ronettes, the Cyrkle, the Remains, Bobby Herb. I'm bored, bored, bored. It feels like they're playing for hours. I'm thirsty and need to pee. Sandy says, "You have to hold it. And don't go in your seat."

The emcee appears on stage. He says the Beatles are having technical difficulties and will be on in a few minutes. People groan. And then, suddenly, everyone begins to scream. You'd think someone was being murdered. But no, the Beatles, in striped suits and big paisley ties, walk onto the raised podium and begin to play "Rock and Roll Music." The audience goes berserk. Girls are sobbing, pulling at their hair, propping each other up as though having just received shocking news. It's like I'd landed on the Fourth of July in a psychiatric institution: flashbulbs popping nonstop in the dark arena and everyone shrieking as if possessed.

What's the matter with these people?

I know most of the songs from Sandy's record player: "Day Tripper," "Baby's in Black," "Yesterday." But the music is drowned out by the screaming. Which continues even when Paul and John are talking, so I can't hear what they say. It's the one part of the concert that interests me. This summer I've been speaking—or trying to—with a British accent. I think it makes me intriguing. At least I don't sound like I'm from Detroit. It drives Sandy nuts. She says there's no way I could have acquired a British accent; I've never even been out of the country except to Canada. And that was just across the bridge into Windsor, Ontario. I tell her I don't know how it happened; I simply woke up one morning speaking like this.

Last summer, it was a Brooklyn accent.

Sandy's standing on her chair when the Beatles sing, "I Wanna Be Your Man." Bev, too, is on her chair, yelling, "I love you, Paul, I love you!" She tugs at Sandy's sleeve. "How's that?"

"Great. Keep it going."

Sandy looks down at me expectantly. I stick my fingers in my ears. "I have a headache!" I shout. "I'd rather be reading a book!"

Later, in the car going home, Sandy says, "Do you always have to be such a spaz?"

———————

In my family, the children all have definitions, like a vocabulary quiz in school.

Sandy: pretty and artistic.

Beverly: beautiful and athletic.

Lynda: smart.

I'm the only one who doesn't have an "and." Ida, who was born last year, is just The Baby. But that doesn't count; she hasn't had time to establish herself yet. Sandy has thick, curly auburn hair that she rolls around empty frozen orange juice cans every night or carefully wraps around her head in small sections and secures with rows of shiny metal clips. It takes hours to do this, but her hair is beautiful in the morning: straight, silky, swingy. She has long legs. She looks great in clothes. I have stubby legs, lank hair, an overbite. I wear pointy blue glasses with sparkles on them.

Dad says, "Bev's going to look like Sophia Loren when she grows up."

I ask, "Who am I going to look like?"

He doesn't answer.

Sandy calls me "ibid" because I use big words and am argumentative. She finds those traits useful enough when she's in trouble and hires me with her allowance money to plead her case for a lesser punishment. But when I turn my words against her for giving me an Indian burn or inflicting other forms of torture banned by international human rights treaties, Sandy's suddenly all sarcastic. "You're just like Dad," she says.

It's a common refrain in our family, but with different meanings. My grandmother Bubbe says it in an accusatory tone, usually followed with: *You make your mother work too hard; she's going to get sick.* Bubbe's from the Old Country. She wears dentures that don't fit very well and clicks them like castanets. So what she says sounds like this: "You just like your fadder," *click, click, click.* "You make your mudder sick," *click, click, click.*

Bubbe is Mom's mom. Mom had rheumatic fever twice when she was a kid and almost died. The doctor says that she's just fine, but Bubbe worries that Mom's always on the verge of croaking. She fears Mom will drop dead from, say, doing laundry or blowing her nose. Zayde, my grandfather, stays quiet. He smells of Listerine and boiled cabbage. Little tufts of gray fur sprout from his ears. At our Passover Seder, after Zayde has had a few glasses of schnapps, he whips off his glasses to show me the scar above his left eyebrow he got from a saber wound as a soldier in the Tsar's army. When Bubbe has been clicking away too long with her worries about Mom, he leans into her face and says in his thick Russian/Yiddish accent, "You talk too much, they lock you up."

On Sundays, Mom takes us to visit them in Oak Park, the first suburb to the north of us. We pass street after street of neat little bungalows and ranch houses, each with a small square of lawn in the front and a fenced-in yard in the back. They border Oak Park Park, whose real name is David H. Shepherd Park, but no one calls it that. A couple of aluminum folding tables covered with plastic and a few card tables are set up in the shade of the enormous oaks, outposts of my grandparents and their Yiddish-speaking, penny poker-playing friends.

Bev and I kiss them: Bubbe in a cotton shift fitted tightly around her stout little body and wedgy, open-toed sandals with white anklets; Zayde in shirt-sleeves and a straw fedora with a black band around the base. Then we examine the table for something to eat. It's the same thing every week: hard-boiled eggs with salt, mashed tuna salad, potato knishes. Immigrant food. Bubbe says, "Esn, mayn kind." I take a knish. It's so dry that I pretend I'm choking and have to run to the drinking fountain near some swings.

Bev and I climb to the top of the monkey bars. Mom waves at us to join her and Bubbe in the shade. She's wearing red lipstick and the white sunglasses that make her look like a movie star. I shake my head, then mouth: *I can't.* Now Bev and I are hanging by our legs on the cross bars, looking at Mom and Bubbe upside down. They're probably talking about the same things they talk about every week: the heat, the price of cantaloupes, Zayde's sister in the wheelchair who has a boyfriend. Bubbe thinks she's a *kurveh*, a slut.

"Bubbe says you can do anything you put your mind to," Mom bellows at me, hands in a kind of megaphone. "She says you could even go through the eye of a needle if you wanted."

What, I wonder, *does she mean? That I'm determined? Obstinate? Exceedingly tiny?*

Dad is the oldest child of Nanny, my other grandmother, so you'd think it would be a compliment when she says I'm just like him. Nanny and Papa are American. Their house smells better than Bubbe's and Zayde's, and Nanny's food is better. She makes scrambled eggs with ketchup on top that she calls rock 'n' roll eggs, in honor of the Beatles. Papa lets me sit on his lap and take little sips from his beer mug. He gives me a piggyback ride to inspect the branches of the Queen Anne cherry tree in the backyard.

Nanny is digging in her garden, her big breasts squeezed together in a tube top, little droplets of sweat popped out above her upper lip. She says, "Aren't you getting too big to be riding on Papa's back?"

I say, "Sssh! I'm admiring the lushness of the Rwanda Highlands!"

She says, "Smart aleck! You'll grow up to be a lawyer just like your father."

Nanny's proud that Dad's a lawyer. She's proud of her other two sons, too: Uncle Todd, a professor of molecular biology, and Uncle Eugene, who's studying for his doctorate in art history in London. Mom didn't go to college, and Nanny says mean things about her. She thinks Mom isn't smart or capable. It makes me mad; I don't like her criticizing my mother.

That doesn't mean I don't agree with her. Mom's life seems to me relentlessly uninteresting. She shops for groceries. She cooks dinner. She does laundry. She orders around the housekeeper— whom Nanny calls "the colored girl" and Bubbe, "die shvartze"— when she comes to wash the floors and iron the clean clothes. She talks on the phone in Yiddish to Bubbe. The high point of her week is going to the hairdresser's to have her hair washed and curled and sometimes tinted. Perhaps she leads a secret, adventure-filled life while we're at school, but I've never seen any trace of it.

So when people say that I'm just like Dad, I take it as high praise; I'd rather be like him. Dad goes downtown everyday to the Penobscot Building, with the big red flashing ball on the top, to his law office. Sometimes he travels around the country selling the prints that Uncle Eugene sends back from London. He listens to classical music on the stereo with his headset on, wildly conducting while my sisters and I leap around the living room like demented ballerinas. He talks to me about articles I've read in the *Detroit News*.

Mom says, "You're becoming an intellectual snob, just like your father."

———

Dad reads books. Mom doesn't. Sandy reads Nancy Drew mysteries. They're stupid and boring. Who wants to be a sleuth riding around in a roadster? My preference is for a profession with a uniform. For a while, I wanted to be a nurse like Cherry Ames. I read all twenty-five or so of the Cherry Ames books: *Cherry Ames, Student Nurse; Cherry Ames, Senior Nurse; Cherry Ames, Army Nurse*; and so on.

The Summer of My Brooklyn Accent, while Mom was pregnant with Ida, I decided to do night duty. I took an old white shirt of Dad's and embroidered RN in red thread on the breast pocket. A piece of white cardboard with a dark blue stripe drawn across the front and an elastic band glued to each end was my nurse's cap. (This was back when members of the profession wore something other than what looks like their pajamas to work.) I attached a piece of paper to a clipboard with the hours of the night written in the left margin. Mom was exhausted from the pregnancy and went to bed early one night. I put on my uniform and set up a plastic TV table in her room with a pitcher of orange juice, a flashlight, a thermometer, and my watch. Every hour I woke her to take her temperature and give her orange juice. She was pretty good-natured about it, especially as she had to read the thermometer for me.

I scribbled down the temperature readings by the dim glow of the flashlight. There was nothing else to do until the next one. It made me think that perhaps nursing was the kind of career that one should do in tandem with something else to fill up the time, something like woodworking or accounting. Dad came upstairs after the 11:00 p.m. reading. He said, "What are you doing here? Why aren't you in bed?"

"I'm the night nurse, and your wife is my patient."

"Don't be ridiculous. Go to bed."

"But I still have all these hours to fill in my chart."

"Lynda, I said go to bed."

Dad has a ferocious, hair trigger temper that's set off by—what? Everything and nothing. You just never know. Looking at him in the gloom, his stocky frame eerily illuminated by my flashlight, I was no longer Lynda Schuster, Night Nurse; I was Lynda Schuster, Girl About To Be Thwacked. We're all scared of Dad. Nobody tries to stand up to him, let alone talk back.

I get tired of Cherry Ames after that. *Department Store Nurse* and *Dude Ranch Nurse* don't hold much promise of a glamorous life. I switch to biographies. I read about Albert Schweitzer and am certain that I want to be a medical missionary in Gabon, with a sideline in lowland gorillas. That is, until I discover Marie Curie. Test tubes, Bunsen burners, crisp white laboratory coats, death by radiation poisoning—I've found my calling.

As a warm-up to becoming a scientist, I try my hand at inventing. I build a specially modified dumbwaiter for our house: a piece of plywood with holes punched at all four ends, twine threaded through the openings, then gathered together. Dad won't let me pound nails into the banister, so I attach the ends of the twine with Scotch tape to the upstairs rail and gently lower the plywood. Sandy looks at the thing, suspended and twirling, and gives it a yank. "Is this how you use it, Ibid?" she asks, as the dumbwaiter crashes to the floor.

Undeterred, I reattach it to the banister. But anything heavier than, say, a single-ply tissue makes it fall down. After a few days, I give up and move the dumbwaiter to my favorite tree in the backyard. The contraption's design flaws, while dashing my hopes for induction into the Inventors Hall of Fame, are a good excuse for getting out of the house. Inside, Mom and Dad are always yelling at one another and at us; sometimes Mom cries. It's hard having to be so careful around Dad. One minute he's great, playing badminton with us or letting us ride on his back when we go swimming in the murk of Kensington Lake. The next minute he's baring his teeth like a wolf about to attack and hitting us with a newspaper the way he hits the dog.

I tie the dumbwaiter to one of the tree's branches that extends out from the cleft where I sit, hoist up a pile of books and fly away to my future self. I'm Amelia Earhart, Florence Nightingale, Sonja Henie. I no longer feel the hard, black bark cutting into my thighs where my shorts end. I'm Albert Einstein, Alexander Graham Bell, Ludwig von Beethoven. I open my stamp book and am in the Central African Republic, fending off nightmarish beetles. In Colombia, where an erupting volcano is spewing life-threatening lava. In Rwanda, amid a stampede of elephants and water buffalo. And best of all, in Qatar.

My beacon in the night.

Fast-forward several years to another summer. I'm fourteen, going on fifteen. Dad now travels the world, buying and selling art. He's just returned from a trip to the Far East. He was away for weeks and never even sent a postcard. He and Mom spend a lot of time in their bedroom, shouting at each other behind the closed door. Sandy is out with her friends and doesn't hear it, but Bev and I do. We creep around the house, trying to find a place where their voices don't penetrate.

One afternoon when we're all watching television, Dad says that he has something to tell us. We sit at our usual places at the kitchen table. The last time we had a meeting like this was six years earlier, when Mom found out she was pregnant with Ida and Dad said: We have a surprise for you. Think of something you guys have always wanted. And Bev said: A color TV?

This time, Mom's face is blotchy and red, like she's been crying. Dad's is calm.

Dad says, "Your mother and I are getting divorced."

Sandy asks, "Why?"

"Because I've met someone else," Dad says.

"Are you in love with her?" Sandy asks.

"Yes."

"Do you still love Mom?"

"No."

Mom's crying. Sandy's crying. I'm crying. Bev's crying. Ida, who's too young to hear this, is playing outside.

Mom says, "Won't you stay, at least for the girls' sake?"

Our kitchen table is rectangular with a fake wood inlay that's sort of pointed at each corner. The points seem to jump and dance through my blurred vision. "Where's your pride?" I shout. "Didn't you hear him? He just told you he doesn't love you!"

Then he's gone, off to London to live with his new girlfriend and run the art gallery that he and Uncle Eugene have opened. And we're left with my mother's hurt and anger and panic.

She turns on us. Now she yells about everything, denying us every request, her favorite word "no." It's not so bad for Sandy, who goes away to college. Ida, still in elementary school, is on her own little planet. Bev and I are the ones who feel the frontal force of

Mom's fury. She shuts down our worlds as if to punish us for the sudden diminishment of her own.

I yell back. I hate her. I hate her for not being interesting or clever enough to hold on to Dad. I hate her for thrashing about wildly like a drowning woman and trying to take us down with her. I won't let her. I won't stay here and let her life become mine. I don't want the once-a-week visit to the hairdresser, the Sunday afternoons at Oak Park, the hard-boiled eggs with salt, the price of cantaloupes. I don't want to have children. I don't even know if I want to get married.

I want to get out, to see the world, to live a life of adventure.

And I will, through the eye of a needle, if I must.

Although in this case, it's through working afternoons and weekends in a bakery. While my peers are experimenting with drugs and sex, I'm shoveling eclairs into small white cardboard boxes and plotting my escape. Friends who are a couple of years older and wise in these things tell me that you can live and study on a kibbutz in Israel for free in exchange for work. You just have to get there.

They shove copies of *O Jerusalem!* and *Exodus* my way, whose romantic renderings of history—to say nothing of Paul Newman's baby blues in the film version of the latter—seize my imagination. (Palestine and Palestinians conveniently don't figure in the fantasy at the time.) I speed through my classes and spend my free periods trying to convince the principal to let me graduate early. Tired of my whining, he finally agrees that I can leave ahead of schedule, but I will not receive my diploma until the following year with my class.

Mom says, "So you won't go to your graduation and have a party?"

I say, "No. I don't like those sorts of things. And that's not until next year and I don't know if I'll be back by then." (Half-truth.)

"But I'd love to give you a party."

"Mom, that's not me."

"Then what are you going to do?"

"Visit Dad and stuff." (Half-truth.)

Mom turns away, her head shaking slightly as it does when something upsets her. She's dating now, which makes her marginally happier. But she and Dad continue to play out their antipathy for one another through me and my sisters, manipulating us like Monopoly tokens to land on Guilt or Hurt or Spite. *I can play this game too,* I think.

Officially, I'm going to London to study for exams to attend Cambridge. That's Dad's idea. Come live with me, he says, and you can go to university here. Dad's ticket gets me part of the way to the Middle East. Unknown to him or Mom, before leaving I withdraw from my bank account the $763 I saved from working in the bakery. That will get me the rest of the way.

This isn't total subterfuge; for about one minute, I consider staying in London. I love everything about it—at least, the ballet-theater-restaurant-gallery-going existence my father is living. His Dutch girlfriend, Gerrie, tries to be nice in a tall, blonde Valkyrian sort of way. She takes me to castles and museums and swanky cafés for iced coffees. But Dad has moved on to his cosmopolitan phase, which leaves little room for a mouthy, resentful teenager. Especially after the note I leave on Gerrie's pillow:

> *Gerrie: Please be vigilant about using birth control. My sisters and I can't accept another sibling at this point. Lynda.*

The afternoon I slink off to the Israeli embassy to sign up for the kibbutz and buy a cheap student-fare ticket to Tel Aviv, I have ecstatic visions of life about to unfold. Then reality intrudes. Riding the Underground back to the flat, I'm sweaty-palm scared over my impending declaration of independence. My anger about him busting up our family not withstanding, Dad still possesses an absolute power to terrify me.

He and Gerrie are having drinks on the terrace. When I finally screw up the courage to tell him that I'm not going to Cambridge, that I'm instead going to Israel to work on a kibbutz, Dad's upper lip starts to curl in that snarly-beast way it does just before he hits us. But he's still in the keeping-the-bathroom-door-shut stage in his relationship with Gerrie, still trying to impress her. She doesn't know about his temper.

He says, "You're going to be wasted there."

And with that, I'm gone.

CHAPTER TWO

CENTRAL AMERICA, 1981

After the Yom Kippur War ends and I'm declaring my desire to stay forever on the kibbutz to anyone who'll listen, Simcha, my adopted mother, wastes no time in setting me straight. She's seen too many youngsters beach themselves on her shores full of similarly fuzzy-headed and romantic notions. Sure, my job picking apples in the orchards might seem fulfilling, even exotic, for now, but what will happen when the thrill of Granny Smiths is gone? "Go figure out what you want to do with your life," she says.

Which is how, inadvertently, I find myself sitting in the coffee shop of a faded downtown hotel in San Jose, Costa Rica, several years later, taking deep breaths through my mouth and trying not to become hysterical. Or pass out from hyperventilation. I've been working for the *Wall Street Journal* for barely a year, and this is the third day of my first foreign assignment. Costa Rica is teetering on the brink of bankruptcy, the *Journal's* two million readers back home are waiting to read about it—and I'm wondering why I didn't become a dental hygienist.

My eleven o'clock interview, a young political scientist with stringy hair that hasn't been washed since the time of the Spanish conquistadores, refused to talk about anything except US imperialism. Then my twelve o'clock stood me up, so I went slinking back to the hotel. Its coffee shop opens onto a public square and a procession of underfed shoeshine boys who shuffle past slowly, mournfully eyeing my feet and the contents of my plate. Which only adds to my already considerable angst.

My stringer, a brash kid from the States who does odd jobs for several newspapers and boasts an extravagant body odor, suddenly appears from behind one of the potted plants. "Tim, what are you doing here?" I say.

Tim says, "That's a nice hello."

"Sorry, not a great morning. Who are you here for?"

"Dial Torgerson of the *Los Angeles Times*. Know him?"

"Not personally, but I've read his stuff."

"He called yesterday from Mexico City and asked me to set up a few appointments. He's supposed to check in around now. Wanna meet him?"

Of course I do. I'd read about Torgerson's exploits when I was in journalism school and remember in particular how he foiled the Israeli military censors' attempt to quash a report of war atrocities by flying to London and filing his story from there. It caused a huge furor, and his subterfuge seemed to me a noble thing, the intrepid escapade of a *real* foreign correspondent. Nothing like the journalistic feats I've racked up in my year covering agriculture out of the *Journal's* Dallas bureau: reporting on sheep auctions in Oklahoma, wheezing in Kansas wheat fields, wading through rice paddies in Arkansas. It wasn't so long ago that I was standing in corn that spread out for acres, peering through the towering stalks and trying to take notes—*green leaves, brown tassels, bugs*—when a combine harvester chugged up. The driver leaned out the cabin window and shouted, "Ever been in one of these?"

I shook my head, stunned by the machine's size and noise.

"Well then," he said, "hop on up, lil' lady!"

I did, and we spent the afternoon puffing through the field, talking commodities prices, real estate, Ronald Reagan, and the soap operas the farmer watched on a tiny television mounted on the dashboard as he slayed ears of corn. I may as well have worked as a parakeet trainer, for how well those stories prepared me to cover a foreign country.

Given Torgerson's resume, I expect to be introduced to your quintessential foreign correspondent: tall, handsome, trenchcoated. Instead, I'm shaking the hand of a small, wiry, middle-aged man in a blue seersucker suit and ugly, squared-off black shoes. What hair he has left is silver, and he walks with a peculiar, slightly rolling gait. (The result, I would later learn, of a car accident that almost killed him when he was twenty-five.) His voice is deep and resonant and lingers over each syllable like a radio announcer's.

Dial says, "So, what's a nice Jewish girl like you doing in a place like this?"

That's the best a wordsmith of his caliber can manage?

"Woman," I say.

He looks confused.

"We're called women nowadays."

Not exactly a transcendent moment.

Still, Dial suggests that we all meet for dinner later, after I've finished my interviews and Tim has taken him around San Jose. I hurry out of the hotel, hail a passing taxi and stutter out an address in Spanish. I hardly speak the language. I had asked the *Journal's* foreign editor for lessons to burnish my high school Spanish, but he refused, offering French instruction instead. When I pointed out that Spanish was generally recognized as the region's language, the editor—known throughout the paper for his idiosyncrasies—lowered his voice. "Schuster," he said, "the idea is to maintain a certain distance from the story."

I'm not sure he intended that space to be the size of the Grand Canyon.

The cab crawls through downtown San Jose's narrow, crowded streets. We pass vendors hawking lottery tickets, pyramids of fresh papaya, cups of crushed ice drowning in tooth-dissolving syrups. There are boxy little houses, colored pink and blue and framed by orange and purple bougainvillea. Converted US school buses, the main mode of public transportation, are painted brilliant reds and indigos with eyes, eyelashes, and mouths drawn on the front fenders, giving them the look of motorized drag queens. *Just what I wanted,* I think, *so why am I not enjoying this?* My mind shifts back to my little outburst of bravado with Dial at the hotel; that's what happens when you feel like a fraud. Or like a toddler: a toddler stuck in her Terrible Twos, desperately wanting to take control of her world, but lacking the experience and confidence to lurch bravely forward. While clad in a disposable diaper.

———

Fraud or toddler, I had never seriously considered journalism as a profession. My embrace of it happened almost as a fluke. Following Sim's admonition, I wound up at a Midwestern university, one sufficiently distant from Mom so that I couldn't easily go home on weekends. The shadow of hurt that flitted across her face when I talked about Sim was enough to keep me away—although I could have just shut up and not been such a jackass. But I was too absorbed in my own plight, trudging through thigh-high snow to classes under the cotton-wool sky of an endless winter, to consider anyone else's feelings. I knew what I wanted: a life that would allow me to see the world and witness history in the making. How to get there, having neither sugar daddy nor personal genie, was another matter.

Still thinking I'd go back to Israel, I majored in Near Eastern studies and in my last year applied to a doctoral program. Not long after receiving my acceptance letter, though, I awoke one night hyperventilating: I was too young to die in academia. Chickening out like that at the last minute certainly made me feel better, but it also made me lose all my scholarship money. Now I needed to learn a trade to support myself—and fast. That's when, flailing about for an alternative, I stumbled on a description in the university course catalog for a master's degree in journalism: no prior experience needed, plenty of spaces still available, two years of studies and you're out covering the world.

Or, at least, waste water hearings at local City Council meetings.

The first day of class was terrifying, until I realized that most of the students were, at heart, pretty much like me: cowards or procrastinators, or just not good enough to get into the snooty journalism programs. One man had had a job cleaning out rat cages. Another wrote poetry. The exception was a short, buxom, dark-haired woman who showed up wearing a tight banana-colored tank top without a bra. *Screaming Yellow Tits,* I thought. Her real name was Marsha, and she had been working on her school newspapers since prekindergarten. Marsha was the type who, in another era, would have shouted in a gravelly voice into the receiver of a rotary phone, "Sweetheart, get me Rewrite. And be quick about it!" Think Katharine Hepburn or Rosalind Russell in those 1940s movies about snappy girl reporters—but about half their size and minus the shoulder pads. Also, add in the braless breasts.

I immediately attached myself to Marsha, figuring she'd be an excellent role model. Which she was, and ultimately, a friend as well. Good thing, too, because we had to put out a paper, as it were, every day on deadline in our workshop. That meant thinking up stories, reporting, writing, and critiquing them—all in about an eight-hour stretch. The head of our program, a small, balding man who had worked for one of the newsmagazines when people still read them, would hear me moaning that I didn't know what to do about a particular source or a hole in my story and bark, "Do everything, Schuster!" But here's the thing about journalism that amazed me: people *want* to talk to you. (Unless, of course, it's a perp or celebrity, in which case your right hand will forget its cunning and your tongue cleave to the roof of your mouth before you'll get any quotes.) Whoever figured out the psychology of journalism all those centuries ago was brilliant: it succeeds by tapping into some very basic human traits, like a person's sense of injustice. Or his ego. Or his desire to avoid doing work. Whatever the reason, people wanted to tell their stories. And once they got going, they would often confide remarkable things having absolutely nothing to do with the topic at hand: how interesting urology seems, for instance, or that a friend's friend let her pet pig sleep in bed with her—when all you really needed was a quote about the new County Commissioner.

I loved it. I loved everything about it: the reporting, the writing, the opportunity to see and learn about new things. How could I not? Marsha's enthusiasm for the profession verged on obsession. She and I never stopped talking shop. After one particularly grueling day, I drove her home from the journalism department in my beat-up Ford and we sat in her driveway, chewing over stories and our respective futures. Marsha had it all planned out: cover a national political convention by age thirty, then get married and start a family. She wasn't buying the you-can-have-it-all daydream for women, even back then. "And you, Schus?" Marsha asked.

"By thirty," I said, "I definitely want to be a foreign correspondent"—and to keep her company, mumbled something that sounded like marriage and children. About the domestic stuff, I still wasn't sure, but there was a glimmer of hope for the working abroad bit. Because it turned out that I had some talent for the profession; it's always better to be doing a job at which you're modestly good. And the best part was that occasionally, just occasionally, the reporting and writing might pay off in some small improvement for the greater social good—what kids nowadays in their college application essays so earnestly refer to as "making a difference."

We all went off to internships in the summer: Marsha to the The *Washington Post* to cover cops and courts, and I—because the head of my program knew the managing editor—to the *Jerusalem Post*, Israel's English-language daily. I worked on the night desk. This being a time when dinosaurs roamed the earth, the newsroom was filled with reporters madly banging out stories on manual typewriters, then ripping out the completed pages and dashing over to hand in the hard copy. I was one of several grunts, our desks arranged in a U around the chief copy editor, who doled out stories for us to correct with No. 2 pencils. The editor, an American woman with the shoulders of a defensive lineman and the demeanor to match, barely tolerated having to entertain an intern. *"Try learning the use of the semicolon!"* she'd bellow, flinging the page I'd just proof-read back on my desk. Much as she intimidated me, she also taught me my craft.

We'd work until the paper was put to bed, usually midnight or a bit later; afterward, I'd trail the handful of younger editors to one of the few bars still open at that abandoned hour. Knocking off work in Jerusalem was nothing like calling it quits in, say, Scranton. We'd all jump into a taxi—and suddenly be zipping past the massive sandstone walls and watchtowers of the Old City, built by an Ottoman sultan half a millennium ago and romantically spotlit against the night. It was as if you had said to your coworkers, "Fuck the karaoke, let's try that *Arabian Nights* thing instead," and were magically transported back through the ages.

During the day, I scoured the country for transplanted Michiganders to interview ("So, uh, do you miss snow?") and other stories with a Midwestern angle to send to a Detroit paper. Most weekends I spent on the kibbutz, drinking tea with Sim. I could hardly believe my good fortune that summer, especially when, as a kind of last hurrah after finishing the internship, I decided to try my luck at being a war correspondent. Israel had invaded southern Lebanon the previous year to push Palestinian forces away from its frontier after repeated terrorist attacks. The Israelis ultimately withdrew, handing over control of the region to its ally, a Christian Lebanese militia. Now the Israeli military was escorting the foreign press on tours of the area. *Why not me?* I thought. *I'm foreign.* I took a bus to the northern border crossing, armed with my reporter's notebook, my little Instamatic camera, and a letter from the Detroit paper that said I was writing for them, and presented myself at the ramshackle hotel that was the jumping-off point for the excursions. No official accreditation from the Government Press Office, no permission from the Ministry of Defense—just the dog-eared letter, my engaging personality, and my winning smile.

"Get lost," said the military press officer. "This isn't the amateur hour."

I cajoled, begged, beseeched the man to take me across the border. I briefly considered crying as well, but back then we were all riding the wave of women's liberation and you didn't do things like that for fear of wiping out. I was desperate to see war again. The press officer remained unmoved until a reporter and cameraman from the Australian Broadcasting Corporation sauntered in and then, inexplicably, allowed me to tag along. We climbed into a military jeep, drove through gates of concertina wire—and suddenly were in Lebanon, bouncing over the hilly, gutted roads of a combat zone. We passed through entire villages, ghost towns really, whose inhabitants had fled the fighting and streets were now strewn with rubble from rockets and shelling. Houses had been ripped open so that you could see inside the rooms, some with only one wall still standing, their doors riddled with bullets.

This being my first foray into war reportage, I observed the methods of my more experienced companions closely. The reporter asked a few questions and took notes, but as broadcast journalists, the Australians seemed most interested in finding exactly the right backdrop to film their stand-up. When the enormous, crumbling remains of a Crusader castle, perched on a distant hilltop and looking like a leftover from the set of *Robin Hood*, suddenly came into view, the cameraman yelled: "That's it!"

The reporter stood by the roadside, the castle framed perfectly in the background. He smoothed down his hair and, at a signal from the cameraman, began, "Since its incursion into Lebanon, the Isra—"

"Stop, stop!" the cameraman shouted. "There's a goat in the shot." He motioned to the animal, obviously a member of the herd methodically ravaging a nearby hillside, that had wandered over to investigate the microphone cord.

The press officer shooed away the goat, and the cameraman said, "Let's try it again."

"How does my hair look?" asked the reporter.

"Fine. Let's just get this over with."

The reporter affected the solemn countenance appropriate to someone bearing witness to war, raised the microphone to his mouth and began: "Since its incursion into Lebanon, the Israeli military . . . "

"Shit, there's the goat again," said the cameraman, snapping off his machine.

The press officer suggested that we find a site devoid of livestock. We ate up a lot of time bumping along the narrow, undulating roads in search of scenery—the equivalent, for a print person, of sitting around and painting your toenails. Interviews were what I needed. Of course, when we finally got around to those, there was that sticky little language problem. I had studied classical Arabic, which, in this case, was like being dropped into south-central Los Angeles knowing only Shakespearean English. I could vaguely understand when people spoke slowly, particularly if they limited themselves to conjugating lists of verbs. When they really got going in dialect, though, for all I knew they were saying that the goat back along the road was the press officer's girlfriend. I didn't care. The tour was obviously a dog-and-pony show; what was interesting was the way people lived their lives in the midst of conflict. Like the man who drove a Sherman tank of World War II vintage home at the end of the day, parked it in front of his house, nimbly hopped down and disappeared inside for the night—as if commuting to work in war were no different than, say, carpooling with your bowling buddies in a minivan. Or the wedding procession we happened on, the bride and her bridesmaid holding up the skirts of their long, satin gowns and gingerly picking their way in high heels among exploded shells.

I got lucky on that reporting trip: my story about life in a war zone ran as the cover story for the Sunday magazine of the Detroit newspaper, which brought the number of clippings I had by the end of my program—foreign stories all—to a grand total of seven. (Unlike Marsha, who had a clip book the size of a Gutenberg Bible.) I sent them, along with job application letters, to forty-three newspapers and received forty-two rejections: *Dear Ms. Schuster: Thank you for your interesting clips from overseas, but have you done police beat?* Granted, my experience was thin, maybe even verging on anorexic, but didn't behaving like an ass to get across an international border into an area of conflict count for anything? Couldn't these editors see that such a skill might be transferable, that I could similarly humiliate myself, say, before a cop and get him to show me the blotter? *How can they be so blind?*

Meanwhile, Marsha landed a job on a small West Coast paper, and the others in my program likewise got offers. I was resigning myself to a life on the local shopping news when the forty-third newspaper I'd applied to, the *Wall Street Journal*, which back then prided itself on molding promising young journalists, offered me a job. Police beat be damned; the editors liked my stories, especially the one from Lebanon.

Girl goes off to war (okay, only for a couple of days); girl gets job at fancy newspaper. There seemed to be a lesson here. So during my interview in New York with the paper's high priests, when they asked which of the *Journal's* many bureaus most interested me, I said, "Oh, I don't want to work domestically. I only want to be a foreign correspondent." They nodded understandingly, and promptly dispatched me to their outpost in Dallas—which, to a New Yorker, probably *is* foreign. Right off the bat, the bureau chief didn't trust me. The woman I was replacing went to the same university as I, had swanned around the office saying that she only wanted to be a foreign correspondent and—wouldn't you know it?—quickly got hired away by a newsmagazine to work abroad. I must have seemed a clone of my predecessor to the bureau chief, a *Journal* lifer who viewed defectors from the paper as deserving of a firing squad without the blindfold. Every story I proposed was suspect, as if writing about an air conditioning repairman in the midst of a crushing heat wave were really a ploy, somehow, to become Beijing bureau chief for *The New York Times*. His antipathy was such that after doling out the sexy business beats—highly valued at the paper—to the other five reporters, the bureau chief told me to come up with my own. That's when Neil, a former bureau chief himself who had been demoted to lowly reporter and stewed at the ignominy of it in the cubicle next to mine, suggested agriculture. "Go cover shit, Schuster," he said. "It's a great story."

Then—as often happens in this kind of tale—I got a break. For reasons shrouded in obscurity, time, and the paper's only grudging interest in stories not having to do with money, the Dallas bureau was responsible for reporting on Central America. The correspondent who covered it abruptly got transferred to Los Angeles; the other reporters were engrossed in their business beats, which they didn't want to relinquish.

"You're the only one left," the bureau chief said generously. "Besides, I know you'd kill for it."

Oddly, I wasn't so sure. These were the early days of the Reagan administration, when the United States was becoming deeply involved in the region's conflicts, providing overt and covert aid to help defeat communist guerrillas and governments backed by the Soviet Union. Which meant that with barely a year's reporting experience, I was suddenly responsible for one of the hottest foreign stories of the decade and competing against the heavy hitters of my profession. Now that I truly had to deliver, all the cockiness that had gotten me over the Lebanese border, that fueled my indignation at being rejected for jobs, melted away. *Maybe the editors at those forty-two newspapers were right*, I thought. Winter wheat was one thing, but an entire region rapidly becoming engulfed in war?

Dial, Tim, and I meet for supper after our interviews at a pseudo-French restaurant near the hotel. The tablecloths are white, with white linen napkins that a white-aproned waiter opens with a flourish and settles on our respective laps. A caged scarlet macaw provides a distinctly un-Gallic soundtrack of shrieks and whistles in the otherwise empty dining room. After we order food—steaks for them, snapper for me—Dial studies the wine list through reading glasses that give him googly eyes. "Chilean," he says with satisfaction. "The best you can hope for in these parts. Always go for the Chilean."

My knowledge of wine is on a par with my proficiency in animal husbandry, so I tuck that little tidbit away for future use. Striking what I hope is the nonchalant pose of the world-weary foreign correspondent—*should I lean back or to the side?*—I ask Dial how long he's been in Mexico. Last I read—*do I sound like a stalker? a groupie?*—he was in Jerusalem.

"For a few months. Much as I love old Jerusalem, four years was enough. It's a very tough post. You work all day and half the night, file your stories, then get called at three in the morning because of the time difference by some junior deskman who wants to know if you can get more comment from the prime minister. At three o'clock in the morning."

"So you asked for Mexico City?"

"It was that or Moscow. Those were the only two bureaus open. And a good friend who works for the San Francisco paper warned against Moscow. Apparently because I'm divorced, the authorities wouldn't try to compromise me with an agent provocateur, which I found rather disappointing."

Tim sniggers, but I nod sympathetically, as though recalling the postings I, too, had turned down for fear that no one on a government salary would attempt to get into my pants. I gulp down the glass of wine. My tolerance for any kind of alcohol is that of a middle schooler and it's beginning to show. One minute I'm blithely expounding on the weirdness of being based in Dallas—where, for instance, it's illegal to possess a realistic-looking dildo—and the next thing you know, I'm spilling my guts about how hard it is to figure out why the Costa Rica story is important to American readers, a requisite for any *Journal* article. Dial scribbles madly on a cocktail napkin. He says, "Here's a bit of advice from an old wire-service reporter," sliding the napkin across the table.

I read aloud, "'You'll never get your ass in trouble if you take the "why" out of the story.'" We all laugh. *Well, that certainly made me look professional,* I think. Then Dial begins to talk—and it suddenly doesn't matter where my ass is. Dial bewitches me with tales from the Middle East, Africa, the Maghreb. He's a hypnotic storyteller with an actor's phrasing and a Southerner's ear for language (his father came from Mississippi and was a writer). Platters of food come and go, untouched. Which is strange, given that nothing short of getting sucked up into the vortex of the coming apocalypse would ordinarily stop me from eating. But I've never stumbled across such a meld of wit, intelligence, and charm.

Tim, meanwhile, stolidly makes his way through every course— dessert and coffee included—while we ignore him. I don't want the meal to end; I'm gobsmacked. It's a word I'd been waiting all my life to use, but how often, truly, is one overcome by wonder? It isn't an everyday feeling like joy or sadness or indigestion. You're not going to be gobsmacked by your butcher or grocer—unless you're the kind of person whose passions are aroused by, say, a superlative broccoli floret—and most definitely *not* by the callow youths of adolescence and early adulthood. I always worried I wouldn't recognize the signs, but this, undoubtedly, is it. Hours later, when we're kicked out of the restaurant—the waiter put a cloth over the macaw's cage for the night, our final eviction notice—the whole world seems transformed. The mundane has become magical: the moonfaced vendor trying to sell one last lottery ticket; the little dog trotting purposefully down the echoing avenue ("On his way to a dog meeting," Dial says); even the policeman, leaning against his squad car under a streetlight, squinting at a comic book.

We agree to meet for dinner again the next night at a Chinese restaurant. I spend the day squirrel-brained, barely able to focus on my interviews, my mind drifting to our impending rendezvous. *Do you find love, or does love find you?* The sappiness of the question aside, it's one I've never really had reason to consider. Suffice to say that my love life, heretofore, has been mostly uninspiring—more an indictment, perhaps, of my judgment than of the opposite sex. Michael, the British boyfriend on the kibbutz, fell under the heading of "Fun While It Lasts": I wasn't going to follow him to England, and he wasn't going to follow me to wherever I landed, so that was that. In college, my insecurities that anyone could find me attractive were such that I picked boyfriends the same way I picked electives: for their novelty value—like the Jewish jock studying exercise physiology (I'd never met a Jewish jock)—or because they fit into my class schedule. Those criteria insured that I had a better chance of growing a dorsal fin than finding someone who would leave me impassioned and soaring. As for my current situation, you could argue that I continue to set myself up for failure. We're in the throes of the country's craze for *Dallas,* the soap opera about a family obsessed with Big Oil and even bigger hair—and I'm the only Northerner in the entire nation who hasn't bought cowboy boots and learned the Texas two-step. *In Dallas!* As a result, the best I've been able to do, dating-wise, is the owner of a bathroom fixtures company who, I'm sorry to admit, liked to talk about toilet flush-handles and bidets in a high-pitched baby voice he thought was cute and broke up with me when I said that it wasn't.

By the time dinner rolls around, I've worked myself into near delirium. I'm dimly aware of the half dozen or so people at our table, local journalist friends whom Tim brought to the restaurant. I'm dimly aware of plates of Chinese food that keep passing by on a turntable. But all this is backdrop to Dial. We talk the entire night, moving from the restaurant to a bar—where we jettison the others—to the deserted hotel lobby, after the bar closes. Dial tells me about his teenaged son and daughter who live in the States and how guilty he feels about not seeing them enough. I tell him about my parents' divorce and living in Israel. He tells me about how his son, when he was young, bit him in the crotch. I tell him about Marsha and her screaming yellow tits. He makes me laugh. I make him laugh. We talk and talk and talk. Okay, and maybe we make out a little, too. We lift our feet for a small man in a dark blue overall who's washing the lobby floor—and suddenly realize that it's dawn. Tim will be here in a half hour to take Dial to the airport.

I race to my room to change my clothes—I don't want Tim to know that I haven't been to bed yet—and brush my hair, which looks as though it spent the night in a blender. Tim's translating the bill for Dial at the checkout desk by the time I get back to the lobby. "Ah, Ms. Schuster," Dial calls out, "just in time to say goodbye." He's wearing the blue seersucker suit and ugly black shoes again. "I'm afraid I have a plane to catch. But I'm sure we'll meet up again sometime soon in one of these world capitals." He kisses me chastely on the cheek, gathers his bag, and walks out the door with Tim.

That's it? No whispered words of love or lust or just plain like? No clasping of my hand an extra beat or two and spelling out his affections, Helen Keller–style, in my palm? *How could you be so stupid?* I think, trudging off to interview the vice president. *How could you believe, for one minute, that someone like him would honestly be interested in you beyond, maybe, a one-night stand?*

I figured the vice president would give me thirty, perhaps forty, minutes, after which I could mope back in my room, but he has a grand tour planned for the entire day. We bump for several spine-jangling hours across mountains that have glossy-green coffee plants and floppy-eared banana trees terraced precariously down the sides. Why kick yourself for being such an idiot when you're already sustaining a whiplash? And with a vice president, no less! Also, the vice president, a large man with thinning hair and a belly that strains the buttons of his white guyabera shirt, doesn't stop talking for a minute. That makes concentrating on self-loathing difficult. We turn onto trails of rock and gravel and bounce through tropical forests, the vice president shouting above the cascade of stones ricocheting off the car about how immoral the neighboring countries are for spending their money on weapons for war. *The whole region is going to go up in flames!* He drags me to schools and a couple of clinics and an alcoholic rehabilitation center in microscopic towns, some with only a few houses, where the trails turn to mush in the rain and the Range Rover gets stuck so that I have to jump out to help push— and still he keeps yakking.

"My government may have gone into debt, but this—" he says, gesturing expansively to a sodden burro morosely chewing the road- side vegetation "—this is what *our* money bought!" I'm pretty sure he means the tiny shack of a preschool, barely visible through the rain behind the dripping, disconsolate beast—but we're plowing through the muck again and the vice president has moved on to more talk of war.

When I return, exhausted, to the hotel, there's a message to call the bureau chief in Dallas. He wants to know when I'm going to file the story on Costa Rica's ailing economy and leave for Honduras to report on a bank failure. We have our usual sort of conversation: he implying my incompetence, me being defensive, each of us talking past the other. I hang up feeling, as always, like a puppy flicked on the snout for failing to pee on the newspaper. The phone rings again.

"Ms. Schuster, this is Mr. Torgerson calling from Port-au-Prince, and I haven't been able to stop thinking about you since I left this morning."

"Likewise, Mr. Torgerson," I say, my heart doing a little samba.

"I apologize for leaving without telling you how much I enjoyed our evening together, but I didn't want young Tim to suspect anything. I enjoyed it so much that I'm hoping to cajole you into meeting me in Mexico City this weekend."

"I can't, I'm sorry. I have to finish this story and then go on to Honduras to report another. You could meet me there. I'll be in San Pedro Sula on Friday."

"Well, I don't know how I'd justify it to my editors in Los Angeles. It'd seem a circuitous way to return to Mexico." He pauses. "I suppose I could tell them I'm checking into a possible banana strike that would have grave implications for the commodities markets."

"Really? Are you sure you want to do that?"

"My dear woman, I wouldn't miss this for the world. I feel so reassured and pleased after hearing your voice over all these satellite reaches, knowing that you're there and that I'll see you again soon. I only hope I'm not being presumptuous."

Cue birds singing sweetly in nests. Cut to sun breaking through clouds. Pan rainbow arcing across sky.

"You're not," I say.

"Until Friday, then."

Under the best of circumstances—having, for example, three years to complete an assignment—I'm a slow writer. There are reporters who can vomit out their stories on deadline, with time left over to read *War and Peace* or whip up a set of curtains for the sewing room. Not I. My motto: another day, another graf—as in paragraph. The thing about writing is that it's so squirrelly. The blank page sitting in the typewriter with its throbbing whiteness presents boundless choices: definite or indefinite article? Personal or possessive pronoun? Noun or noun phrase? *And that's just for the first word!* When I say that I love the writing part of journalism, I mean the finished product—not the process. The process has all the pleasure of getting your gums scraped by a periodontist. That front page stories—leders, in *Journal*-speak, and what I'm supposed to be writing—can be upward of two thousand words increases the pain exponentially. The first time I attempted a leder, I was marooned for weeks in the bureau's writing room, a small, airless space. Every few days Roger, a fellow journalist, would stick his head in the door. "How ya doin', Shooey?" he'd ask, using the nickname he and the other reporters— men all—have bestowed upon me, and which sounds suspiciously like a pig call. "Have you died back here?"

So of course I choke. The pressure of wanting to prove myself and of the impending rendezvous with Dial provokes a monumental case—even for me—of writer's block. I type and retype the same sentences for hours, ripping the paper out of the roller, wadding it up, and throwing it onto the floor. I just can't get the first take, those ticklish initial three hundred or so words that are supposed to suck a reader in and tell him what the story's about and why it's important. As with most fixations—the size of your behind, for instance, or the guy sitting across from you with the eye twitch— once you're locked in, there's no turning away. I'm going to live or die by that first page. The room acquires a desperate, last stand look with trays of decomposing food from room service stacked on chairs and the coffee table, dirty towels strewn across the bathroom, knee-high eddies of papers swirling around the desk. And then—wouldn't you know it?—I start getting a sinus infection. By the morning I'm supposed to file my story, I'm nowhere close to finishing. The only way to stall for more time is to go to Honduras: I can pretend the flight got delayed or, better yet, canceled, and that way remain incommunicado with the bureau chief for another twenty-four hours. (This was back when the quaint notion of being unreachable existed.) I send a telex, saying that I'm going to file from Honduras and book a ticket to the capital, Tegucigalpa.

Then the plane really *doesn't* show up. The ticket counter is deserted, and no one at the other airlines knows anything about the flight. I sit with my typewriter on my lap trying to work, but am distracted by the departure announcements—all of which sound as if they're going to Augustino. *Why is every airplane flying to Augustino?* I wonder. *And where is it, anyway?* I blow my nose and hear, for a moment, the velvet-voiced announcer say, "con destino"—destined for—and the name of a city. My ears immediately clog up again, and all the planes resume their Augustino journeys. But it doesn't matter; mysteriously, the ticket counter suddenly opens—hours after the scheduled check-in time—an aircraft appears, and we're herded on board. I spend the flight trying to equalize the pressure in my ears and think thoughts that don't have the word "fired" in them.

It's remarkable how total panic, maybe bordering on hysteria, can concentrate the mind. I don't even bother unpacking when I get to the hotel room in Tegucigalpa, just set my typewriter, notebooks, and a stack of paper on a table in front of the window and start churning out paragraphs. Every so often I look up and see hills littered with wretched little shacks and hanging laundry, and ancient buses trying to make hairpin turns. A muddy stream runs under the hotel; a few women with their skirts hiked up around their knees are washing clothes in the water. *That's you if you don't finish,* I think. I pound away into the night, downing bottles of mineral water from the minibar and lining up the empties on the air-conditioning unit. Toward dawn my head droops onto the typewriter for just a moment to rest—and I awake a couple of hours later with the outline of several keys impressed on my cheek like a miniature checkerboard.

The story is done. I pencil in a few changes and hurry to the telex office downtown, a dark, medieval-looking section of the city with narrow, cobbled streets and stone edifices. The operator flips through the nearly seven pages of copy and informs me, through the little hatch where I passed him the story, that he has a backlog and can't send something of such length for at least a day, maybe two. This is beyond imagining, especially in my feverish state. My body begins to shake, my voice cracks like a bar mitzvah boy's, and I'm about to throw myself entirely on the operator's mercy—or as much of myself as I could squeeze through the hatch—when I remember my expense account. *Tip him!* I shove the man a wad of lempiras, the local currency, and add in, for good measure, a note to the bureau chief blaming the delay on my flight and giving him the hotel's telephone number. The operator moves my story to the top of his pile. I float back to my room feeling triumphant and professional, but really, how accomplished can one be with lava flows of snot streaming from the nostrils?

As it turns out, the bank failure that I have to report on next is a tangled mess of shady entrepreneurs, bad loans, corrupt officials—your usual business story. It's like tuning into a long-running soap opera for the first time and trying to get straight who's screwing whom. The thing you have to watch out for in writing about bankers, in my limited experience, is that they will avoid answering any question—except, maybe, about the weather or the current time—by boring you into submission. One minute you're asking about how a particular institution's books were cooked; the next thing you know, the financier is talking LIBOR-OIS spreads and confirmed irrevocable letters of credit—and you've closed your re-

porter's notepad, your mind having drifted to your upcoming gyne-
cological exam. So of course I still have more work to do when I fly
to San Pedro Sula, the country's commercial capital on the coast
and site of my romantic assignation.

At the hotel, I spy Dial across the cavernous lobby, talking to a
woman at the check-in counter. Once again he's in the seersucker
suit and black shoes—obviously his traveling clothes. (This was a
time when, astonishingly, people dressed *up* for their trips.) He has
a neat leather carryall slung over his shoulder and a typewriter case
in his hand—the epitome of professionalism. I, by contrast, look
like a refugee from the siege of Stalingrad. Not knowing what to
bring for my first foreign reporting trip, I brought everything: a suit
valet stuffed so full it resembled a body bag for a pituitary giant,
along with a suitcase that could double as a life raft for about half of
economy class, were the plane to go down. I run to embrace Dial—
although with all the weight I'm hauling it's more like a waddle—
and he plants a perfunctory kiss on my cheek. *Again?* He locks his
arm in mine and strolls me across the lobby, behind the bellboy
struggling with my luggage.

"I told the receptionist that we were married and didn't want to
arouse suspicion by acting too affectionate," he whispers. "The story
is we want a suite, but each need to be charged for half to use on
our expense accounts. It's going to look awfully strange back home
if one of us doesn't have a hotel bill."

I want to ask him about the subterfuge, impressed as I am with
all his forethought—but instead we jump into bed. And stay there
for the weekend. From time to time I arise to blow my nose and do
an interview about the bank failure by phone, hoping that the
source speaks English or only first-grade Spanish. Dial dictates a
telex to the hotel operator, reassuring his editors in Los Angeles

that he's still trying to track down the banana strike. Then we go back to bed. "That's what room service is for!" Dial says gaily. It doesn't escape my attention that he's old—okay, maybe just older, but when you're twenty-five, someone in his early fifties does seem fairly ancient. Truth is, I don't care; never have I felt so loved. (Although later, his teenaged daughter Jordy will say with dismay, "How can you kiss him? He has wrinkles!")

On the last afternoon, we emerge from our room for some air on the balcony. The view is of emerald mountains, lapis skies, bushy-headed palms—your everyday exquisite tropical vista. There's a Swiss Family Robinson–sized tree growing to the side of the balcony, almost within reach, where Dial says he wants to build a little house without telephone or telex so that none of our editors can find us. *Even his DIY projects are romantic!* I think. The sun starts to set, turning the sky an iridescent purple-pink that makes everything look shimmery and me feel giddy and besotted—or maybe it's just extreme dehydration.

"I'm admiring the pale fire of your cheekbones," Dial says, stroking my face. "I was thinking about them in a little restaurant in Port-au-Prince earlier this week. Want to hear the rest of a middle-aged man's meanderings?"

I nod, a junkie for his words.

"Over my second cup of coffee, I was thinking about how much we had shared in so little time in Costa Rica. It was only two days, but a very rich two days. First we discovered that we had the love of Jerusalem in common and that we could laugh together."

I laugh, and he says, "See, I told you. Jerusalem and laughter are very important in relationship building."

"At the French restaurant," he continues, "and again at the little bar after that dreadful Chinese dinner, we found we could charm one another. At least, you certainly charmed me. I didn't know that I was reaching you, but apparently I was, or you wouldn't be here. I remember thinking, *How lovely she is to talk to.* And then we discovered this," he says, embracing me.

I would swoon if I weren't already seated. Instead, my nose begins its deluge again. "Romantic, eh?" I say, honking furiously.

Dial says, "I'm sorry you're so sick. Don't worry, if you go deaf from this infection, I'll learn sign language so we can talk. Little things don't bother me."

On my way to the bathroom for more tissues, I notice an envelope that's been shoved under the suite's door. It's for Dial. He pulls out a telex and reads, "'ProTorgerson, exGibson. AP reporting Salvo army in major battle with guerillas eastern province. Acknowledge receipt and book yourself on aircraft soonest. Regards.'"

"Who's Gibson?" I ask.

"The foreign editor."

"What does it mean?"

"It means that I'm going to El Salvador, not home to Mexico City."

This bit of information puts me in two minds. On the one hand, I'm envious. This is the reporting life I'd always imagined: urgent cables in the dead of night (okay, maybe the dead of dusk), the scramble to find airplane connections, hurried preparations for going into a war zone. Because the *Journal* considers itself the paper of daily record only for breaking stories about business, we normally don't cover spot news of this type. Any foreign articles I write, especially for the paper's front page, require careful plotting and pleading and promising of firstborns to the higher-ups to justify the time and expense.

And yet, *He's going into a war zone!* My mind turns back to the interview with the Costa Rican vice president when we traveled upcountry, and his admonition about the whole region going up in flames. I say, "You'll be safe?"

Dial says, "Lynda, it's war."

Which is about as reassuring as being told that a charging elephant is a pachyderm.

But that's barely on my mind the next morning after he departs for San Salvador and I board my flight back to the States. As the plane takes off, with one hand I'm cradling my ear, which feels as though there's a troupe of miniaturized Cossacks inside doing a kazatsky. With the other, I'm clutching a little note that was waiting for me when I checked out:

Dial Torgerson fell in love at 11.37 p.m., Thursday, Oct. 1, in San Jose, Costa Rica.

CHAPTER THREE

CENTRAL AMERICA, 1982

Of course, Dial is fine on his Salvador trip. The concern I had about his safety is testimony to how quickly life can shift when you're young. One minute you're a rookie full of angst and insecurity, about to embark on your first overseas reporting assignment—and the next thing you know, you're still a rookie full of angst and insecurity, but now with war and love rolled in. Not to mention lingering mucus.

When the bureau chief calls me into his office for a debriefing on the trip, I make a big show of blowing my nose loudly and piling up used tissues in a little pyramid on the armrest of my chair. Message: she's a trooper, able to soldier through even the worst of tropical diseases. His probable interpretation: she's a disaster, incapable even of leaving home without coming down with the Black Death. After I retreat to my cubicle, I see him through the glass windows of his office frantically wiping down the chair. Then I go off to an ear, nose, and throat doctor, who Roto-Rooters my sinuses and pumps me so full of drugs I have absolutely no chance ever of playing major league baseball.

The Costa Rica story runs soon after on the front page. Miraculously, I receive a herogram telex from the paper's managing editor in New York: *Nicely done piece on Costa Rica today.* And another when the second story appears: *Compliments for a fine piece on the Honduras bank collapse and its ripples.* High praise, indeed, in *Wall Street Journal* world. I'm walking around on a cloud of pink fuzz, especially when the bureau chief pins the messages on the bulletin board in the back of the newsroom. By day's end, though, the other reporters have penciled snarky little comments on them. It's junior high all over again with them—minus the mildewed braces and bra snapping. When I was covering agriculture, a story of mine about shrimpers in south Texas that ran on the front page described how, "shrimp boats, anchored two and three deep, bob with upturned prows like eager women vying for attention in a beauty contest." Okay, maybe it was a *bit* overwrought. But was that cause for Brent, who works across the room, to appear suddenly at my desk, story in hand, and begin bouncing up and down? "I'm bobbing, Shooey," he said breathlessly. "Is my upturned prow getting your attention?"

Steve, another reporter, joined in, the two of them jumping in place like Masai warriors. "We're eagerly bobbing for your attention, Shooey!" Neil, sitting in the cubicle behind mine, told them to knock it off. I think he felt sorry for me being the only female reporter in the bureau.

This time he says from behind the partition, "Nice Central America stories, Schuster." Neil has a Donald Sutherland–like lisp and gray, patchy beard. He was one of the last people in the country to contract polio and wears a brace on his withered leg. I always know when he's about to sit down or stand up because of the brace's *click-click* as it changes positions; when the mood strikes, he leaves it off altogether and uses crutches instead. Neil doesn't talk about what caused the *Journal's* gods-on-high to throw down thunderbolts and transform him from bureau chief to mere reporter—but whatever the reason, it's my gain. Hearing him work a source is a master class in newsgathering. He's an ingenious journalist, all expletives and drawl on the telephone, genteelly intimidating the hell out of the person on the other end to give him the information he wants. But it's his writing that leaves me in awe: astonishing, lapidary prose in the great tradition of Southern writers.

"Thanks, Neil, coming from you it means a lot," I say, then notice what he's done to a picture taped above my desk. It's of Jordanian Bedouins, resplendent in flowing burgundy robes and bandoliers across their chests, astride bedecked camels in the desert. The photograph—a pale substitute, really, for *being* in the Middle East—is from an oil corporation's glossy annual report; we're supposed to scrutinize the booklets to make certain that companies haven't buried bad news amid the agitprop. Neil has drawn a tidy little speech balloon issuing from the mouth of one of the Bedouins: "I'm going to make your earth move, Jew woman."

A few days later, we're driving back from lunch in Neil's silver, souped-up sports car, what Steve calls "the pimpmobile," and Neil's raving about the latest book he's been reading, *Pissing in the Snow*. "Nice title," I say. "What's it about?"

"A collection of Arkansas pornography."

"Great, just what I always wanted to read."

"But it's a *classic* of Arkansas pornography!"

To change the topic, I tell him about Dial—obviously leaving out the prurient details of the San Pedro Sula rendezvous but including the romantic, mushy parts. I'd been desperate to talk to someone in the bureau about how I'd fallen in love, bursting almost. Neil snorts when I get to the bit about Dial being fifty-three. "That's how old I am, Schuster," he says, pulling into the *Journal's* parking lot. "Let me tell you something. A man my age is interested in someone as young as you for only two reasons: sex and ego."

But all I hear from Dial is love. In a letter he posts from El Salvador, Dial writes:

I'd like to wake up in the morning speaking French, playing the guitar and married to Lynda Schuster. This is not a proposal, merely something admissible, as they say in court, to prove a state of mind. But if anyone asks you if my intentions are honorable, you can smile a secret little smile and say, "Well, he has his impossible dreams." Relax, you will not be pressed.

Married? I'm about three seconds into my brilliant career—who wants to think of being married? Being cross-eyed in love, yes. Deeply in lust, ditto. But married—that's the antithesis of the glamorous, globe-tripping life I'm trying to construct here. Marriage is hearing the lock clink into place on the dungeon door as someone turns the key from the outside. Marriage is having cement poured into your shoes with your feet stuck in them. *Marriage is my mother!*

Who happens to call in the midst of these mental histrionics.

"Hi honey, it's Mom. How are you?"

"Fine."

"I read your stories from Honduras and Costa Rica. I'm *so* proud of you."

"Thanks."

"I hear you met someone down there."

She probably got that from my sister Bev, whom I called as soon as I got back to the States. I yammered on and on about how Dial isn't a daddy thing, really, because even though he's actually older than Dad, he's a hundred times nicer and recites whole chunks of poetry from memory and is *totally* romantic! At which point Bev must have telephoned Mom to tell her that I had lost my mind.

You'd think by now, having grown up and landed a plum job and fallen in love, I'd be inclined to cut my mother a bit of slack. Nope. The thing is, I've been dragging around the baggage of my anger about what she wasn't and isn't for so long that, in my twisted little mind, it's come to resemble an attractive, monogrammed Louis Vuitton rolling duffel that I can transport everywhere and is the star of the luggage carousel. So I'm not about to give it up. This is part payback for her perceived shortcomings, part insecurity, stupidly convinced as I am that being open, even in the slightest, might make me vulnerable to becoming just like her.

I say, "Yeah, well, it's nothing important."

Silence. Her hurt is palpable.

She says, "Oh, okay. Where are you off to next?"

"Nicaragua, I think."

"Nicaragua! Well, stay safe. Call me when you get back."

Nicaragua, because those herograms from New York buy me, grudgingly, a quick reporting trip to Central America from the bureau chief. Still suffering the effects of a massive earthquake a decade earlier and a more recent civil war, Managua, the capital, looks the way I imagine parts of Europe after World War II—if you added in palm trees, volcanoes, and a lake with tropical fish. Just trying to find a street address amid the rubble requires the skills of an oracle. The Marxist leaders of the revolution who overthrew the country's brutal dictator promised the usual stuff to win popular support—democracy, pluralism, press freedom, a rainbow every third Tuesday—then promptly set about clamping down on everything after taking power a couple of years ago. The city has the feel of a bad Cold War spy novel. Blondish Eastern-bloc security goons, immediately recognizable in their cheap leather jackets and sunglasses, lurk in bars and hotel lobbies, scrutinizing patrons from behind days-old newspapers. There are Big Brother–type billboards on all the roads, reminding citizens of their Marxist goals—FOR THE DEFEAT OF THE EXPLOITING CLASSES AND THE VICTORY OF THE EXPLOITED CLASSES!—and extolling the successes of the glorious revolution—98% OF THE HOG INDUSTRY HAS BEEN NATIONALIZED! Even the language has been Sovietized: women now address their husbands as "compañero," although this apparently hasn't convinced the men to do something truly revolutionary such as, say, wash the dinner dishes.

The place is creepy with bored, trigger-happy soldiers. Every newspaper thinks President Reagan won't stand for another virtual Cuba in the hemisphere and is on the verge of sending in the Marines, including *The New York Times*. I run into the reporter they've got on a deathwatch at my hotel. Despite being a veteran correspondent and rather debonair, Warren is nice in a non-patronizing sort of way, even tossing me a spare tube of toothpaste from his balcony above my room after I've run out. *New York Times toothpaste!* He's particularly sympathetic when I return from a day of interviews to find that my room has been rifled: clothes in disarray, suitcase over-turned, papers strewn about the floor. Nothing was stolen; this isn't your usual hotel burglary. Warren thinks they were probably after my notebooks, which I—in my customary paranoia —always carry with me. The authorities clearly don't like us, he says, adding that his phone seems to be tapped. In my case, it doesn't help that the *Journal's* editorial page, notorious for opinions that would make even a troglodyte blush, had run a piece a day or two earlier sug-gesting, in essence, that Reagan nuke the Marxist government. When I call the foreign minister's office to try to set up an inter-view, his personal secretary says: *"Wall Street Journal?* Did you come by nuclear submarine?" before hanging up on me.

The following morning, my fixer Martin and I leave for a small town up north, near the border with Honduras. Martin is a young, Ivy-educated scion of a wealthy family, precisely the sort that the new government is targeting. Rather than decamp to Miami with his bitter cohort, though, Martin decided to stay and cash in on his communications degree by working with clueless foreign journal-ists like myself. It's his suggestion that we go north for a story I want to do on how the revolution is faring in the rest of the country.

At the town's only hotel, the manager says I can have a standard room, whose bathroom is down the hall, for the equivalent of four dollars a night or the deluxe room, with self-contained toilet and shower, for six. Being as I'm on expense account, I splurge on the latter. The minute I get into bed, though, exhausted from the jour-ney and several rounds of interviews, the electricity goes out. *Not a problem! Who needs to see when you're going to sleep?* Besides, I have my trusty flashlight—a Dial-recommended item which I added to my packing list—in case I need to pee in the night. Every noise seems amplified in the inky blackness, and I'm distracted by a scurrying sound on the wall next to me. I flip on the flashlight: the wall is Times Square on a Saturday night for insects of every size and stripe, crazily scurrying in all directions, some of which decide that my mattress is part of their party plans and fling themselves with abandon onto the blanket. I hastily drag my bed to the middle of the room, a move that deters all but the cockroaches. These are hardened, post-revolutionary bugs the size of Matchbox cars, which I spend the night hitting, whack-a-mole style, with the end of my flashlight as they breach the sides of the mattress. The siege goes on for hours. Toward dawn, carefully picking my way among the roach carcasses, I go to use the deluxe toilet that's standing in the open air on the other side of the room and—wouldn't you know it?—find a rat casually reclining on the seat.

"I am not spending another night here!" I say by way of greeting in the morning to Martin, who also looks a bit beleaguered.

To that end, I embark on the journalistic equivalent of speed dating, bombarding each interviewee with questions—"So what do you think of the revolution? Has your life improved? Worsened? Do you have giant-sized cockroaches in your home?"— and barely allowing the poor person a chance to breathe before dashing on to the next. Anyone with the misfortune to cross my frenetic path is fair game. Old, young, rich, poor—even the mute and the unborn. The pull of reportorial duty versus the terror of creepy-crawlies, to say nothing of rodents, is no contest: vermin win hands down. Still, I try to seek out opinions both for and against the government and end up hearing stories about war that are deeply poignant, heartbreaking even. A woman tells how the former dictator's henchmen burned her husband's furniture factory, his eleven delivery trucks— and then burned him alive on a deserted highway because of his support for the revolution. *How do you live with something like that?* I think, wanting to hug or somehow console her, but knowing it would be unprofessional.

In moments like these, I hate being a journalist. And yet I wouldn't have the opportunity to learn of such things, or disseminate them, if I weren't. There's one other thing that catches my attention while interrogating the townspeople: an often-repeated rumor of antigovernment rebels training just over the border in Honduras. This might just be wishful thinking by those who feel betrayed by the revolution, but I file away the tidbit anyway to check out later.

By the twenty-fourth interview, I sound like a bleating sheep with a serious nicotine problem; the fingers on my writing hand are permanently fused to my pen. Martin, meanwhile, has slowed to a tortoise shuffle. "Please, let's go," he says. "It's dark, we can't see anything, all the shops are closed. You're not going to find anyone on the streets to talk to. Besides," he adds, sotto voce, "I think a security guy is following us."

Let him *spend the night in the deluxe room!* I think, loading up the car for the drive back to Managua. It's funny how quickly one's outlook on a particular place can shift, given the right circumstances. Just yesterday I was moaning to Martin about what a dump the capital is—and now, having returned from the Eighth Circle of Hell, the city seems positively alluring. Those charming Orwellian billboards! Those adorable soldiers with itchy trigger fingers! Those quaint leather jackets on the ubiquitous spooks!

And one wholly unexpected, heart-thumping addition to the list, waiting for me in the hotel lobby: Dial.

Is there anything more romantic than your lover turning up after he's covered another firefight in El Salvador? I wonder, maturely resisting the impulse to jump on Dial while ascending in the elevator to our room, my thoughts racing in bodice-ripper sound bites. *Am I testing the limits of his passion in a war-torn region by not having bathed for two days?* The latter question I manage to address by showering before he has a chance to consider it; the former I leave to ponder later, after lovemaking. But later, of course, I'm glued to my desk, banging away as always on my typewriter. I look up to see Dial on the balcony, lighting a small candle in the potted palm. He smiles and says, "Come out here for a minute."

I say, "What's that?"

"Our menorah. And this is for you," he says, handing me a small box. Inside I find a delicately wrought watch and a note: *With much—all—love to Lynda. Chanukah 1981. From he who found grace in your eyes. Dial.*

"So much better than latkes!" I say, embracing him. "And you're not even Jewish! Thank you, it's beautiful. Now I'll think of you every time I'm late for an interview. As if there's ever a time I'm *not* thinking of you. But I would have gotten you something if I'd known you were coming." It occurs to me that I'm not even supposed to be in Managua, that I would have stayed in the north were it not for the hideous swarms; what would he have done if I hadn't returned?

"I would have pursued you," Dial says. "That's what. And if you disappear in the mountains of Guatemala on assignment, I'll be there looking for you. Or you become smitten with a Cossack like Natasha in *War and Peace*, I'll find him and fight him with sabers. And win."

Oh my heart, my beating heart! "You don't have to worry about a Cossack, Torgerson. A Gurkha, maybe, but not a Cossack."

The next morning, Dial is up early to catch a plane to Mexico

City. By the time I make it downstairs to the restaurant, he's eating breakfast with Warren, the *Times* correspondent, who's still waiting for Reagan to send in the Marines. Sliding into the booth, I pick up a fork and spear a mouthful of Dial's fried eggs before deciding what to order. Afterward, when I walk outside with Dial to the taxi stand, he whispers, "Lynda, you can't just eat out of my plate like that, people will know we're sleeping together. We have to be careful. Reporters are the biggest gossips in the world."

Who would have thought bad table manners a sign of intimacy? I wonder. Then again, would I honestly have stuck a spoon in Warren's cereal? Sipped from his coffee mug? Bitten off a hunk of his Danish? Okay, maybe the Danish—but not without asking first.

And then Dial is gone, leaving me slightly chagrined but also breathless and disoriented, reduced to humming pop tunes I'd always derided as silly or trite. It's this way every time we part; Dial calls it "our psychotic state." That the lyrics to, say, "Do That to Me One More Time" now seem ineffably sweet, even meaningful, surely indicates some sort of mental disturbance. I pour out my feelings to Simcha—unwilling as I was to acknowledge them to my own mother—and she writes back: *When did you get to be so damn clever anyway? I knew that fifty-three-year-old men were sensitive and stimulating, but I didn't think you had found out already.*

Truth be told, I barely know him. Our assignations are most likely made even more intoxicating by being compressed into the briefest of moments; I've had lower gastrointestinal tract infections that lasted longer than the time we've spent together. Somehow I have to figure out a way to steal more days, maybe even a whole week, with him.

———

Inadvertently, my foreign editor arranges for us to do just that. After I finish writing my Nicaragua stories, the *Journal's* page-one editor invites me to do a copyediting stint at headquarters in New York—an honor, Neil says, that's usually reserved for more experienced staffers. In this Paleozoic era, the *Journal* looks nothing like other newspapers in the United States: no color, no photos, just a few graphs and an occasional drawing of a business magnate or financial guru executed in tiny, gray dots. They resemble something a pointillist painter might have done had he awoken one morning and said, "Screw the gorgeous colors; I'm going totally drab." So aside from snippets of international and business news, the front page is essentially comprised of three stories: two leders and one, more light-hearted column. These are the *Journal's* sacred spaces that its hundreds of reporters around the world vie for. To work on page one is to be ushered into the Holy of Holies, to be made privy to the secrets of accepting or rejecting a story proposal, and to the rituals of editing the final product. I spend most of my time doing the latter. It requires telephoning some of the paper's most incandescent luminaries, reporters whose very names make me fall on my face in awe, to question their prose: "Uh, I'm really sorry, but could I please bother you to explain what you mean in the third line of the sixth paragraph of the second page?" That aside, I like being in the New York bureau. Its vast acreage of cubicles is the closest thing the paper has to a central newsroom and is in stark contrast with Dallas, where you can't leave your desk to pee without the entire place passing judgment, Greek-chorus style. Here you can disappear into your allotted space and plot a bloodless coup, say, or develop an alternative dandruff shampoo. It could be weeks before anyone noticed.

The other good thing about being in New York is getting to meet the top editors, many of whom I know only by name. They pass me around like a silky new puppy, taking me to lunch and engaging in long, earnest discussions about what the paper expects of its young reporters. This is a perfect opportunity to lobby for more time in Central America, particularly El Salvador. The country's civil war is heating up *and* it's about to hold elections, sponsored by the United States, that hundreds of journalists from around the world will be covering. I hastily write up a half dozen story proposals to send to the managing editor, his deputy, the page-one editor and the foreign editor—especially the foreign editor. Until now, we've only ever talked by telephone. The conversations have been rather bizarre, mostly, given his habit of not immediately answering a question. These aren't momentary hesitations in which he's gathering his thoughts, but eerily long pauses so pregnant that a good-sized mammal could gestate in the time it takes for him to respond. Which is fine if you're sitting across from the man and can see him cogitating—but not when you're on the other end of a phone hundreds of miles away and don't know if he's dropped off to sleep or stopped breathing.

At breakfast at the Yale Club—even though he's a Harvard man—the foreign editor seems interested in the El Salvador stories.

"How many reporters will be down there?" he asks.

I say, "Gazillions. The *LA Times* will have three or four, and *The New York Times* and *The Washington Post* probably more, just on principle. I know this isn't exactly our kind of story, but we're going to look pretty stupid if we don't have at least one person on the ground."

"And how much time do you think you need?"

Deep breath. "Oh, I don't know. Everyone else is going for about six weeks."

I take it as a good sign that he neither chokes on his coffee nor falls to the floor, rolling around on the richly patterned rug and laughing wildly at the idea of a *Journal* reporter covering a foreign story for so long. Also, I have to be very careful here. I can't look as if I'm doing an end-run around my bureau chief, whose idea of a protracted overseas reporting trip is one that lasts for about four-and-a-half minutes.

He says, "The paper's changing and there is more of an appetite for foreign pieces. But we don't want you doing bang-bang. No blood-and-guts. We want *Journal* stories."

"Of course," I say, envisioning pieces in which guerrillas provide projections for the annual Gross Domestic Product in the territory they control. As always, though, beneath my facade of swagger and self-confidence is a considerable nugget of self-doubt that now swells to the size of a prize autumnal pumpkin. Even if I don't have to report on military battles, I've never actually been to El Salvador, let alone truly worked in a war zone. (My public relations junket in Lebanon notwithstanding.) But the lure of covering such a story is irresistible—all the more so after Dial sends me a letter with a plan for how we can virtually live together during the time:

> *I'll get a hotel room to serve as an office with maybe one single bed in it, and reserve the adjoining room with a double bed. But when you get there, you'll have to have a separate bill for the adjoining room for propriety's sake. I'm smiling to myself as I sit here typing, thinking what it would be like to have you there for a week, two weeks or even parts of THREE weeks—it seems riches beyond the dreams of amorous.*

Thrilled as I am, it's still first-day-of-school scary when the foreign editor tells me I can go. "Take a month if you need to," he says. "And don't worry about your boss in Dallas; I'll handle him. Oh, and you'll be filing your stories directly to me in New York." *Now the bureau chief will probably be gunning for me, along with the guys in uniforms.* As I'm walking out the door, wondering if bulletproof vests come in bra-cup sizes, the paper's publisher—himself a former foreign correspondent —throws a last bit of reassuring advice my way: "Don't bother dying down there. We wouldn't even appreciate the kind of story that could get you killed."

Every news organization in the galaxy has lit upon this tiny nation, which could fit nicely into the state of Massachusetts with a little room left over so as not to inconvenience the residents of Cape Cod. I'm waiting for the elevator in my hotel, newly checked-in and completely nervous. The glitterati of journalism are all here, including the news anchors from the major US television networks who wander the mobbed lobby in full-dress makeup; think a youngish Tom Brokaw with enough foundation on his face to make a Miss America contestant envious. I try not to gawk. They're broadcasting the morning and evening news programs from the building's rooftop and, presumably, have to be ready at a moment's notice in case there's an outbreak of information. The door to the elevator slides open. Inside, reporters are crammed together shoulder-to-shoulder; a photographer for one of the weekly newsmagazines, multiple cameras hanging from his neck, is talking to a *New York Times* correspondent.

"Blood," he says, "and I mean *blood*. Everywhere. It was amazing. You couldn't walk two steps without slipping in it."

I let the door close and take the stairs.

The television hacks and wire services have offices on the second floor. Their rooms are choked with newspapers, filing cabinets, wall-sized maps, police band radios, clattering telex machines, tattered lists of telephone numbers and flight schedules, caches of water and canned goods, people yelling into telephones. In the midst of the chaos, I register with the Salvadoran Press Corps Association (SPCA). This gets me a laminated card with my photograph on it, identifying me as an international journalist, and worn on a cord around my neck. It's supposed to make me bulletproof, like some sort of Committee to Protect Journalists fetish—but given the high regard for press freedom in the country, it feels more like a bull's-eye hanging right over my heart. Things lighten up a little when I get to the sixth floor, where Dial made our reservation, and a tall blonde woman wearing a flowing muumuu and large glasses bursts out of one of the rooms. "Hi, Swedish Television," she says, shaking my hand, then jogs down the hallway bellowing: *"Does anyone know the president's full name, please?"*

Dial isn't in our room, but there's a note taped to the mirror above the desk: *Back soon to our little abode, where we shall steal time together from the world like great burglars.* It's the first thing, really, that's made me smile all day, especially given the travails of getting here. El Salvador's international airport had exuded all the welcoming warmth of a penitentiary: halls littered with large men in sunglasses and machine gun–festooned soldiers, scrutinizing every passerby. The fellow ahead of me in the line to clear customs was abruptly hustled away by soldiers after an official, pawing through his suitcase, pulled out a sheaf of papers that were apparently deemed objectionable. *Just wait until he sees my light reading material!* To add to the pleasure of arriving in a police state in the throes of civil war, my cabbie decided to make the twenty-five-mile drive to the capital at breakneck speed. "It's a bad sign that the road's deserted," he shouted, careening around lush, verdant mountainsides with the wind whipping through the open windows—no air conditioning—and me bouncing around the back seat like a hot little kernel of popcorn. "That's when the guerrillas are most likely to strike."

But six stories up, all is quiet, peaceful even. A panel of windows at one end of the room provides a good view onto the city. Several high-rises dot the skyline, but it's otherwise mostly flat-roofed buildings the color that teeth get after not being brushed for a couple of days, piled on one another like Lego blocks and spread across the undulating green hills. My mind turns back to a BBC radio broadcast from Guatemala I heard some time ago in which the reporter, with a thrilling, plummy British accent, began: "You don't have to leave your hotel room in Guatemala City to understand how tense and dangerous the political situation is." At the time, I howled at the radio, "That's because you're too chicken to go outside!" But now I see his point. *Maybe I can cover the story from up here!* I'm considering all the possibilities of reporting from a hotel window, and unpacking the small shipping container of newspaper clippings, books, and other background material that I brought, when Dial walks in.

"You made it!" he says, enfolding me in his arms. He's in his full-on foreign correspondent's regalia: non-wrinkle, short-sleeved shirt with his passport, notebook and glasses tucked neatly into the breast pocket; synthetic trousers with a permanent crease that he can, in his words, wash while wearing in the shower and then step outside to drip-dry; running shoes. My Prince of Polyester! "Come look at our little home for the next month," he says, taking me by the hand and walking three steps to complete the grand tour of what amounts to your standard hotel accommodation. He opens a communicating door to the next room; it's been turned into a kind of command center for the *LA Times*, a miniaturized version of the SPCA office. But what really catches my eye—wonder of wonders—is the direct telephone line to the United States that Dial, like the other large news organizations, had installed. He and his reporters won't have to go through the hotel's telephone operator. For the rest of us, the war could be over and the guerrillas moved on to, say, studying for their real estate licenses by the time we get a connection.

"Does this mean we're not going to worry about keeping our relationship quiet anymore?" I ask, noting the room's single bed that may placate the Puritans and accountants back in Los Angeles but won't fool anyone here—especially when it remains unused.

"I think if both our offices are pleased with our respective work, we won't have any trouble over the conveniently close living quarters," he says. "They can't challenge us for waking up together, or for suspecting us of waking together, as long we produce great things. And if they don't like it, I'll quit and become a junior draftsman."

I say, "Electrical or mechanical?" And then we jump into bed. Not the single, of course, but the double one, after discreetly closing the door to the connecting room. This doesn't need to be our usual making-up-for-lost-time marathon, though; we have whole weeks stretching magically before us. Besides, Dial has to manage all of his people, divvying up coverage. And I have to throw myself into reporting to catch up with everyone else.

Right off the bat, it's the ubiquitous poverty that gets to me: the little kids with stomachs swollen and hair made thin and dull by malnutrition; the teeming, fly-infested hovels; the feces floating in puddles of standing water. That, and the lack of institutional remedies. There's no independent judiciary here, no free press, no viable political opposition. The oligarchs and their military men control everything, as they have since the days of the Spanish conquistadores; you almost expect to round a corner and come upon a tribunal for the Inquisition. Just about anyone who tries to work for peaceful change—priest, peasant, teacher—is silenced. "Offed," as my colleagues so elegantly put it. Twenty thousand people have died in the civil war over the past two years, many at the hands of right-wing death squads that roam the country.

At an office that compiles human rights abuses, I run into a peasant woman who came from the countryside to search for her three married daughters. Soldiers destroyed part of her village and murdered scores of residents whom, the officers claimed, collaborated with the guerrillas. The woman says her daughters were kidnapped by troops after they shot and killed her sons-in-law and burned her house. She now sleeps under a tree with her fourteen grandchildren. Sobbing, the woman flips through an enormous photo album of victims of the violence, gruesome pictures that are truly difficult to look at, to see if she can identify her daughters among them. I take down her story, then hurry back to the hotel room. And weep.

Luckily, Dial isn't around to witness my little breakdown; it feels embarrassing and not at all professional. I suspect this isn't the way most seasoned reporters spend their free time, a hunch that's confirmed a few days later when, on impulse, I stop a veteran British war correspondent, a friend of Dial's, in the hallway of our floor. "Uh, Paul," I say, "do you ever, I don't know, *cry* after covering a story?"—and he looks at me as though I just asked if he likes dressing up in women's clothes.

What makes this overwhelming, crushing abjection of the majority even worse is the contrast with the obscene wealth of the country's privileged few. They reside in the hills of the capital's northern reaches, a planet away from the squalor that most people are stuck in. Up here, the air is clean, the roads well tended, the neighborhoods quiet and beautifully landscaped. Once you've finished admiring the fuschia- and peach-colored bougainvillea and stately trees, though, you start to notice other things, too: the jagged shards of glass, like a set of bared fangs that top a mansion's concrete-block security walls, for instance, or the gun turret cunningly built into the corner of another estate's walls as if it's nothing more than an architectural flourish. My taxi honks twice at the gates of a landowner I'm going to interview. A guard peers through a slat, then opens a door in the wall. Two men wielding submachine guns emerge and walk slowly around the taxi before one asks for my name; that information is relayed inside, and the gates slowly swing apart.

A uniformed maid ushers me through a marble-floored foyer to a living room that, in a pinch, could be traversed in fifteen minutes on foot. A wall of French doors at one end leads outside to an elaborate garden and swimming pool; an armed guard leans against the trunk of a palm, cleaning his fingernails with a small knife. *He probably picks his teeth with it, too,* I think. The landowner is a short, compact man dressed, for some reason, entirely in brown. This includes a tasteful little leather pistol holster that's buckled around his ankle, a gun tucked neatly inside, which I see when he sits down on the sofa across from me and his pant leg rises. We talk about the violence in the country and the economy, but I find it hard not to stare at the holster. It's like trying to avert your eyes when someone's private parts are showing. Also, I don't know if this little flash of firepower is inadvertent, the equivalent of a slip peeking out from under a hemline—or if it's meant to convey a message. If the latter, he's certainly got my attention. I'm all compassion when he talks about the difficulties of farming thousands of acres of coffee in the midst of a war—that is, until he offers his opinion of the peasants who toil his land and make the harvest possible. "Nothing more than donkeys," he says, "who don't deserve anything."

Personally, I'm beginning to sympathize with the rebels.

I obviously don't agree with their Communistic bent or their violent tactics, but can understand why they took up arms. Professionalism—or my approximation of it—compels me, though, to try to write evenhanded stories that spell out the complexities and resist the temptation to editorialize. At least, that's what Marsha and I learned in journalism school. But this place is a writhing snake pit of competing ideologies that I, in my stunning naïveté, never anticipated. On one side you've got the leftist journalists, some of Dial's younger reporters included, who consider the guerrillas to be gentlemen and professors; they shun me like I've got Ebola and am bleeding from the nipples, on the assumption that anyone who writes for the *Journal* must subscribe to the editorial page's Neanderthal politics. Which is laughable, really, because the *Journal's* editorial writers are apparently convinced that my reporting is too liberal precisely because I *do* include the leftist point of view. They publish, as corrective, a piece virtually calling me a liar. *In my own paper.* (The foreign editor kindly cables me a copy.) On the other side, you have the diplomats over at the US embassy, busily cooking the numbers of civilians killed by the government-backed death squads to make the weekly reports they have to send to Washington—grim-grams, the reporters call them—more optimistic to justify their policies. Under their creative accounting, the generals are on the verge of becoming Quakers.

"Lynda," says one of the diplomats after I've filed several stories, "why do all the children you write about have to have distended bellies?"

"Well, Gale, maybe it's because their bellies *are* distended."

Tonight, like most nights, Dial leaves me in the room thwacking away at my typewriter, trying to make sense of all this. I'm too jumpy to join him and the journalistic hordes for dinner. After an hour or so, though, I need a break and wander downstairs to the hotel bar, which is jammed as usual. Off to the side, a television reporter is interviewing one of Dial's reporters under a halo of bright lights. *The broadcast people must have run out of Salvadorans to talk to. Next thing you know, they'll be interviewing the furniture: bragging about an exclusive with the floor lamp or scoring a one-on-one with the sofa.*

At least this business of journalists using each other as sources is more decorous than what happened last night. I was sitting at the bar, talking to a couple of US Marines about the pack mentality of the press, when one of them said, "Watch this." Winking at his buddy, he whipped out his walkie-talkie and whispered a message to his home base to send him an emergency signal. Thirty seconds or so later, the transmitter emitted a shrill and persistent alert that reverberated throughout the bar and the dining room next door. The two Marines dashed out of the hotel to their vehicle in the parking lot—followed by scores of reporters abandoning their drinks and meals and scrambling for their notebooks, the television types shouting at their cameramen to grab the equipment, everyone struggling to push past one another. Only to return an hour later, after trailing the Marines to their house and realizing they'd been had.

I slide onto a barstool, next to a television correspondent for one of the major networks whom I barely know. She's older than I am, maybe midthirties, tall and somewhat voluptuous. Turning to me, hands gripping a half-drunk beer, she says, "I miss my son."

Why is she telling me this? "I'm sorry. Where is he?"

"New York."

"Who's looking after him?"

"My husband."

"What does he do?"

"Works for a news agency."

"So at least your son's with one of his parents."

"That isn't the point." She's almost hostile in her intensity. "He's only six years old. I just got done talking to him, before he went to bed."

We're interrupted by John, the United Press International bureau chief and SPCA head, who's handing out T-shirts to everyone. They're white with PERIODISTA—NO DISPARE! ("Journalist—Don't Shoot!") in blue lettering on the back, and on the front, I SURVIDED (sic) THE SALVADORAN ELECTIONS.

"No wonder UPI is going broke," I say. "They can't spell."

The television correspondent doesn't even crack a smile.

That went over well. "How often do you talk to your son?"

"Every night. But I really, really miss him. I don't want to be here." Looking around to see if anyone's listening, she lowers her voice to a whisper. "I don't want to die. I don't want even to have to *think* about the possibility of dying. But I can't let my producer hear this." She waves away the bartender. "Do you have any kids?"

"Nope," I say glibly, grabbing a handful of fried plantain chips. "And I don't intend to."

"You have no idea what it's like once you have a child," she says, shaking her head. "There is nothing, and I mean nothing, better in the entire world."

How could having a child possibly be better than this? I wonder, returning to my room and piles of discarded story drafts. *To be covering the hottest story around* and *waking up every day for a month with your lover!* Just this morning, before we got out of bed, Dial was saying what luxury it is to know I'll be beside him when he awakens so he can tell me his dreams. "Like the one I had last night," he recalled. "I dreamt I was covering a press conference where the Pope announced he was quitting to marry a nun."

"Yes," I said, giggling and snuggling next to him. "Go on."

"As usual, I showed up without a notebook and the only thing I had to write on was a slab of frozen fish."

"Fish! You're such a carnivore, you'd think it would be a side of beef."

"I know. Anyway, I was taking notes carefully on this piece of fish, but the TV lights were very hot and it began to thaw and bits were flaking off and then it began to smell. People around me were saying, 'He's writing on a fish!' and finally made me leave."

"This is an anxiety dream if ever there were one," I said. "I can't believe that you, of all people, would have anxiety about performing your job."

"I just hide it well. I don't think you ever quite lose it completely, no matter how experienced you are. Anyway, I remember reaching down and picking up a scale on my chair that had a few words written on it and fitting it carefully back into my fish. Then, carrying it very gingerly with two hands, I went to look for a telephone so I could dictate the story."

We still had to race off to interviews once we'd finished dissecting his dream, but knowing that we'd see one another again in the evening—and in the morning and evening after that. His ties hanging in our closet, his scrap of hotel notepaper with Spanish vocabulary words (*cabida = capacity; cumplir = to achieve*) taped to the mirror: it's the closest approximation we've had of living together, albeit in about two hundred square feet of space. I love the almost-domestic rhythm to our existence. There's the usual nine-to-five routine that includes, say, nearly getting kidnapped by guerrillas or being followed by right-wing goons brandishing rifles out the tinted windows of armored station wagons, after which we'll go to a nearby stadium to run around the track. I tried jogging on the road once with Swedish Television, she in tiny shorts and a tight T-shirt, but all that expanse of majestic Nordic flesh was too much for the Salvadorans; there were three near-collisions before we completed even half a mile. Besides, the gunfire that's often heard on the streets is scary. From our hotel window I've seen local runners, an obviously adaptive species, come to a dead stop at the sound of nearby shooting—and simply turn and start jogging up the thoroughfare in the opposite direction.

The stadium's small and run down, nothing fancy. Outside, a few peasant women sell refreshments: sodas, papayas, and coconuts they hack open with machetes, the region's universal bottle opener, and stick with a straw. There aren't many people on the track at our usual hour. It's mostly paunchy, middle-aged men encased, despite the heat and humidity, in velour running suits, resolutely making their way around the pockmarked blacktop. Once, on the innermost lanes, members of a high school hurdles team were doing practice drills, shouting, "*¡Puta!*" (whore) at each other for encouragement. Dial and I will run a dozen or so laps, and while I'm stretching afterward, he'll sprint one last time around, knees and elbows pumping high.

"They make that same distance longer every year!" he invariably gasps, his T-shirt plastered to his chest with sweat. We'll return to the room to shower and make love, then order tea and apple pie to eat while watching the sky and distant volcanoes at dusk turn astonishing shades of indigo and purple. It's all sublimely romantic.

Although we're circumspect, Dial's reporters, who come and go from the office next door, must be at least vaguely aware of us in our snug little love nest. Out of the blue one evening, Dial warns me against hubris. I don't know whom he's worried about appeasing: the gods for our stunning good fortune or some of his snarkier colleagues. Before I can ask, though, he says, "I told one of the guys that we're in love and planning on getting married."

"We are?" I say. "Getting married, I mean. The being in love part I already knew about."

And then, oddly, I don't run from the room shrieking. I don't even flinch. Most uncharacteristically, I let it—almost Zen-like—wash over me. Living with Dial in this fashion has sparked a major epiphany, one that occurs to most women by, say, age fifteen: maybe I *don't* have to be my mother! Maybe I can be in a relationship, married even, and still have my brilliant career covering horrifying events. Especially as those two things together have made me happier than I ever imagined possible.

That's because the paper is running my stories as fast I can finish them, even the leders. No more waiting around forever in the front page queue and hoping that none of the people I quoted have expired in the interim; war, as the grizzled old-timers like to say, is the quickest way to get fronted. And here's the astonishing thing: the stories are apparently good. At least, the Big Boys in New York think so. I'll come in from a day of reporting, covered in three layers of dust, to find the little light illuminated above my room mail-box: a herogram from the managing editor, page-one editor, foreign editor. Even my bureau chief! On top of that, Warren, the *New York Times* correspondent whose editors finally tired of waiting for the Marines to invade Nicaragua and moved him here, says in passing, "Nice piece in the paper today." And for one full minute, sixty sweet seconds, I don't feel inadequate. I feel like I belong. It's an exhilarat-ing sensation, especially to be doing work that seems so vital. *The eyes of the world are upon us*, I think self-importantly on the way out to cover another election rally, then catch a glimpse of myself in the lobby mirror: hair like a beaver's lodge, sweat-stained shirt, pants streaked with grime.

Too bad this is what they see.

And suddenly, in almost an instant, the exhilaration is gone. Four Dutch journalists are killed on a remote road en route to film rebel encampments. The military says they were caught in crossfire, but this has the smell of the right-wing death squads all over it—espe-cially as the Dutchmen were known to be sympathetic to the guer-rillas. Officials from the US embassy hastily arrange a meeting with American reporters in the dining room of our hotel to discuss how to stay alive. Dial decides to skip it; he has an interview with some-one who viewed the journalists' bodies. I go downstairs a few min-utes early and notice a television producer, one of the many who work out of Miami, perched on the edge of the little fountain in the lobby. Barefoot and dressed in patterned pajama bottoms, he's throwing crumbs into the fountain.

"Don, what're you doing?" I ask.

"Feeding the fish."

"What fish? I've never seen fish in the fountain."

"I put goldfish in there."

"Why?"

"I just thought it would be nice to have a few fish in the fountain."

"But why?"

"I dunno. Something different." He stares at the orange-red glints darting through the water. "This country sucks," he mumbles, then pads off to his office.

The dining room is crowded and noisy. At least the organist, who performs so loudly at lunch that nobody can carry on a conversation, isn't playing. I sit at a table with another television producer, one of Don's competitors but older, who is methodically demolishing a hamburger. His correspondent, a tall, nervous fellow with glasses, crouches next to him, whispering furiously. From what I can discern, the correspondent heard something on the police-band radio about rebels moving up the Pan-American Highway and thinks they should investigate it in the morning. The producer doesn't even bother looking at him as he breathlessly suggests several story angles—just stares straight ahead and chews. Finally turning to the young man, the producer pats him on the head and says through a mouthful of fries, "You go wash your hair and leave these things to me."

The officer from the embassy's press office, usually unflappable and cheerful, is ashen-faced. "Can I get everyone to take a seat and quiet down, please?" she says, looking around the room. "I want to start out by saying that the ambassador is very concerned about what has happened, as are we in the press office. We take this matter very seriously.

"We're also very concerned about a list that has just surfaced that names thirty-five people, mostly journalists, who are supposedly targets of death squads. As many of you know who have seen the list, a lot of the people named aren't even working in the country right now. So at this moment, it's hard to ascertain its veracity."

The producer at my table interrupts to ask if the embassy thinks the military-backed death squads are now deliberating targeting journalists. The officer repeats the official line that reporters face danger from both sides when covering war; the two go back and forth at each other until someone tells the producer to shut up. The officer looks down at her notes.

"I will reiterate that all of you who are American citizens should register with the consulate so that we know you're in the country. We can be much more effective in an emergency if we already have your particulars.

"Also, be sure to use the buddy system. Always travel with someone else. If you're going up-country, check in with the SPCA office and let them know your itinerary and estimated time of return. If you're late coming back, the SPCA should contact us."

A reporter at the back of the room raises his hand. "What can the embassy actually do if we're picked up by the military or the police?"

"Well, we can make sure, through our representation, that you're afforded all the rights and privileges granted to any Salvadoran citizen . . . "

What a relief to know that my very own diplomats can make certain I'm tortured or mutilated or outright disappeared, just like the poor people of this country! "Forget it!" shouts the reporter. The rest of the officer's response is drowned out by hoots and catcalls, and the meeting disintegrates into chaos.

I'm in our room when Dial returns from talking to the journalist who'd seen the Dutch corpses. He pours himself half a glass of Nicaraguan rum and takes a long drink. "How'd it go?" I say.

"The bodies apparently had multiple gunshot wounds to the chest, arms, and legs at close range," he says. "One of them had half his head blown away."

I shudder. "Crossfire, my ass. They were murdered by the army's henchmen."

Dial is silent, his thumbs beating a little tattoo on the side of the glass. I love his hands: big, beautiful paws with broad, flat nails. Butcher's hands, he calls them.

"They were laid out in new jeans. Someone thought to go out and buy them new jeans."

The lamps dim suddenly, then go out completely. The city that only seconds ago was spread out below our window in a glittering needlepoint disappears; the guerillas must have hit the power station again. Dial gropes his way across the room for a couple of candles.

"What did the embassy people say?" he yells from the next door office.

"The usual. 'We'll be standing there, politely reminding the Salvadoran military of the Geneva Conventions on press freedom, while they're stretching you on a rack'. It was a joke."

"Well, that was worth missing."

"Oh, and my managing editor called. He said I don't have to stay if I don't want to."

Dial returns, lit candles in hand. "And do you? Want to stay, that is."

"Of course I do," I say. *But I am scared shitless.*

"You know, Alan left," he says, referring to a *New York Times* correspondent. "His name is on the list."

"But ours aren't, so I guess we're safe. Some people think the whole thing's a hoax."

"Lynda, how can you be safe covering a war?"

In the flickering candlelight, I can see his finely etched profile. The shadows smooth out the lines in his face, erasing the years in a temporary deception that grips at my silly little heart.

I say, "Promise me we won't die here."

"No, no," he says, embracing me so that I can smell his musky, animal-ardor scent. "It would be a waste to die in a stupid mess like this."

That night, I can't sleep. As if the Dutch journalists dying weren't bad enough, there's heavy gunfire close by, closer than I've heard since arriving. I don't want to wake Dial, who can slumber through a troupe of Sousaphone players slow-stepping across the room. Instead, after fruitlessly trying to calculate the trajectory a stray bullet might take— cosines? tangents? Pythagorean theorem?—I grab my pillow and crawl under the bed. *This is probably as effective*, I think, *as a duck-and-cover drill under a school desk to survive a nuclear attack.*

People turn out in huge numbers for the election, despite clashes between the military and the rebels, who boycott the vote. At one place north of the capital, where the army killed about a dozen guerrillas in a skirmish, voters simply step around the blood-soaked ground as the line slowly snakes into the polling station. My taxi driver ties a fluttering white rag to his radio antenna: this identifies us as neutral and, if we're lucky and the shooters aren't nearsighted, might keep the car from being used for target practice. I continue reporting for several more days, after which the foreign editor tells me to go home to Dallas. Dial's bosses make him stay on. I don't want to leave him or the story, but at least we managed to string out five whole weeks together—a new world record.

The bureau chief is a changed man when I return: warm, funny, at times even complimentary. *Have I suddenly sprouted a penis?* I wonder. From now on, he says, you can pretty much focus on Central America. And just like that, I'm a real foreign correspondent, flying around the region for weeks at a time on scary airlines, mostly, whose acronyms can be made into catchy little phrases that include such words as "crash" or "dead." Even more astounding is that I churn out stories, lots of them. It's not as though the spigot marked "insecurity"—an industrial-sized valve, really—got turned off; rather, there's more a rerouting around it, a kind of cerebral outer-loop bypass. My production is such that my sister Sandy, when I call her, says Mom has created a little shrine to my articles in her living room—something simple, as I envision it, perhaps in gold or silver plate with a bit of incense and maybe an offering of fruit.

Life is perfect! I think. And then, worried that I'm indulging in the very hubris Dial cautioned against, consider spitting through two fingers—*ptuh! ptuh!*—like my peasant grandmother to keep away the evil spirits, until I recall that she also, for instance, recommended bathing newborns in urine to promote good health. But, really, how can I *not* feel that everything is perfect? Especially after reading the letter Dial sends from El Salvador:

It was here that I composed for you my first letter of love and trivia,
way back in October, when I came here newly and madly in love.
How long ago that seems, so many miles and so many feelings and
so many capitals. And what changes in my life, my ways of living it,
my perceptions of myself and where I stand in time and place—and

all because of you. Sometimes I wonder: could I ever go back to being that old me? Now that I've gotten back to feeling, to really caring, I don't think I could ever return to my old ways. To measuring myself out in coffee spoons and two-week increments, to pleasant-enough times with friends who never learned that when I tell the truth, my eyes tear over.

The only what's-wrong-with-this-picture moment comes from Dial's bosses. They unceremoniously order him back to Los Angeles for a "priority conference" after some of the reporters who were in El Salvador for the election complain about our relationship. Conflict of interest, they say. Which is absolute horse doo-doo: our papers play to entirely different audiences; we write very different stories. To say nothing of how meticulous we were about keeping our expenses separate, right down to the one telephone call I made on the *Times*'s direct international line and paid for *in cash*! Dial, who is deeply angered and humiliated, writes a long memo to the paper's executives refuting the charges and informing them at the end that, anyway, we're planning to get married.

After that, Dial starts carrying around his divorce papers on the off chance I'll marry him when our assignments overlap. He brings them to Guatemala, where I don't want to wed because the military dictator is not only savage but unhinged. He brings them to Panama, where I don't want to wed because of the country's long history of being ruled by army strongmen. He brings them to Argentina, where we both wind up, serendipitously, to help cover the Falklands War. (The *Journal's* South America correspondent missed his motorcycle and needed to go home for a while.) I *really* don't want to wed here because this, undoubtedly, is the stupidest war ever. One minute there are a million people on the streets of

Buenos Aires demanding the resignation of the ruling generals, who have murdered thousands of political opponents and ruined the economy. The next thing you know, in a blatant diversionary tactic, the same generals have invaded the Falkland Islands: a bleak, wind-swept outcrop in the South Atlantic controlled by the British but claimed by the Argentines, with a population of three thousand people and five hundred thousand sheep. *And it works!* Down come the banners calling for the generals' heads and democratic elections. Up go the massive Argentine flags and patriotic slogans. The people are whipped into a wild, nationalistic fervor—until the British sail across the ocean to reclaim the islands, and the poor Argentine soldiers start coming home in body bags. I promise Dial we'll wed before my next birthday.

Which is why he calls at the end of August while I'm on assignment in Tegucigalpa. "Lynda," Dial says, "I cannot not be married to you any longer."

"I hope you're not pregnant."

"You're turning twenty-six in three days," he continues. "If you're a woman of honor, you must marry me. I'm flying down tomorrow from Mexico with Jordy and two rings, and we're going to get married."

"But I have interviews all day," I say, stupidly.

"You can still do your interviews. Just be back at the hotel by five."

Married! I set out early the next morning, but can barely focus. My mind keeps drifting; instead of taking notes, I find myself scribbling: *Lynda Schuster Torgerson. Mrs. Dial Torgerson. Señora Lynda Schuster de Torgerson.* I think, *My initials will be LST!* Then I recall that was some sort of boat used in the Normandy invasion of World War II. During a short break at noon, it dawns on me that I have nothing to wear to my wedding. After making a few inquiries, I'm directed across the main plaza, its phlegmatic fountain dribbling forth a bile-colored rivulet, to what is probably the city's only boutique. Where I'm stymied. I have a hard time matching my socks, let alone an entire outfit, and in the end decide to go virginal: white blouse, white skirt, knitted white belt—an ensemble that makes me look more like a tiered wedding cake than a blushing bride.

For my last interview, a man I don't know but whose car was described to me, picks me up at an appointed street corner and drives a circuitous route to a house on the outskirts of the city. The rendezvous is with representatives of the Contras, the guerrilla group trying to overthrow the Nicaraguan government that I'd heard rumors about the first time I visited the country. *Maybe a mani-pedi would have been a better idea on my wedding day,* I think, as we career through sketchy, labyrinthine neighborhoods. It turns out to be a remarkable interview, though. Just yesterday, I had lunch with the US ambassador who, while sweating in the considerable heat and eating lasagna that smeared around his mouth, refused to admit the Contras' very existence, let alone that the US government is providing them with aid. And now here they are, putting the lie to his words. Suddenly I look at my watch. It's 4:50 p.m. "Gentlemen, I'm very sorry but I have to go," I say. "I'm getting married in ten minutes." Not the usual sort of information imparted to guerrillas, but they take it in stride and even offer congratulations when they drop me at the hotel.

Dial is sitting on the edge of the bed in my room, dressed entirely in white. His knuckles are a matching color. "I didn't think you were going to show up," he says. Chattering about the Contra interview, I change into my wedding outfit; then Dial, Jordy, and I crowd into a taxi, along with a journalist friend enlisted as a witness, and drive downtown to the four-hundred-year-old City Hall. The toothless registrar, whom Dial bribed to perform the cere-mony—you can only get the certificate on Thursdays, and today is Tuesday—is waiting for us outside. He leers at Jordy, then at me, and says in a spray of Spanish, "Which one of you is getting mar-ried? Ha! Ha!"

We troop inside the building, an elaborate colonial relic with beamed ceilings, gilded moldings, wood-framed windows. The reg-istrar motions Dial and me to stand next to a kind of lectern. *If I faint right now, could the ceremony continue at floor level?* I think, hold-ing Dial's hands tightly. *Am I really doing this?* The registrar mumbles something unintelligible; for all I know, he's pledging me to a life of indentured dishwashing.

"Sí, quiero," I say, the equivalent of "I do."

My knees are shaking, and Dial has to steady me as I sign the register. Then he repeats the oath and signs; when he looks up, his eyes are filled with tears. It's such an overwhelming moment that we almost forget the matching rings that Dial brought from Mex-ico, delicate bands of twisted, burnished gold. We laugh and kiss and pose for Jordy to take pictures, but only one photograph comes out and even that's strangely overexposed. Dial stares steadfastly into the camera with an ebullient smile, while I, demure in vestal, all-cotton confection, avert my face; behind us, the room is suffused with a swirling pinkish aura that brings to mind poltergeists and other supernatural ephemera.

That's it? I think, as our little wedding party files outside to wait for a taxi in the rush-hour traffic. *No speeches from the registrar about the sanctity of marriage? No band breaking out in a rousing fanfare to celebrate our union? No line of well-wishers, or just passersby even, bestow-ing their congratulations?* I spent more time today with a group of guerrillas than at my own nuptials. But really, what can you expect of journalists on deadline?

Back at the hotel, we buy the only bottles of champagne to be found and share them with a Honduran air force colonel who is sitting at the bar. He regales us with an anecdote of how his helicopters came under fire that day after making a wrong turn into Nicaraguan air space. "Only a few lost!" he says merrily. We finish off the bottles—Dial furiously scribbling notes on a cocktail napkin—and retire to the room to call our families. Dial's son, Chris, is positively ecstatic upon hearing the news. Not so my father, who asks whether we *had* to tie the knot. Then I call Mom. The telephone line is bad, and I have to shout over what sounds like copulating gerbils.

"Hi, Mom. I'm calling from Honduras. How are you?"

"So nice to hear from you! I'm just fine, dear. And you?"

"I'm married."

Dead silence. Only now does it occur to me that maybe the woman who, for all those years, changed my diapers, cleaned up my vomit, cooked my meals, listened to my grievances, wiped away my tears, watched me grow—might have wanted to be informed that I, her daughter, was planning to get married.

CHAPTER FOUR

MEXICO, 1983

Several months later, Dial writes from Guatemala:

> *The thought came to me when I was trying to call you this morning that I still think of you as a lover, not as a wife. Although I left the message at your office: tell her that her husband called. The fact that we're married doesn't change at all the way my heart leaps up at the thought of hearing your voice, or the disappointment which comes if I don't get to hear it. Nor does it change the way I miss you in the morning when I awaken and you're not there.*

He addresses it to Señora Lynda Schuster de Torgerson, Reforma

46, Mexico. That's my office in Mexico City. An airless cubby small enough to make even a monk feel claustrophobic, it's tucked into a corner of the Associated Press bureau and requires six flights of winding, lung-popping (especially at this altitude) stairs to reach. There's an elevator, but I've been loath to use it ever since an electrical power surge trapped the watchman between floors overnight, so traumatizing him that he now refuses to ascend anything higher than a footstool.

The AP has a half dozen or so reporters here, babbling away in Spanish and typing frenetically on their computers under yellow fluorescent lights. Being in the same space as a news agency is useful, allowing me to be among the first to know if, for instance, Armageddon occurs, but most days I keep my door closed to block out the noise. This sometimes endangers my computer, though. When the tiny window fan falters and my office gets too hot, the display monitor goes all frizzy and begins pulsating, like something out of a 1950s flying saucer movie. Then I have to figure out a way to file my articles to New York through the AP—just about the only vestige of my old life working in Central America.

I no longer cover that beat because—yet again—the gods, miraculously, smiled upon me. This happened not long after our wedding, and I discovered that a journalistic marriage differs little from a journalistic romance: everything is dictated by the story. Our honeymoon was a reporting trip to Honduras's interior, where we became hopelessly lost and ended up at the Pacific Ocean, staring across an inlet at Nicaragua. Dial had to hurry back to Mexico two days later, after the president decided to nationalize the banking system. We resumed our random-molecule existence, me despairing that we'd ever have a life together, when the *Journal's* Mexico correspondent suddenly asked to be transferred back to the United

States for the sake of his newly pregnant wife. The managing editor tracked me down in El Salvador to offer the post. I immediately telephoned Dial at home in Mexico City to tell him the news; there was a loud *clunk,* as if the receiver had been dropped on the floor, and I heard him call out from a distance, "I'm doing a one-man cha-cha-cha down the hallway in celebration!"

After the verdant, rain-scrubbed purity of Central America, Mexico City is a dump. Smog stains the sky a permanent brown-pink, as if some crazed preschooler who hadn't yet mastered combining crayon colors was let loose across the heavens. This is a city that's sniffed before seen: its cloying, sickly-sweet odor steals into the cabin of inbound airplanes while the jets are still thousands of feet above the ground and nowhere close to landing. Once visible, though, the metropolis spools out endlessly for miles in every direction, eighteen-million-people wide. Only during Semana Santa, Holy Week, when seventeen million of those people evacuate for the seashore and the smog lifts, do you suddenly observe two snow-capped volcanoes, Popocatépetl and Iztaccihuatl, and realize how beautiful the place must have been once.

The neighborhoods in Mexico City all seem to have a theme. The refrigeration district—FREEZERS AT DOUBLE-DISCOUNT PRICES!—is just beyond the airport; the furniture area after that; and so on. Our apartment is in Colonia Juarez, near the downtown. Its motif is Europe. The streets all bear names of cities on the continent: Varsovia (Warsaw), Londres (London), Hamburgo (Hamburg)—although it would take a bottle of tequila, with maybe a hallucinogenic mushroom or two thrown in for good measure, to notice any resemblance. Tourism also seems to be part of the idea. But that's confined to the Zona Rosa, the district of nightclubs and restaurants and street vendors, most of them indigenous, whose buckets of flowers for sale are wild explosions of color on the otherwise dingy thoroughfares.

Our apartment is light and airy and looks out on several tireless cars beached on cinder blocks across the street. We furnish it with the appliances I shipped from Dallas, along with white tufted sofas purchased in the furniture section of town. After only a few weeks, though, the upholstery begins to exude the smog scent, a kind of atmospheric body odor. Our housekeeper, Flor, scrubs the fabric with laundry soap, but within a month, maybe two, the stink returns. The sofas probably bore Flor, who is small and moonfaced and wears her black hair in pigtails entwined with red ribbons; interest-wise, they cannot compete with my shoes. Any time I pop into the apartment unexpectedly, she's curled up cozily in the bedroom closet, gently caressing the flats and pumps with a cloth. Not so Dial's footwear, which remain oddly untouched and with a permanent coating of dust.

Covering Mexico full-time elevates me in *Journal*-world. My editors consider it important because of the country's foreign debt crisis, something that evidently threatens the very stability of our solar system, if not the Milky Way. This is a story reported by eating lunch. Just about every day, I meet at one grand restaurant or another at the request of the major players—bankers, economists, officials from the Ministry of Treasury, representatives from multinational lending agencies—to yak about debt-to-GDP ratios and the Exchange Stabilization Fund, which I pretend to understand and, more importantly, care deeply about. When what I'm really concentrating on is, say, my source's widow's peak and trying to decide, in an effort to stay awake, whether it's his hair or just an excellent toupee. *How did these people find the time to create such a huge financial mess?* I wonder, stumbling away from yet another five-hour marathon of four courses and two bottles of wine, followed by coffee and brandy. And whiskey.

It seems crazy to admit, but I miss the adrenaline-stoked adventure of reporting on Central America's wars. There, at least, the danger to your life is from something truly dramatic like bombs or bullets, not elevated cholesterol or alcohol poisoning. But it's not the perilous part that I miss, it's the people: talking to them about their lives and sending out their stories to a world I imagine, in my crusading pompousness, as otherwise unknowing or indifferent. Mexico, a country with a rich history and culture, has plenty of such tales—but I'm stuck listening to Citicorp and Chase. Worst of all, I miss Dial. Oddly, I see less of him now because he has to spend so much time covering the conflicts in El Salvador and on the Honduran border with Nicaragua. But at least we have a home together.

And, as he likes to remind me, we get to keep our underwear in the same chest of drawers.

Dial says, "So when are you going to pull the plug?"

We're on the balcony of our apartment, painting bookshelves ordered from the States. Dial managed to steal a rare weekend at home. In a raggedy, salmon-colored T-shirt and baseball cap with BEETHOVEN emblazoned across the front—a gift from Jordy—he slowly stirs a can of primer. The blare of Mexico City's perpetual traffic jam surrounds us in a schizophrenic mash-up.

I say, "What do you mean?"

"I mean, when are you going to have your IUD removed so we can have a baby?"

Deep breath. "I don't know," I say, and escape to the kitchen to fetch him a cool beer.

Babies? I think, pawing through drawers to find where Flor hid the bottle opener. *Getting married was one thing, but babies? Helpless little things that spit up and cry and can't even tell you whether theirs is an existentialist or gastric crisis?* I know that he adores Jordy and Chris and that their childhood was the happiest time of his life, which is probably why he longs to have another. But I don't feel the same pull. If we have to have something small and warm in our lives, why not a hamster? That, at least, doesn't conjure up visions of Detroit and domesticity and my mother's existence, all things I thought I had so cleverly excised with my glamorous life as a foreign correspondent.

Not that I've kept Mom and the rest of my clan from him. We've been to Detroit a few times now, most notably to be remarried by a rabbi in my sister Sandy's living room with Jordy and Chris and my family in attendance. A less-than-joyous occasion, to be sure. Sandy, a militant vegan, took it upon herself to order the wedding cake. "Carob?" Dial said, incredulously. "When you can have *chocolate?*" My grandmother Nanny sat in a rocking chair for the entire event, swaying and muttering under her breath about Dial's advanced age, *older even than the bride's father!* Dad—now wedded to Gerrie, his Dutch girlfriend, and again living in Detroit with my new sister, Tamara—drank too much and had an ulcer attack that laid him out on Sandy's sofa. And then there was Mom: glowering nonstop at Dad while trying to play mother-of-the-bride and, at the same time, sidle up to me. When all I wanted from her was—what? To go back magically in time and be the mother I'd always hoped for? Transform herself into someone whom I, in my utter lack of charitableness, most likely would never even acknowledge?

Dial said it was like wandering into the middle of a Tolstoy novel. Back on the terrace, I hand him the frosted mug and kiss the nape of his neck, red and rough like a farmer's from too much time in the tropical sun.

"Thank you," he says.

I say, "What about my brilliant career?"

"What about it?"

"Won't I have to take a lot of time off if we have a baby?"

"Oh, don't worry about that. I'll take a leave of absence to write a novel or something and to watch the baby. Or maybe I'll leave the *Times* altogether."

"There's always that junior draftsman thing," I say, replacing the lid on the primer container. "Seriously, you'd give up journalism?"

"If we could swing it financially and it would mean we could have a child together, then yes. I've done it before, you know."

"Done what?"

"Taken time off. I did it to be with Chris, when he was little."

"Why?"

"Well, now he's nice and charming, and all the mothers of the girls he dates love him. But he was hyperactive as a kid and used to throw all his food on the wall. He drove Ellen (Dial's ex-wife) crazy. I'd come home from work and find the two of them glaring at each other from across the room. So I took a year off to build a house and be with him."

"Did it help?"

"I think so. Maybe he just got older and outgrew it. Anyway, we certainly got closer."

Dial wipes the brown stain off his hands and takes a sip of beer. "I remember that he sent away for a Jolly Green Giant kite that year. We got it in the mail a month or so later, and went to a hilltop on a windy fall day with four balls of string. The Jolly Green Giant went out into the afternoon, a ball of string at a time, until it was a thousand feet away. We could feel the tug of it, like a giant fish we'd caught in the sky." Dial stares off into the polluted distance. "When we reeled it back in, I said, 'Chris, you must remember today, because in all your life you'll probably only have three or four great kite-flying days.' And he said, 'I love you, Dad,' and I almost cried."

He swallows hard. "The next week, the Jolly Green Giant got stepped on, and we never had a kite-flying day like that again."

His story puts to shame any counterargument; how could you have an anecdote like that about a rodent, even one with a running wheel? I suddenly notice the time. "I've got to go," I say. "I have to file the labor union story for tomorrow's paper."

Dial isn't leaving for Tegucigalpa until later in the afternoon. He washes the paintbrushes while I change clothes and is standing at the French doors, admiring his handiwork drying on the terrace, when I come to say goodbye. Putting my arms around him from behind, I bury my face in his solvent-scented shirt. "I love you," I say, the words muffled.

He whirls around. "Don't worry about having a baby," he says, holding me. "We have world enough and time."

A couple of nights later, I'm sitting in a gaudy nightclub in the Zona Rosa, watching a drunk American at the next table pour a thin stream of margarita into the cleavage of his companion. She whoops and, giggling, reciprocates with a good measure of her drink that lands across, rather than down, his shirt. The man loudly signals the waiter for more margaritas: the couple take a few sips, then pick up where they left off basting one another. The woman collapses in a marinated heap on the floor.

The club is half empty, despite being home to the oldest mariachi performer in Mexico. I have an interview with him, an attempt at a feature story that doesn't have the word "debt" in it, but not until after he's finished two shows. This requires sitting through hours of his music as backdrop to smashed American tourists, who inexplicably prefer wearing their tequila to drinking it, and to the assignations of several middle-aged Mexican men with slicked-back, Brilliantined hair. They're out with young women, some no older than teenagers—undoubtedly their daughters' ages—and nervously wave away the roving photographers trying to take their pictures as souvenir. *What a nice keepsake that would make,* I think, *for the wife waiting at home.*

I don't get back to the apartment until well after midnight. As usual, I call Dial to say goodnight. The Mexican telephone system, which hasn't seen much improvement since Alexander Graham Bell's initial invention, requires numerous attempts to connect to Honduras; when I finally reach the hotel in Tegucigalpa, the receptionist lets the phone in Dial's room ring several times, then comes on the line to say that Señor Torgerson must be out. Now I remember: when we spoke last night, Dial said he was going down to the Nicaraguan border for a day or two and would leave his things at the hotel. I tell the receptionist to leave a message in his mailbox saying that his wife called.

Then I pour myself a glass of grape juice and settle in to read a *New York Times* that's only a week old, a rare find. The telephone rings. *It's Dial,* I think. *Maybe he didn't go to the border after all. Maybe he went to the hotel bar for a nightcap and just got my message.*

But it's Eloy, the Associated Press bureau chief. He's crying, sobbing almost, which prompts an odd reaction in me. In a freeze-
framed instant, I think: *Hang up the phone. It's one o'clock in the
morning, the AP bureau chief is on the line, and he's crying. You know exactly what he's going to tell you. But if you don't hear it, nothing will have
happened. So hang up.*

"Hi, Eloy," I say.

"Lynda, has anyone phoned you tonight?"

"No, I've been out."

"You need to call the *Los Angeles Times.*"

"What happened?"

"Just call them."

"Eloy, you know how hard it is to make overseas calls from here.
What's happened?"

"It's Dial." Eloy's weeping so hard I can barely understand him.
"He's had an accident."

"Is he alive?"

"No, Lynda, he's dead."

Four words, and just like that, the earth shifts ninety degrees
beneath your feet. Had Eloy said, "Yes, Lynda, but he's hurt," my
world would have remained essentially intact, my life continuing on
the same trajectory. But he didn't, and everything changed.

I somehow reach the *Los Angeles Times* and am connected with the
managing editor. He reads me the paper's press release, something
about a rocket-propelled grenade being fired from Nicaragua's side of
the border—the Honduran government's initial explanation of what
happened—that killed Dial and a photographer and decimated their
car. The editor is startlingly laconic, as though reporting on traffic
congestion or the weather. After reciting the statement, he tells me
that the foreign editor is trying to get to Honduras and hangs up.

I'm left in the stillness of the night, not knowing what to do.

The telephone rings again. It's the duty officer from the State Department in Washington, informing me of Dial's death. Oh, and by the way, the officer says, the Honduran government is going to bury him in Tegucigalpa if his body isn't claimed by three o'clock this afternoon. This is too much—as if just being told that your husband is dead isn't sufficient. "But there aren't any commercial flights to Honduras today!" I scream at the man. "I can't get there by three o'clock! Stop them! You must stop them!"

The rest of the night is a delirium of telephoning. I call every foreign correspondent I know in Mexico to see if anyone has a way down to Honduras. They don't. I call the television correspondents based in Miami, trying to hitch a ride on one of their small planes. No one can land in Mexico. A kindly reporter pages through several US directories, reading off the telephone numbers of air charter services in Miami, Dallas, Houston, and Los Angeles. I call them all and finally find one open at this late hour, but the company doesn't have permission to land in Mexico. I call the press attaché at the US embassy here and insist that he wake up the ambassador to get me landing rights. I call the *Los Angeles Times* again to demand—from a junior copy editor, the only person still on duty—the use of the corporate jet. I call the *Journal* to demand the same, but no one answers. I call the US consular officer in Tegucigalpa to beg her not to let Dial be buried there. I call Jordy and Chris, who are very sweet and brave, no easy thing; their mother died of cancer exactly two months before. I call Mom. I call Dad. I call Sandy. I call Bev. I call and call, in between crying, unable to stop this mad frenzy of dialing, afraid of being alone in our hushed apartment.

The weird pea soup glow of a Mexico City dawn begins to filter through the window. I will never again see a sunrise with him, polluted or otherwise—an unbearable realization. I stumble downstairs to look for a taxi; I need to talk to Lilia, my secretary, who doesn't have a telephone. The cab driver shudders when he sees my swollen, mascara-streaked face.

At Lilia's house, I pound on the door, softly sobbing, "Wake up, please wake up." Workers glance at me as they pass on the street. Lilia finally answers, and I fall into her arms; from now on she— thankfully—is in charge. She drives us back to the apartment and within a couple of hours has found a Mexican air charter company to fly me to Honduras. Also, and not without difficulty, she manages to procure landing rights for both Tegucigalpa and Los Angeles, the latter being where Chris and Jordy live and where I want to bury Dial.

The apartment fills with journalists come to help. Eloy brings hundreds of dollars in cash to pay for the aircraft's refueling along the way; the charter company said I couldn't use a credit card. Chris, the The *Washington Post*'s correspondent, offers himself as escort for the journey. His wife, Carole, follows me from room to room with a spoonful of scrambled egg. "Eat," she urges. "You must eat." Various reporters from American papers and news services enfold me in hugs, whispering their regrets in my ear. I, meanwhile, am fixated on finding proper widow's attire. Maybe this focusing on the trivial and controllable is a normal response to shock, like worrying about a zit when you've been diagnosed with bubonic plague. All I care about right now is black clothing. In my bedroom, I dump the contents of my drawers on the bed and empty the closet, but only come up with thick, black-patterned stockings, of a type suited to an evening out in the Arctic. I'm struggling to pull them over my sweaty legs when Lilia yells from the living room that I have to hurry. It's time to go.

Besides the three o'clock deadline to arrive in Honduras, the reason for the haste is that Tegucigalpa's airport has no runway lights. We need to be airborne, on our way to Los Angeles with the body, before dusk. I make two last calls before ducking out the door: to the *Journal's* managing editor in New York, to inform him of my itinerary; and to the consular officer at the US embassy in Honduras, requesting that she have Dial's body waiting on the airport tarmac.

And that she please keep away the press.

There's less room inside the six-seater jet than I imagined. Even though Chris and I sit on opposite sides of the aisle facing the cockpit, our arms are practically touching. I don't even bother to fasten my seatbelt. For the first time in my life, I understand the allure of suicide. To obliterate memory, to slip free of crushing, merciless pain, to feel nothing—all seem irresistible. I can't even watch the flight attendant serve Chris a beer without remembering the way Dial gripped his glass with both hands, thumbs tapping his endearing little tattoo on the sides. *Let's just end this now*, I think, with every bump and stomach-clenching dip the airplane takes.

The urge for oblivion only intensifies as we approach Tegucigalpa. The plane passes over the familiar squat houses clustered on hillsides, banks hard, and lands on a runway flanked by lines of drying laundry. It's well before three o'clock, but the place is deserted. No hearse, no body, nothing; only shimmery undulations of heat rising off the tarmac. Then I notice the phalanx of television cameramen on the airport's observation deck. The same deck where, on a similar sun-splattered afternoon a few months ago, Dial caught a strand of my hair between his fingers and kissed it, murmuring, "See how it glows golden-red in this light." I look away.

Al, the *Los Angeles Times'* foreign editor, suddenly appears on the tarmac, unshaven and bedraggled; he too has been up all night. The US ambassador to Honduras is with him. He'll later become President George W. Bush's ambassador to the United Nations, then to Iraq, as well as the first ever Director of National Intelligence. For now, though, Honduras is his concern, which is why he and I aren't on good terms. Maybe he felt offended that after feeding me lasagna in his sweltering residence, I still didn't believe his denials about the Contras. After my story appeared, the ambassador flew to New York to complain to the *Journal's* editors—not to dispute the piece's accuracy, just its right to exist. Unhelpful, the ambassador said. The hug he gives me is little more than perfunctory, the bodily equivalent of an air kiss. He explains the hearse's absence: to enter California legally, Dial's body must be in a hermetically sealed casket. Such a box won't fit in our little plane, which means we'll have to spend the night in Tegucigalpa and take a commercial flight to Los Angeles tomorrow.

I can't spend the night here. I can't stay in the city where Dial and I were so recently married. I can't sleep in the hotel where, on our wedding night, we turned off the lamps and opened the curtains and gazed at the hills aglitter with thousands of little lights. And awoke the next morning to a rooster sounding like it had whooping cough and a billboard below our room that read: DON JUAN—BEST FOOD IN TOWN—COME ON DOWN. I communicate this to Chris in furious whispers, trying not to cry. I really don't want to cry in front of the ambassador.

The embassy's consular officer materializes, asking for our passports. Chris walks to the terminal with her and the ambassador.

Alone on the tarmac, I feel another wave of weeping beginning to crest and look heavenward to hold it back, taking deep breaths. The sky is a dazzling azure. *How could he die here, of all places? How could he die at all?* Just then, the consular officer returns to say the ambassador will try to work something out about the casket. In the meantime, though, we need to go to the embassy to collect Dial's things and sign documents. Knowing my desire to avoid the press, the officer directs her driver to a back entrance of the chancery. Here's sweet irony: the journalist not wanting to talk. But what can I say? They're colleagues, true; some are even friends. Seen now from the other side, though, they're intrusive and unfeeling, contemptible almost.

The officer brings me the worn leather carryall that Dial left in his hotel room. Alone, I bury my nose in every shirt, every pullover, trying to detect his salty-sweet scent. Not a single stitch of natural fiber in the entire lot. He was always trying to convert me to his synthetic ways. "See how easy they are to wash!" he'd say, stomping shampoo suds on his clothes in the shower like harvested grapes. After they'd dried, he'd roll the shirts and trousers up tightly and squeeze them into the little carryall, proclaiming, "An entire wardrobe and nary a wrinkle!"

My reverie is interrupted by Susana, Dial's Honduran stringer, who was the last person to see him alive in the capital. Always small and thin, now she looks positively spectral. "Lynda, I was supposed to go with him," she says, embracing me. "I should be dead now, too."

I stare at her, dumbfounded. "What do you mean?"

"Dial had an interview with one of the Contras here in Tegucigalpa who told him there was going to be a big attack down by the border and that he should go there to see the fighting," she says.

"Dial got all excited and started poring over a map with this guy. Then he said to me, 'Go rent a car.'" She pauses to blow her nose. "I was going to drive; you know how Dial always gets lost driving in the countryside. And a photographer was coming along to take pictures.

"So I went off to rent a car and met Dial back at the hotel to give him the keys. We agreed to go at five thirty in the morning, but as I was leaving, he suddenly said, 'I think you'd better stay behind tomorrow.'" Susana can barely breathe, she's crying so hard. "I said, 'No, no, you need me along.' And he said, 'No, you stay here and keep pestering that damned army colonel we've been trying to see with the questions I have.'"

The consular officer pokes her head in the door to say the ambassador managed to get the rule about the casket waived; I can take Dial home in a body bag. But we have to hurry if I'm going to leave before sunset, and there's paperwork to finish.

I can take Dial home in a body bag, I think. *What's wrong with this sentence?*

Susana grips me in a fierce, breath-sucking hug. "Don't look at his body," she whispers in my ear. "I had to identify it at the morgue. This isn't the way you want to remember him."

Then she's gone. I'm shaking so violently the consular officer has to guide me through the small mound of documents, indicating where to sign. I stuff Dial's clothes into the carryall and suddenly realize his passport and notebook, always so meticulously stowed in his breast pocket, are missing. The officer says they didn't find them on his body.

Al and Chris are waiting for us in the embassy's minivan. The sun is casting long shadows across the runway by the time we reach the aircraft; television cameras still line the observation deck. A hearse draws up, and two men pull something from the back that looks like a sleeping bag. The realization that Dial—or what remains of him—is in there makes me break down, my face in my hands. Al whispers, "The TV crews are filming you," and gently leads me around to the other side of the plane, out of sight.

It takes a few minutes for me to regain my composure; we walk back once the hearse has departed, but a producer I know and her cameraman pursue us across the tarmac. "Jesus Christ, he was your friend too, Viviana," I shout. "Can't you be human for once?" She motions to the cameraman, who snaps off his equipment.

The pilot offers his apologies and helps me into the plane. The body bag is lying on the floor in the aisle; I virtually have to step over it to get to my seat. The sight is devastating: to behold your husband stowed on the floor like carry-on luggage is beyond comprehension. The pilot starts the engines and taxis to the end of the landing strip. I stare out the window at the fast-fading light, blinking hard to hold back the tears. The plane gathers power, hurtles down the runway, and ascends, leaving behind the hovels, the swaying clotheslines, the children wildly waving goodbye.

Airborne, the flight attendant fills enormous tumblers with vodka and a splash of tonic for Chris and Al. They down the drinks like soda. She offers to make one for me, but I refuse. I can't stop looking at the bag: every curve, every projection, is outlined under the thin material. *There's almost nothing inside*, I think. And it takes all the restraint I can muster to keep from getting down on the floor, putting my arms around whatever remains of Dial and holding him one last time.

After a while, my companions fall into an intoxicated sleep. The sun hangs just below the port window, the sky smeared an incandescent purple-pink. Al stirs suddenly, opens his eyes, and says,

"My God, it's my thirty-first wedding anniversary," then goes back to sleep.

Dial and I never even made it to one year.

On and on we fly, hurtling through a dusk of matchless beauty: the glory of the heavens at my elbow, the pieces of my husband at my feet.

PART TWO

CHAPTER FIVE

THE MIDDLE EAST, 1984

The airplane to Beirut stops at the far end of the runway, miles, it seems, from the terminal. "Our insurance company won't let us get close to the building," the flight attendant explains helpfully, while I'm waiting at the forward door for a mobile staircase to be pushed out to the aircraft. "It's been hit by gunfire too many times." I'm the only passenger to exit the almost-full plane, which is continuing on to Damascus. *Maybe the crew can call a cab to take me to the terminal,* I think, standing on the tarmac and squinting at it in the distance. "Good luck!" the attendant yells, throwing my bag down after me, then hastily pulling shut the door.

At the front desk of the sole hotel still functioning in West Beirut, the manager politely asks, "Would you like a room on the car bomb side or the rocket side?" In the midst of a nasty civil war like Lebanon's, this is the vague equivalent of offering a view of the mountains or the pool. The current weapon of choice being a vehicle packed with plastique—two hundred and forty-three US Marines have recently been annihilated in their barracks by just such a device—I opt for a room on the rocket side, but on the highest floor. This is based on the truly laughable assumption that I can ride any bomb explosion down as the building collapses.

The traffic jams here—a constant in a city where the fighting has obliterated most signal lights and turned streets into small canyons—just about send me over the edge. Any of the stalled cars around me could be wired as mobile missiles. I nervously try to make eye contact with the driver in the vehicle to the left, then the one to the right, as if showing how friendly I am might make him pause before pressing the detonator. *She looks nice,* he'd think, *maybe I'll wait until the next intersection.* This absurd attempt at bonding does nothing, of course, to placate all the other irate drivers, any of whom, in a blinding, eardrum-erupting moment, could blow everything to smithereens. Part of me wants it to happen: never to have to feel or think again—it would be so easy, welcomed even. But another part, the primal survival mechanism, is terrified, imagining me and everyone else splattered across the wide boulevard.

This is where my editors send me to recover after Dial's death.

I probably could have requested a slightly more cheerful place, but dealing with the aftermath of retrieving Dial's body left little time or energy to think. The Dallas bureau chief called almost immediately after we landed in Los Angeles. He was astonishingly kind; maybe tragedy brought out the best in him.

"I've always known you could finesse just about anything, Lynda," he said. "And I knew you'd be able to get through this, too. Although the past twenty-four hours must have been hell."

"Thank you," I said. "I wasn't worried so much about the past twenty-four hours as I am about the next twenty-four years"—and immediately regretted this little leak of self-pity. *Don't start*, I told myself, *or you won't be able to stop*.

How could I feel sorry for myself when Chris and Jordy, just like that, lost both their parents within the span of a couple of months? Jordy, who had much of her father in her, was mostly stoic, but not Chris. He wanted no mention of a deity at the funeral service. "After all that's happened," Chris said, "I'm not sure I believe in God." Then, because I couldn't bear to do it, he and his stepfather went off to pick out a cemetery plot and casket. What does one look for in the latter, anyway? Sumptuous finish? Sleek design? Comfort? Meanwhile, Jordy, who had just earned her driver's license, offered to help me find a dress for the funeral.

At an upscale department store, I mechanically flipped through a rack of suits, not focusing on any of them. Just ten months ago, I was shopping for my wedding; clotheswise, at least, being a widow seemed easier than being a bride. *Something simple in sackcloth*, I thought. A saleswoman spied us from across the room; Jordy intercepted her before she could descend on me and whispered in her ear. I heard her gasp, "But she's so young!" The saleswoman directed us to another rack, speaking slowly and over-enunciating. This seemed to be the new default in talking to me, as if losing a loved one caused hearing impairment or regression to second grade language skills. I knew that people meant well and were trying to convey sympathy;

they probably just felt awkward. Death *is* awkward. Even talking about sex with a middle schooler is less weird than considering personal extinction. Still, the saleswoman was helpful, expertly zeroing in, amid the prints and patterns, on a basic black dress. My new go-to for funerals: what every twenty-six-year-old needed!

Back at Jordy's and Chris's house, I suddenly noticed my wedding band. *What should I do with it? I'm no longer married.* In a panic, I called the funeral home; perhaps I could bury my ring with Dial's?

After a long pause, the mortician said, "There isn't a ring."

"What? You mean someone took it? Maybe between the time he died and when his body was recovered?"

Another pause. "No."

"Then what?"

The mortician cleared his throat. "There are no hands."

There are no hands. Undertaker-speak. Not, "He doesn't have any hands," or "His hands were destroyed," but a sentence lacking— quite literally—a subject, as if Dial had been reduced to mere parts. *There are no hands.* There was no more Dial, so why should such a small detail have felt so haunting?

On the morning of the funeral, I awoke to find that I had my period. Oddly, this seemed more real than Dial's death. Here was something palpable, concrete, conclusive: I would never have a child with him. Ironic, too, given our last conversation in Mexico City, the one about me pulling the plug and getting pregnant. My resistance now seemed so cavalier and foolhardy; I would readily agree to ten babies, somehow nursing them all simultaneously, sow-like, if it meant I could have him back.

The little chapel where the service was being held quickly filled with reporters and editors from the *Los Angeles Times* and other California news organizations. As the relatives of the deceased, we had our own seating area of several pews off to the side at the front, shielded by a curtain. I almost fainted when I first saw Hunter, Dial's brother, whom I'd never met. *Maybe this was all a mistake!* I thought, stunned by the uncanny resemblance. I could barely take my eyes off him, even when my family trooped in.

The *Los Angeles Times* had, most kindly, flown them out from Detroit. Of all people, you'd think my parents and siblings would've been able to be themselves in my presence—but there they were, talking in hushed tones and tiptoeing around like beginner ballerinas. Dad, who'd always had an extreme phobia about death, apparently warned my sisters to be careful when speaking with me. What was he afraid would happen? That I'd start sobbing? Openly mourning? Isn't that what you're supposed to do when someone dies? Or did he think it was infectious?

Mom, meanwhile, was even more at a loss than usual trying to engage me. She threw her arm around my shoulders and asked, "How are you?"

"How do you think?" I said.

She flinched. "You know that I love you."

I didn't respond. Her arm on my shoulders felt like a log. Obviously, she just wanted to comfort me; even I could see that. But I figured that grieving gave me license to be especially dismissive and, if not outright self-pitying, then at least self-indulgent. Why should I bother with compassion for her when the gods had treated *me* so cruelly?

Jordy, Chris, and I sat together in the front pew during the service. Through the mesh curtain, we had a good view of Dial's casket: highly varnished wood with a single rose placed across the lid. That was it, as far as flowers went. I had requested people send money to a fund for Central American war refugees instead of floral arrangements. Close as we were, though, I could barely hear the proceedings. A couple of rows back, my nephew Jacob, Sandy's infant son, was crying, screeching almost. Sandy made no move to take him out of the room, and I was too paralyzed to turn around to ask her to leave. So during the eulogy, I just joined in: howling like a dog at the moon, baying at the universe's injustice, all pretense at self-control and decorum out the window.

I had asked a *Washington Post* reporter, who worked with Dial in Jerusalem and now covered Central America, to make the speech. Which was beautiful, from what I could discern. Then again, he'd only known Dial in that fleeting, superficial way of foreign correspondents: more bonhomie-of-strangers-singing-around-a-campfire, than devotion-of-brethren-bound-by-a-blood-oath. *Should I have asked an editor who was with Dial on the city desk instead? One of his friends?* But who *were* his friends? What did I know of him, honestly? We'd been together for so little time, not even two years. His brother's looks certainly blindsided me. As did the letters from assorted women around the world that had been arriving almost daily at the kids' house: *Dear Lynda: I don't know you, and you don't know me, but I loved Dial, too.*

My husband, the heartbreaker? And this was supposed to be a consolation?

Afterward, we all trudged up the cemetery hill for the graveside rites. Wooly-headed from all the crying, I had a vague impression of trees, blinding sunshine, cars whizzing by on the freeway below. Then the coffin was being lowered into the ground. *Why did everything with Dial always happen so quickly?* I stared at the casket, not knowing if I should whisper something or touch it one last time. Instead, I kissed the rose I'd been clutching and gingerly laid it next to the other one on the lid.

And then had to grasp Jordy to keep my knees from buckling.

Later, I went to talk with Neil, who had flown out from Dallas. The *Journal's* managing editor had called when I first arrived in Los Angeles, asking whom I wanted to represent the newspaper at the funeral. "Neil," I said immediately, only to hear later that the managing editor was offended. So I had to call back to invite him as well. *Hell, bring everyone!* I wanted to shout. *We'll make it a party!* Then, always the soul of sensitivity, he told me there had been a bet going in the New York newsroom the day after Dial died as to whether I'd make the three o'clock deadline to claim his body in Honduras—but didn't say whether he'd made or lost money.

Neil, who had sat next to the managing editor during the service, now stood by himself off to one side. He was wearing a three-piece suit; I'd never seen him so dressed up.

"You look like a banker," I said.

"Thanks," he said. "It's my funeral outfit."

"Did the service sound awful, with my nephew screaming his head off like that?"

"Nah, it seemed kind of appropriate. You know, young life and all that."

"Thanks. I really appreciate you coming."

"It was nothing. I even sat next to the big boss."

"I saw," I said. "And you didn't knife him. I'm proud of you."

"Inflicting bodily harm did cross my mind. But this didn't strike me as the right venue."

"Neil, am I going to be okay?"

"You're going to be just fine, Schuster," he said, balancing on his cane and enveloping me in a one-armed hug,

It certainly didn't feel that way, especially when I had to wade through the hundreds of letters, telegrams, and telexes that came to the kids' house, where I was staying for a while. Notes from journalists in Atlanta, Beijing, Boston, Buenos Aires, Cairo, Chicago, Dallas, Houston, Jerusalem, Johannesburg, Los Angeles, London, Manila, Moscow, Nairobi, New York, Rio de Janeiro, Rome, Tokyo, Washington; from the Foreign Correspondents' Associations in Hong Kong, Israel, El Salvador, Florida; from the US ambassadors in Mexico and Honduras, the US embassies in Nicaragua and Panama, the consulates of Australia, Britain, France, and Israel in Los Angeles; from senators, congressmen, and the vice president of Honduras; from bankers, businessmen, and the Anti-Defamation League of B'nai Brith; and from total strangers, like the woman whose husband had been killed forty years—*forty years!*—earlier in World War II and wrote, *I know your pain so well.*

I read every last one, and cried over them all. *When* does *the pain stop?* No one had ever died on me before—Bubbe and Zayde excluded, but they were old—so I was clueless as to how grief worked. Why wasn't this taught in schools? Home economics, personal hygiene, driver's education—all that I got in preparation for adulthood. But nothing on death.

It would have been difficult enough if Dial had succumbed to, say, your garden-variety malady or an accident. But at least I'd know the circumstances of his death, a small solace. In this instance, though, my misery was compounded by each new detail that kept cropping up. Not long after the funeral, for one reason or another I called the Los Angeles coroner who examined Dial's corpse. We got to talking about what happened to Dial and the photographer; when I mentioned the Honduran government's explanation that they had been killed by a rocket-propelled grenade, he cut me off. "Impossible," he said. "That would have created a downward explosion. The way the bodies were mutilated indicated a massive upward momentum of the charge."

The way the bodies were mutilated.

His assertion squared with what Juan, a friend and reporter for
the Miami paper, discovered when he and his photographer went
to the site of the attack. There they saw the demolished white
Toyota rental. The force of the explosion had shot it into the air,
then split the body in half; the motor, blown out of the chassis,
landed a football field away. The blast left a crater six feet in diam-
eter. More significantly, they also saw landmines embedded in the
road. They took pictures of everything and showed them to officials at the US embassy in Tegucigalpa, who suddenly decided,
along with the Honduran government, that the occupants of the
car weren't killed by a grenade, but by a Nicaraguan-planted land-
mine.

Other military analysts, though, who saw the photographs believed the charges were of a type used only by the Contras—the
US-supported guerrillas. *My tax dollars at work?* That possibility
alone was horrifying, but then I learned the mines were command,
not pressure, detonated. Which meant this wasn't a random accident of war. Several other vehicles drove the very same route as
Dial, before and after him, on that day. Someone had been sitting
by the side of the road, waiting for Dial's car to pass—and pushed
a trigger.

Why would anyone want to murder him? I wondered, opening a
small parcel that had just arrived, bearing a Miami postmark. Out
popped Dial's passport and notebook, caked with dried blood and
bits of desiccated flesh. The odor alone, to say nothing of the grisli-
ness, made me run, retching, to the bathroom. *The bastards had his
things all along!* But which bastards? The package had no return
address, and all the pages were ripped out of his notebook.

I called the *Los Angeles Times* to ask if the paper intended to investigate the deaths of their reporter and photographer. The editor said, very politely, the matter was closed; the management accepted the findings of the US government. *Closed?* I wanted to scream. *How could it be closed when it was unclear who killed them, let alone why?* Talk about callousness! Here was a quick lesson in being on the receiving end of journalistic priorities: two deaths, tragic as they might be, weren't going to rise to the level of, say, a Watergate or Pentagon Papers investigation. No matter that he was one of theirs, Dial was now yesterday's news; the world had already moved on. And this was even before cable television reduced our collective attention span to that of a cicada. *If that's the way they're going to be, fine,* I thought. *I'm a journalist. If they won't investigate it, I will.*

In high dudgeon, with a pinch of hysteria thrown in for good measure, I called my foreign editor. Before I could get a word out, though, he launched into a long riff about me bringing back Dial's body. Keeping my husband from being buried thousands of miles from his home in a foreign land—which anyone in my position would have done— had somehow morphed into a tale of derring-do, an exploit that put me up there with the he-men of war correspondents. As if the bet about whether I'd succeed weren't enough, the worst day of my life had now been transformed into a romantic adventure. Okay, maybe that's what it looked like from where the foreign editor sat in New York. But when he started in on how I was his hero, I had to interrupt. "I want to do an investigative piece about Dial's death," I said.

Long pause—as usual. Finally, he said, "I don't think that's a good idea, Schuster. You're the grieving widow. You lack impartiality."

"I'm still a journalist. I haven't had a pre-frontal lobotomy."

Pause. "Yeah, but people will think you have an axe to grind, that your objectivity's been impaired."

"I don't care what people think. This is something I want to do."

Longer pause. "I understand that. But anything you uncover will be questionable. I won't be able to let you use the *Journal's* name."

"Fine, then I'll take a leave of absence and write it on my own," I said, hanging up. *To hell with all of them! Who needs newspapers anyway?*

The phone rang. It was the *Journal's* publisher. "Lynda?" he said gently. "I understand how you're feeling just now. But have you thought about your personal safety? We're actually very concerned that what you're proposing could put you in real danger."

Do I want to die?

"Here's another suggestion," he continued. "How about if you return to Mexico and go back to work? Go back to work, let some time pass, see how you feel."

And that's all it took: appealing to the chicken in me. After all, where would I be without a respected publication lending its name and reputation—to say nothing of its protection—to my endeavor? I'd probably never get to the bottom of what happened and instead turn into a kind of conspiracy theorist bag lady, prowling the halls of Congress with my sacks of evidence, the scourge of Senate staffers who'd lock themselves in an inner office when they saw me coming and relegate me to the pimply-faced intern in the anteroom, whose job it was to answer calls from irate constituents and keep the crazies at bay.

So I left Los Angeles and went back to Mexico. Feeling—what? Cowardly, mostly. In leaving unanswered the most basic questions of my profession—who and why—I'd clearly failed Dial. But I was also tired, beyond exhaustion, really. And numb; I just wanted to sleep. Chris came with me to help sort through Dial's things in the apartment. On a wet, dreary afternoon, when Dial and I would have made love and then curled up afterward in delicious peace, I instead packed away parts of his life. One by one, I held up articles of clothing for Chris to claim; most ended up in plastic trash bags, destined for charity. Before consigning them to their fate, though, I surreptitiously inhaled each item. But all traces of Dial had been scrubbed, literally, leaving behind only the scent of the laundry detergent that Flor, our housekeeper, used.

After Chris left, I tried to resume working. Focusing was out of the question; I spent hours wandering the apartment, unable to read or write or even eat. *Maybe I can package grief,* I thought, *market it as a diet plan and start a new career.* Everywhere I turned, I ran into traces of Dial. His book in the bathroom, marked where he'd left off reading. His barbells in the little room behind the kitchen, still lined up on the exercise mat. His stainless martini shaker on the sideboard, poised for that moment in the late afternoon when he'd whip off his glasses and say, with a contented sigh, "I think I'm done with work for the day!" I imagined it was the same for anyone who'd ever experienced the sudden death of a loved one: the sensation that the person had stepped out only for a moment and would be back soon. Truth be told, Dial's absence didn't feel much different from our married life together. He could just as well have been on assignment in Central America. One afternoon, sitting in the living room and watching rivulets of rain stream down the French doors, I heard myself say aloud, "I suppose if he didn't die, he would have called by now."

Flor, at the sound of my voice, came bustling in. "¿Sí, Señora?"

Virtually every night I dreamed I heard a telephone ringing from a long way off; when I finally answered it, Dial's voice came faintly through the line. *He isn't dead!* I'd think ecstatically. But I could never understand what he was saying and didn't know where to find him—and would awaken from the dream, sobbing. I became a kid again: a kid with an apartment and work obligations and a perpetual care contract for her husband's grave, who was afraid of the dark and had to sleep with a light on. I probably needed professional help. But here's the thing about therapy: if you're compos mentis enough to think you need it, chances are you don't. And I hadn't lived in Mexico long enough to make the kind of close friends who'd notice the dazed stare, trailing sentences, cornflakes in the hair and diplomatically intervene.

After weeks of shambling about, though, it became obvious even to me that I couldn't function. Latin America was where I'd fallen in love with Dial, where we'd gotten married, where he'd died. I just wanted out—as if going to a place where people spoke, say, Icelandic or Southern Altai instead of Spanish would stop the pain. My editors must have recognized my struggles; they readily agreed to a transfer when I finally got up the courage to ask, almost immediately sending in a covey of international movers.

Now what? I thought, sitting on the floor and watching the packer swaddle a demitasse spoon in three sheets of protective paper. It was a question I assumed had been answered for the next couple of decades when Dial and I married. I never had any illusions about how much time we'd have, figuring he'd die first, most likely when I was middle-aged. That's if we were lucky. My mind turned to a story Simcha had told me about a woman she once met who didn't marry until well into her sixth decade. "'And then we had twenty-five wonderful years together!'" the woman declared. *Twenty-five years!* World enough and time, as Dial had said on that last afternoon we were together. I would have continued with my brilliant career, he would have continued with his, and we would have continued being madly in love: happily ever after.

There wouldn't be a fairy-tale ending now, that much was clear. As to what came next, though, I had no idea. Nor my editors, apparently: they couldn't tell me where I would be going. So after I'd rescued my wastebasket from being triple-wrapped with the trash still inside, and the packers finished cramming everything into boxes, my stuff went to storage, and I went to Israel.

"Tell me," Sim said. "Why did you only spend a day with your family in Detroit before coming here?" We were sitting in the main room of her little house, drinking tea. The window was open; outside, beyond the kibbutz, the approaching dusk was gently softening the hard edges of the Golan Heights.

"My grandfather asked exactly the same thing. He couldn't believe I wouldn't want to be in the bosom of my family at a time of tragedy."

"And why didn't you?"

I couldn't tell her that to stay in Detroit would be like backsliding, like admitting defeat at having tried to break out from there and do something different. "Come on, Sim," I said. "You know how I feel about my parents. Mom was even more clingy than usual."

"You're her daughter and you're hurting. She wants to make you feel better. As a mother, I can understand that."

As could I—in theory. But Mom, more than anyone, represented all that I had tried to jettison. Her mere presence kindled a kind of spitefulness in me—as if it were somehow *her* fault Dial had died and everything had come crashing down. To say nothing of famine, pestilence, and the Chicago Cubs' perennial failure to win a World Series; she was always to blame for my, and the universe's, shortcomings. "I know I shouldn't push her away," I said. "It's almost an automatic reflex. Anyway, I needed to get here and talk to you."

Sim poured the dregs of the teapot into her cup. "You know, one of the things I'm most upset about is that I've been cheated out of ever meeting Dial."

I nodded, feeling the waterworks begin to strain at their valves again.

"I had just dropped a boring, humdrum letter to you in the post box, when Doug came around and asked what your husband's name was because he'd heard the news on the BBC. I went berserk, trying to contact you."

"You know what really haunts me?" I said, unable to hold back the tears any longer. "I don't want him to have felt any pain or suffered. The coroner, when I talked to him, said Dial and the photographer were killed instantly. He said that at most, they would have seen a flash of light." Now I was weeping and could hardly get the words out. "Light travels faster than sound. So by the time the detonation reached their ears, they would have been dead."

"Oh, Lynda," Sim said, patting my hand. "I wish I could take away *your* pain. In the meantime, let me make you some more tea." She grabbed the pot and disappeared into her tiny kitchen.

"You're so British!" I called after her, blowing my nose.

"I can't help it. That's where I was born."

When she'd returned and smothered the teapot with its cozy, I asked, "Will it ever stop?"

"Having been through a divorce, I can testify to the fact that, clichéd as it may sound, time does heal all wounds. It will get better, I promise. You'll wake up one morning and be able to go five whole minutes without thinking about it."

"Then what?"

"I'm divorced, not clairvoyant."

I spent a few more days with Sim, talking and drinking tea as always, and by the end of the stay felt better. As I was leaving, Sim hugged me tightly, saying, "When the Israelites were about to cross the Jordan River into the Promised Land, and Moses handed things over to Joshua, he said, 'Be strong and of good courage.'"

She didn't know I'd just found out I was being sent to Beirut.

I don't think my editors intend any malice in dispatching me to a place that's in the midst of civil war. The *Journal's* Middle East correspondent is being transferred to Washington; the editors need someone to fill in temporarily; I'm available. A perfect match! Especially since working in Beirut is so much safer than, say, wrestling sharks or going down Mt. Everest backward and blindfolded or any number of other things that might be tempting to do in my current state.

Beirut's devastation is unlike anything I've ever seen. After nearly ten years of brutal combat, whole swathes of the city now lie in Dresden-like destruction. Some neighborhoods are abandoned entirely, dead zones really, their burned-out apartment buildings like rows of gap-toothed jack-o'-lanterns sporting spiky rebar hair. Dunes of rubble from collapsed structures, exploded cars, and even huge rooftop air-conditioning units choke the streets, rendering them impassable. The city is divided by a no-man's land, a terrifying place where snipers from the warring militias pick off pedestrians as if they're Pac-Man dots. I try to concentrate on writing about some of the hundreds of thousands of ordinary people caught in the middle of the conflict: Shia and Sunni Muslims, Christians, Druze, Palestinians. They're the unfortunate pawns used by the regional and world powers to play out their geopolitical fantasies of empire and conquest—variations on the same sectarian violence that engulfs the Middle East to this day.

Always gracious, the Lebanese thoughtfully bring their war to you. One evening, I'm sitting on the edge of my bed, talking to a page-one editor in New York, when an explosive device goes off so close to the hotel the concussion almost throws me to the floor. *"Holy shit!"* the editor says from 5,600 miles away. "What was that?"

I don't even want to look out the window. "Oh, nothing," I say, trying to keep the quiver out of my voice. I crouch down next to the bed, as if that will prevent my room from becoming a tomb-in-waiting. "Just your usual Tuesday night mayhem."

Gone forever is the facade I'd once hoped to cultivate of the fearless, globetrotting foreign correspondent, blithely blowing through war zones with a nonchalant toss of the head. Whereas before, in places like El Salvador, I was only intermittently scared shitless, now it's a constant. Okay, this *is* Beirut. But nowhere feels safe anymore. In my naïve, pre-bereavement mind, horrible things only happened *out there,* to people in typhoon-prone countries or trailer parks. *Out there* has become *right here.*

How could I be so stupid? I think, going downstairs to the lobby to send off a telex and ask about the detonation. To expect, or hope, that my youth, my passport, my profession, my lucky pajamas—would somehow shield me from life's inherent randomness and fragility. Why should I be immune to the calamities I spend my days chronicling? In Central America, I'd often felt dishonest, abashed almost, about the way I did my job: convincing people to take me into their confidences, spending hours crying or laughing with them, getting them to open up, to share their stories—and then I'd leave. Bye-bye, tragedy. Hello, privileged life and nice, clean apartment with running water and electricity, where no one was shooting at me or trying to kill someone I loved. Guilt-tinged as that divide was, it appeared immutable.

Bye-bye magical thinking.

Yet some part of me still cares about bearing witness to the world's injustices. Especially in a place like Beirut, where people conjure up remarkable resilience and grace in the face of often unspeakable horror. I'm clearly not cut out for the frontlines, though. Sliding onto a stool at the bar, I hear a reporter, a couple of seats over, say the explosion was a bomb that had gone off in a nearby building. "No biggie, not even casualties," he says dismissively. But who, exactly, *is* fit for this job? For every brave and dedicated practitioner of the profession, there seem to be three alcoholic action-junkies who simply can't stay away from the bang-bang. To say nothing of those who are just plain haunted. Among my fellow journalists, it's hard not to notice all the drunks, busted marriages, abandoned offspring. The bar is a veritable triage ward of the walking wounded and bereft. *I suppose that now includes me*, I think, sipping a beer and watching a plastered *New York Times* correspondent attempt a cartwheel across the lobby.

Here's a heretical thought: What if I had it all wrong? What if it weren't the breaking out and adventure that made me so happy, but something so simple as love? Maybe *that* was the hubris Dial warned against: my childish arrogance. When you're young, it's easy to underestimate how rare love truly is. Dial, with his maturity and experience, could appreciate the miracle, the sheer improbability, of us finding one another. My mind turns back to a story he once told me about being a young reporter covering a convention in a Los Angeles hotel. Standing in the ballroom's kitchen before the luncheon began, he watched the chefs cutting hundreds of grapefruits into halves, which waiters hurriedly carried out to place on tables for the meal's first course. "I wondered what the chances were that two people, sitting next to one another in that huge room, would each get one half of the same grapefruit," he said, kissing my hand. "Somehow, in all the world, I found my matching half."

No more grapefruits for me; citruswise, it seems I've been demoted to lemons. The first week I was here, a *New York Times* correspondent tried to grope me at the bar. *In full view of everyone!* Another man, who claims to be a Polish shipping agent, keeps inviting me to go on a picnic—because who wouldn't want to sit outside on a blanket amid the debris of blown-up buildings and downed pylons, breathing the fresh scent of newly exploded shells and listening to the pleasant whistle of missiles flying overhead? The worst was one night when a Druze general I'd recently interviewed pushed his way into my hotel room, flopped on the floor, unbuttoned his jacket and, lifting his shirt, demanded, "Look at this stomach! Do you see how flat it is? You could punch it and nothing would move! Nothing!" He pulled down his shirt and sat up. "Do you see how young I look?" he said, turning his face from side to side. "Can you guess how old I am? Can you?"

Is it pity that makes them act this way? Charity? Or am I giving off a kind of scent, something subtle perhaps that, if bottled, would have a name like Wanton Widow, say, or Eau de Dissolute?

Whatever the reason, all I can see, stretching before me, are years and years of reporting in places like this. Problem is, I have no Plan B, nothing to fall back on such as masonry or midwifery. *Journalism is it*, I think, draining my beer. I'd like to believe I'm soldiering on, but it's more like a stumble, really. Especially when the

African gray parrot that lives in the lobby decides, as I'm passing its cage, to emit its perfectly terrifying imitation of incoming artillery—and I just about hit the ground.

So I go off to do my job. Which, in the middle of a civil war, usually means trying to get into a place that everyone else is trying to flee. You'd think it would be easy, this going against the flow of humanity: just steer yourself onto the empty, inbound lane of the road and cruise right in. But the country has splintered into a series of sectarian fiefdoms, each with constantly changing allegiances and boundaries that, like relationships among teenaged girls, are hard to keep straight. One minute you and your driver are careening along picturesque roads, high in the Mount Lebanon massif, admiring the cedars and snow-capped peaks in the distance. The next thing you know, there's a submachine gun pointed at the car window, and you're desperately pawing through your bag, saying to the twitchy soldier, "Uh, I know that military pass is in here somewhere!" showing him the pens, reporter's notebook, candy bar wrapper, busted tape cassette, dried-up towelettes, movie ticket stub, emergency tampons, and passes from rival militias that come tumbling out.

The sun is beginning to set by the time we make it to the headquarters of the soldier's Druze militia. This is my profession at its most bizarre: I'm going to ask permission to spend the night in a Christian village that the soldiers have been bombarding for months. Thousands of Christians from nearby hamlets are squeezed in there, having fled their homes because of the fighting and seeking security in numbers from the Druze, a Muslim sect. In the morning, the Israeli army—which had invaded the country for a second time in 1982—is supposed to show up to liberate the Christians and, with the consent of the Druze soldiers who've been trying to kill them, will escort the refugees down to the coast where they'll board boats for the Christian side of Beirut. There's something in this surreal sectarian choreography for all the players: the Christians are saved; Druze transformed into benevolent humanitarians; Israelis re-modeled into guardian angels; journalists confirmed as dolts for trying to make sense of it.

The village is just across a gorge; I can see it from the com-mander's office. Your typical, timeless Biblical-style community: houses of sandy, limestone bricks with arched entryways and red-tiled roofs, terraced up the mountainside. Think Charlton Heston and *Ben-Hur*, minus the chariots. Also add in a sewage system. The commander agrees to allow me entry—although his men will, as usual, be firing at the village. "Probably after midnight," he says.

"Really?"

"Yes, but we'll try not to hit you," he says, pouring another cup of tea.

The mayor of the Christian village is not happy to see me. Every house is already overflowing with refugees from the surrounding area; there's nowhere for me to spend the night. Nowhere safe, that is. There is space in one of the abandoned homes on the edge of town, facing the Druze stronghold across the gorge. The front lines, as it were. "Must be a great view!" I say, trying to sound brave but emitting something closer to a squeak. The mayor takes us to the house, shows me the bedroom, and hastily leaves. As does my driver: he prefers to sleep in the car, parked as far away as possible from the Druze guns. Only as he zooms off does it occur to me, the brilliant and resourceful reporter, that I, too, could have slept in our vehicle.

The electricity in the house is out. I light a lone candle remain-ing on the mantle. The room isn't much: a couple of beds, a night-stand and lamp, a chest of drawers. All the bed linen and pillows are gone, most likely carried off to wherever the homeowners have de-camped. Fully clothed and wearing a hat and mittens, I lie down on a bed, tucking my jacket around me. Sleep would be a good thing. To say nothing of a large, but contained, fire to defrost my toes.

Then the rockets begin. *Right on schedule*, I think, diving, as usual, under the bed. The attack is heart-thumping, pray-to-every-god-in-the-universe awful. Maybe because this is the last night the militiamen will have, quite literally, a captive audience, they seem to be throwing everything they've got at the village. *Think of it as the end of a fireworks display!* I'm trembling like a dog in a thunderstorm, while the poor people here have had to endure this for weeks. And what of the carnage if they actually hit a target! *Don't these soldiers have anything better to do with their nights? Couldn't they take up a hobby instead, something along the lines of stargazing, maybe, or crocheting by candlelight?*

Being under bombardment and a bed, my mind naturally drifts to Dial. Why did he even go down to the Nicaraguan border? He was never one to take undue risk, much less with a photographer. "Don't ever travel with a photog," he once warned me. "They run straight into the danger the rest of us are trying to avoid." But what if Dial were so intent on proving himself, his bosses having accused him of shirking his job because of me, that he allowed his judgment to be clouded? Worse yet, what if he *deliberately* ignored signs of possible peril in the hope of scoring a big story, an exclusive, maybe, to restore his good name?

Wouldn't that mean I'm inadvertently responsible for his death?

Always the masochist! I think, as the tears start streaming. Of course, I could try to convince myself that Dial honestly had no idea, beyond the obvious, of the danger he and the photographer were heading into. *Why not? There's so much else I'll probably never know about his death, why not add that to the list?* I envision it more as a box, though: an open, messy carton, bulging with lies and secrets and unanswered questions that I'm going to have to learn how to carry around forever.

I wipe my eyes and face on my mittens, too scared to crawl out from under the bed to find a tissue. There's nothing like having a good cry when someone's shooting at you. The Druze are still going at it, but I'm calmer now. Calm enough, in fact, to spend the rest of the night on the floor worrying about where bugs go when there's artillery fire.

The next morning, the Israeli Army rolls into town with its trucks and martial swagger. The main square is awhirl with grateful Christians being directed onto the vehicles, Druze soldiers—the very same ones who, not more than a couple of hours earlier, had terrorized the place—aiding the Israelis. I run around, trying to interview people amid the chaos. Fat chance. Everyone just wants to get away from this sulfurous hellhole, with the monkey-grinning militiamen, as fast as the Israelis can spirit them. Standing beside one of the trucks, the Druze commander nods at me. "Did you sleep well?" he asks, and smiles as he walks away.

Unable to pump any more quotes from the villagers or soldiers, I trot off in search of my car. The mayor said he saw it on the other side of town. By the time the driver and I return, though, the square is deserted. No women corralling their children like frenzied hens, no men trying to hoist yet more sacks of household goods onto trucks, no bawling babies. The convoy has departed without us. Which leaves me with one of two choices, neither very appealing: take the winding, hours-long way back to Beirut through the mountains, or try to catch up with Israelis on the faster, more direct, route leading to the coastal highway. After conferring, the driver and I decide on the latter; we're both exhausted and want to return quickly to the capital.

My car is the sole vehicle on the road. It has a proper name, but I know it only by its moniker: Sniper's Alley. We're chasing the phantom Israeli trucks and the promise of safety. I peer into the distance, foolishly hoping to catch a glimpse of them, their sharpshooters riding shotgun. Not even a glint of sunlight flashing off their Uzis. No matter how much I wish it otherwise, they're gone; there's nothing on this road. No traffic, no people, nothing. Only my car, zipping along through the beautiful Lebanese countryside—a sweet little target.

The driver checks and rechecks the rearview mirror. Tiny droplets of sweat pop out on the back of his neck and merge into small streams. Now he glances at me in the mirror. He's waiting for me to say something, but I don't know what to do. Thick pine forests rise up on either side of the road in an opaque green curtain. They make for excellent cover. Anything or, more to the point, anybody, could be hiding among the trees; we'd never see them. If this were a chapter in a textbook on foreign reportage, it would be entitled, "Knowing When to Go." That fine balance between coward and cowboy, between acting the professional and reacting to the hair standing up on the back of your neck. With a bit of dumb luck thrown in too, for good measure.

Did Dial have a premonition driving down that road on the Nicaraguan border? Did he have any inkling he should turn back?

"Turn around!" I shout at the driver. "Turn around quickly! We'll go back through the mountains, the long way to Beirut."

When we finally straggle into the capital late that night, I hear the news. Two people, traveling separately, were shot and killed on the same road to the coastal highway—after my car turned back.

CHAPTER SIX

SOUTH AMERICA, 1985

Simcha was right. I can soon go a whole five minutes, maybe even six, without thinking about Dial and that he's dead and how he died. Of course, then I feel guilty for *not* thinking about it. But what can you do? Here's the thing about grieving: like it or not, the habit of life stubbornly reasserts itself at some point. And all the guilt in the world about being alive and getting to eat and have dental work done and make waxing appointments isn't going to stop it.

It helps that my editors eventually extract me from Beirut. Not being confronted daily with the worst of humanity's tendencies can do wonders for your outlook on life. When you're in the midst of war, it's hard to remember there are places in the world where people are buying bagels with two shmears and looking at lingerie catalogs. Although, I'm not exactly thrilled by my new, permanent assignment covering the southern portion of South America out of the *Journal's* Miami bureau. Returning to Latin America clearly isn't my first choice; it isn't even my last. But really, you can't write off an entire continent because of what happened in one country. I decide to accept it and try to move on. First, though, I have to stop in Washington to interview the experts in my new beat.

Of course, I become hopelessly lost in the State Department's miles of corridors and wings and internal courtyards with an office numbering system so cryptic it's a wonder our diplomats can ever find their way out to the bathroom, let alone to negotiate treaties. *Why don't they provide a compass when you check in at the visitors' entrance?* I wonder, wandering the halls. By the time I locate the Argentina desk officer's cubbyhole, I'm twenty minutes late for my appointment and sweating. "Hi, Lynda Schuster, *Wall Street Journal*," I say, breathlessly. "Sorry for the delay, but this place is a maze. Do you still have time to talk?"

A tall, lanky man in his midthirties rises from the desk to shake my hand. "Dennis Jett. No problem." Dirty blond hair, blues eyes, nice smile. Terrible tie, though, the color of dried vomit. "People sometimes go missing for days in the hallways."

After I've settled into my chair and given him my card and my spiel about what I've covered previously and my new beat, Jett says, "I know you were married to Dial Torgerson. I was very sorry to hear about his death. I knew him when I worked in our embassy in Tel Aviv."

"Really? Did he interview you?"

"No, we met at a little dinner given by a journalist we were both trying to date."

"Successfully?"

"I don't know about Dial, but I didn't have any luck. Maybe he didn't, either, because I remember he said, rather sardonically, how it was typical that our hostess would invite the two men vying for her attention to the same dinner."

That's as far as I want to go with that weird bit of coincidence; discussing Dial with a complete stranger is still difficult. The desk officer gets down to the business of Argentina. It seems like all the same stuff I covered the last time I was in the region: crippling foreign debt and groping attempts at democracy. The generals, who did such a bang-up job with their conflict-of-choice in the Falklands, were left no alternative but to slink off after the war ended and return the country to civilian rule. Jett talks about the seemingly endless ping-ponging between military and democratic governments, and the disastrous effects on the economy. *More lunches with bankers! More soporific insolvency stories!*

"This is very helpful," I say, hastily scribbling it all down. "So besides debt and democracy, Mr. Jett, what else is interesting about Argentina?"

He pauses for a moment. "Well, there's the issue of divorce. Take me, for instance. I'm divorced."

I stare at him for a moment, dumbfounded—especially given what he knows of Dial—then jot in my notebook, *this guy is a jerk,* and close it. Interview over. On to the next.

Later that evening, I walk into my hotel room after landing back in Miami to a ringing telephone. "Lynda? This is Dennis Jett from the State Department. How are you?"

You've got to be kidding.

"Just off the plane," I say. "How did you know which hotel I'm staying at?"

"I called your office."

"And they gave it to you?"

"I told them I'm a government source and have top-secret information to pass on to you."

"And they believed you?"

"I wanted to know when you're coming back to Washington."

"Why?"

"So we can have dinner."

For about one second, I'm more intrigued than irritated. *Dinner with a diplomat! Even one who's a jerk!* Only much later will I realize how completely out of character this was for Dennis, how utterly unlike his usual quiet and unassuming self. Still, you have to admire his nerve. He and Dial both liked that reporter in Israel; maybe he thinks he ought to try me as well.

"I have to go house-hunting for a place to live," I say. "And it's going to take a while to line up more interviews in Washington and convince my bureau chief I have to go back."

"Okay," Dennis says. "I'll be here, guarding state secrets."

I get busy settling into Miami, which I like: all the mystery and dampness of Central America, but in a less democratically challenged package. I find an adorable house, a small Spanish stucco number with arches and tiled floors and gigantic Palmetto bugs, which is just a fancy name for cockroaches. The property to the left of me has majestic royal palms; to the right, the elderly neighbors keep a vintage aluminum Airstream trailer in the driveway out front and sunbathe nude out back. I buy a sporty little blue import, even though I don't know the first thing about driving a stick shift, but it's on sale and really, how difficult can it be to learn? The first morning I take the car to the office, I have to leave it on the street and run upstairs to ask one of the reporters to drive it up the parking structure's ramp because I keep stalling out. But the bureau's half dozen or so journalists are friendly and accommodating. Even Gary, the investigative reporter, who spends most of the day yelling at people on the telephone a couple of cubicles down from mine. He's your quintessential crusading hack: gruff, jittery, obsessed, with a seriously compromised sartorial sensibility and thick New York accent. He kept talking about his sauces when we were introduced, which made me think he had a little catering business on the side—until I realized he was saying "sources."

Should I go back to Washington and have dinner with this Dennis Jett? I wonder, unpacking a framed picture of my sisters and placing it on my desk. *Am I even ready to start dating? It's only been a year since Dial died.* Still, a diplomat might be fun; bureaucrat-wise, it beats going out with, say, a budget analyst or contract oversight specialist. And most certainly the men I met in Lebanon.

I saunter into the bureau chief's office. "Got a second?" I ask, trying to affect a nonchalant air.

The bureau chief looks up from a magazine. "Sure."

"Uh, I need to go back to Washington to talk with people in some of the government agencies I missed when I was up there."

"Which ones?"

"Oh, the Foreign Agricultural Service," I say, vaguely. "Fish and Wildlife, maybe the National Oceanic Service."

The bureau chief, one of the *Journal's* legendary writers, narrows his eyes. "Fish and Wildlife?" he says. "National Oceanic Service?"

"Yeah. South America has oceans, doesn't it?"

In the end, he allows me to go—reluctantly. Then I really do have to spend the day listening to bureaucrats yammer on about arcane things that are, at best, a sideshow to my new beat. (Although I do learn a lot about Brazilian piranhas.) All this just to meet Dennis for dinner afterward at a fancy restaurant in a fancy hotel. And on my expense account, no less. He's wearing a blue suit, a modest improvement over the puke-colored tie of our first encounter. Still, he's handsome in an Anglo-Saxon, regular-featured sort of way and clearly has a great body—the result, I'll later learn, of running a score of marathons. The tuxedoed sommelier hands him a wine list the size of the *Oxford English Dictionary*. Dennis quickly flips through the pages. "We'll have this," he says, pointing at something toward the end of the book.

The sommelier glances at Dennis's selection. "Sir," he sniffs. "We usually *finish* the meal with a Sauterne."

"Well, I'm a bit backwards," Dennis says, then recovers nicely by ordering a bottle of white that costs the equivalent of the annual per capita income of some developing countries.

I say, "Okay, now you really do have to pass classified information to me so I can justify this when I file my expenses."

"I can't be bought that easily. It'll take two bottles, at least."

While the sommelier pours the wine, I sneak a glimpse at Dennis's smooth, unlined profile. *So different from Dial's; he's got to be, what, fifteen years younger? Is that good? Bad? Irrelevant?* My little reverie's interrupted by the waiter, a woman, who takes our food order: steak for Dennis, fish for me. After which, to maintain a facade of professionalism, I say, "So tell me more about Argentina."

"It's a seriously fucked-up country."

"That's not very diplomatic."

"But true." Dennis takes a sip of wine. "Did you know that Argentina has more psychologists, per capita, than any other country? By a mile."

"Now there's a great statistic! And what accounts for this?"

"Argentines have a pathological superiority complex. They think they're actually Europeans who should be in Europe, and the rest of Latin America wishes they were."

"Can I quote you on that?"

"You can't quote me on anything truthful that I say."

He may be a jerk, but at least he's a funny jerk.

Maybe it's the overpriced wine, but after that we dispense with the pretense of work and jump headfirst into personal stuff. Dennis tells me about his teenaged son and daughter who live in Virginia and how guilty he feels when he has to go abroad. I tell him about Chris and Jordy and all they've been through. He tells me about how, when he was posted to Buenos Aires, a member of a right-wing death squad gave him his business card, saying, "Anything you need done, we'll take care of it for you." I tell him about the supposed Polish shipping agent in Beirut and his penchant for picnicking under incoming artillery. He makes me laugh. I make him laugh. We talk and talk and talk. Okay, and maybe we make out a little when he drops me at my hotel. All the while I'm thinking this feels a lot like the way Dial and I began—and yet it doesn't. *What am I doing?*

If not outright fireworks between us, there are at least low-level, backyard-grade pyrotechnics, the kind you usually have to cross state lines to buy. Dennis clearly has a wicked sense of humor and a serious addiction to politics—which, besides being upright and breathing, are my prerequisites in a lover. I'm actually humming— humming!—as I open the door to my room. It seems like the start of something, but who knows with a government employee? I'm leaving for a reporting trip to Argentina, so there's no time for any follow-up; when we parted, Dennis said only that he'd be in touch.

———

Buenos Aires certainly looks better than it did during the Falklands War. Most of the massive flags and patriotic banners have been folded up and put away, and the city returned to its former glory of broad avenues, manicured squares, and general mash-up of European architecture. If Madrid married Paris and they produced an offspring, it would be Buenos Aires. The place still feels creepy, though, despite the reversion to democratic rule. Maybe it's because I'm working on a story about the ten thousand or so people whom the generals "disappeared" during what came to be known as its "dirty war" against leftist terrorists in the late 1970s. Guerrilla groups, hell-bent on fomenting a socialist/communist uprising, were operating throughout the country at the time and committing horrific acts of violence. But the generals decided to employ a broad and sweeping definition of terrorist that could include just about anyone with leftist sympathies. Trade unionists, journalists, lawyers, students—all were fair game to be taken away, in full view of families and coworkers, and imprisoned in concentration camps, torture centers, really. Most were never seen again.

One man tells me of being awakened before dawn by a banging on his door. Soldiers had surrounded the apartment building; they burst into his home when he went to check on the noise. Dressed in full military gear, grenades hanging from their belts, the soldiers forced the family from their beds at gunpoint and lined them up in the living room. The officer in charge said they had come for the eldest daughter, the one who worked as a social worker in Buenos Aires's slums. Nothing serious, the officer promised; she'll be back soon. The man's daughter clung to him, crying, begging him not to let the soldiers take her.

What could he do? Soldiers were standing in his living room, pointing submachine guns at his wife and four other children. *Don't worry*, the man said softly to his daughter, *they only want to ask you a few questions. You'll be home in time for breakfast. Here's some money for bus fare so you can come home when they're done talking to you.* And with that, the man gently pried his daughter out of his arms and handed her to the officer.

She never came home.

Years later, the man would learn she'd been transported that night to the basement of the Naval Mechanics' School, the site of a notorious concentration camp, where she was tortured and, ultimately, killed. "I had no idea," he says, blinking back tears. "This was early in the Dirty War, before anyone really knew the magnitude of what was happening. I honestly thought they'd question her and then let her go."

On the way back to the hotel, it's all I can do to keep from weeping. *A parent, unwittingly, sending his own child to her death! How can you go on after something like that? How can you want to go on?* I've worked myself into a full-on Slough of Despond by the time I reach the lobby—but there, stuffed inside my mailbox, is a message: *Señor Jet* (sic) *called; please call back.* Dennis!

"Señor Jett, how are you?" I say, once the hotel operator finally connects us.

"Great! And you?"

"Pretty miserable." I tell him about the interview. "Sometimes I wonder why I do this job. It just makes me so depressed."

"You do it because it's important to tell the world what happened."

"What good is that? All I ever seem to write about are the creative ways human beings find to kill one another."

"Because people in power need to know that they can't get away with this shit. Because governments need to be held accountable."

"But you work for the government."

"And I expect to be held accountable. That is, if my bosses are ever dumb enough to put me in a position of real responsibility."

"For all your actions?"

"Well, maybe not all of them. Just the ones that make me look good."

The rest of the reporting trip is hardly what you'd call uplifting, either. The new government is busily exhuming bodies from mass graves around the country, but most victims will never be found. Hundreds, maybe thousands, were apparently flown out over the South Atlantic or Río de la Plata, drugged, stripped of their clothing—and dropped, still alive, from the aircraft to the water below. First, though, they were usually tortured in any of the hundreds of concentration camps the military secretly operated.

I visit one such site that was housed in part of an enormous police garage, to the city's west. About 150 prisoners were kept in tiny cells, measuring six feet by six feet, each with a couple of concrete bunks. Guards fed them watery soup in the mornings and evenings; once a day, they were taken to the bathroom. The garage sits in a kind of square, surrounded on all sides by modest homes and large shade trees. I go from house to house, knocking on doors, trying to talk to residents about what went on in the building just across the street. The handful or so who don't outright shut the door in my face insist they never heard or saw anything. An ex-prisoner I interview, one of the few who survived, says, "If I could hear children playing soccer on the street from inside my cell, they could hear my screams from the outside."

It's enough to fracture your faith in humanity—or at least, severely sprain it. But now, at the end of every day, there's a telephone call from Dennis that somehow manages to make the world seem whole again. Not to mention droll.

When I return to Miami, he offers to fly down to help move furniture and unpack boxes in my new house. We spend the day finding just the right spot for the wicker settee and unwrapping cutlery and hanging pictures. If you want to know someone's true mettle, try hanging pictures with him.

"Where do you want this?" Dennis asks, holding up a large and heavy oil painting Dad gave me for my wedding.

"How about the living room?"

"Here?" he says, raising it above the couch.

"I don't know. Do you mind trying it over the fireplace?"

"How's that?" he asks.

"Okay, but I'm not sure."

Dennis's arms are beginning to tremble.

"Do you mind trying over the couch again?"

"I think this is good," he says, valiantly attempting to keep the picture steady.

"Maybe. But I'm not sure about the height. A little higher maybe?"

That evening, exhausted by our labors, we snuggle on the newly positioned sofa in front of the newly hooked-up television in the newly arranged microscopic den, watching *Miami Vice*. (Yet another primetime drama about another city I'm living in—and with only marginally better hair.) Out of nowhere, a mouse suddenly darts across the floor. And I, I'm sorry to say, forever disgrace my sex and my profession by leaping onto the couch and acting every bit the damsel-in-distress, shrieking included.

Dennis, meanwhile, gallantly dashes to the kitchen to grab a broom, which he uses to try to shepherd the terrified rodent through the house and out the front door. When that doesn't work—the creature is clearly out of its little mouse-mind with fright—Dennis hastily constructs a pathway from boxes and piles of books that ultimately funnels the mouse out the front door. He returns, triumphant, broom in hand. "My hero!" I say, hugging him.

Then we jump into bed. And stay there for the weekend. From time to time Dennis arises to eat chocolate ice cream out of the container in the freezer, and I get up to use the bathroom—but not without making Dennis first check for Palmetto bugs. Then we go back to bed. At some point the doorbell rings. "Ignore it," Dennis says. "If it's important, they'll break a window." We ignore it. By the end of our little marathon, we are deeply, deeply in like. To say nothing of lust. *What am I doing?*

Dennis flies down again a couple weeks later to go to Yom Kippur services with me. (How do I find these Judeo-Gentiles?) We're standing in the sanctuary of a synagogue, waiting for prayers to begin; next to me, an elderly woman, no more than four feet eight-inches tall, with hair dyed a shade of orange never once seen in nature, furtively looks at Dennis, then at me, then back at Dennis. Finally, she leans in and whispers, "He isn't Jewish, is he?"

I whisper, "No, he's not."

"I knew it! It's okay," she says, patting my arm and returning to her prayer book.

A minute later, she leans in again. "What's his sign?"

"What do you mean?"

"You know, his astrological sign."

I tell her Dennis's birthday. "I knew it! Cancer!" she says. "Very giving. Very, very giving."

Back to her prayer book momentarily, then, "So when's the wedding?"

Afterward, when we're on our way back to my house and I'm already feeling hungry, even though it's only two hours into the twenty-five-hour fast, I say to Dennis: "I just want to go on record that I'm never getting married again. No matter how much I care for you."

Dennis, who's driving my car—I still can't manage the stick shift well and certainly not while fasting—quietly says, "So who's asking?"

"Well, I'm just saying."

If being in love with Dial were, emotionally speaking, like falling off a cliff—Dennis is a slow, inexorable slide down the slippery slope of romance. And I'm grasping at every bush and outcropping along the way to break the descent. Things didn't exactly turn out smashingly the last time I tried this. One part of me wants to find a Jewish convent and hole up there for the rest of my life, safe from ever feeling again. Yet another part longs for love once more— while another doubts I can, in any case, find something comparable to what Dial and I had. So why bother? While I'm busily dividing myself up like a pie, though, Dennis's tenacity is seductive, reassuring even. Reassuring enough to make me stop overthinking the relationship for an entire fifteen minutes at a stretch.

Our liaison continues. He flies to Miami on weekends to see me. I fly to Washington to see him. We talk virtually every night on the telephone which, back then, costs almost as much as the flights. (Economy, not business.) My hesitations notwithstanding, our feelings deepen. Then one morning, I'm walking into the office and the bureau's secretary, a self-proclaimed Cuban-American princess, trills, "Lover Boy telephoned. I left the message on your desk."

The bureau chief is reading in his office and probably won't notice me making a personal call. Besides, as usual, Gary's yelling at some poor sucker on the phone. Nothing short of the Harlem Boys Choir, standing in front of his cubicle and singing the "Requiem Mass," could be heard over his interrogation. I dial Dennis's number at the State Department.

"Hey, it's your hot-wax-and-leather slave," I say.

"Sylvia?"

"Very funny, Jett. What's up?"

"I've got great news."

"Let me guess. You're finally going to pass classified cables to me."

"Something better. I've applied for my next assignment. In Miami!"

"Miami? Did Florida secede?"

"Not that I've heard, but the Department has some weird domestic assignments designed to get us out of Foggy Bottom."

"That's great."

"You don't get it, do you? We can live together!"

"Wait, you're moving in with me?"

"Well, yes. Why else would I do this?"

Living together?

"That's great," I say. *Living together!*

And just like that, everything changes. One minute you're a weekend squeeze, so intent on making love in the limited time available you barely even have a chance to listen to National Public Radio news updates, let alone do anything socially. The next thing you know, you're a full-fledged couple, foregoing sex after finishing the washing-up from an only partially store-bought dinner party that goes late—

because now there's always tomorrow night. Not to mention the night after that.

Now, too, we have long, luxurious Sunday mornings: drinking coffee and eating muffins that Dennis brings back from his run; reading *The New York Times*; figuring out four clues to the crossword puzzle before giving up. A large, lime-green lizard that lives in the bushes outside the slatted dining room windows keeps us company, quietly thinking little lizard thoughts and occasionally inflating its bright red dewlap just for fun. Later, we all watch the Sunday news shows. Every week it's the same:

"These politicians are idiots!" Dennis shouts at the television.

"These reporters are chicken shits!" I shout.

"They're hoodwinking the American electorate," Dennis says.

"They're not asking follow-up questions," I say.

"How did these guys ever get elected?" Dennis says.

"How did these people ever get journalism jobs?" I say.

The lizard blows out its red dewlap.

Since neither of us has to worry about catching a plane home, afterward we go to a movie or spend the evening playing Scrabble and arguing—because we're too lazy to get the dictionary—whether "fece" is a word. "Then what's a single turd called?" Dennis asks.

Plus, we have friends! Swedish Television, in all her Nordic glory, is based here, as are her Italian cameraman—a dead-ringer for a young Gene Wilder—and his Kenyan-born wife. We become res-taurant and movie buddies with *The Christian Science Monitor* re-porters, a married couple who have the same temperament and height differential as us. Roger, another *Journal* reporter from the bureau, lives a few blocks away and turns up every two minutes to show off his newborn son's latest tricks.

I obviously still have to travel to South America, but when I'm home, I love the ordinariness, the quotidianess, the Wonder-Breadness of my life with Dennis. Which is weird, because I thought this was precisely what I was rejecting about Mom's life. Maybe she was onto something there. Or maybe it's a chemical thing. Maybe being in war zones, so far removed from a normal existence, depleted my natural Betty Crocker reserves. *Can you have a domesticity deficiency,* I wonder, *like too little vitamin B?*

Then, one evening at sunset as I'm shutting the wooden blinds in the living room, my mind suddenly turns to a similar evening in Mexico City: I'm in the living room of our apartment, closing the blinds on the French doors; Dial is in the kitchen, gently shaking his post-work martini. Our life together is all there, just waiting to happen. The sensation is so vivid, so redolent of that time and place, it just about sucks the breath out of me and I have to sit down.

Dennis wanders past the living room and notices me in the half light. "Hey, what are you doing?" he asks, squeezing in next to me.

"I don't know," I say.

We sit for a few moments in the gloaming.

"Are you okay?" he asks.

"Yeah. Just sad, I guess."

"About?"

I shrug. "Dial, life, everything."

"What made you start thinking about him?"

"This room, I suppose. These are the same pictures we had in Mexico City, the same furniture. The couch still has the yucky pollution smell," I say, burying my nose in a cushion.

"Well, it hasn't been that long."

I turn to face him. "You don't mind that I still have these feelings? About Dial, I mean."

"Of course not. What I care about are your feelings for me."

"Why are you so patient with me?"

"Because I love you," he says, putting his arms around me. "You *and* your baggage."

Our conversation inspires me to take Dennis a few months later to Detroit to meet my family. Not without trepidation, though, given the spectacle when I introduced Dial to them. There's a dinner at Sandy's house, the usual circus: Dad all bluster and bravado, like a Pekingese with a self-image problem; Mom trying too hard; my Cheshire cat–grinning sisters checking Dennis out. As always, Nanny is in fine form. After shaking Dennis's hand, she says in a stage whisper, "Oy, he's so skinny! Does he eat?" And later, during a lull in conversation at the table, "Oy, he's so quiet! Does he talk?"

Afterward, Mom plops herself next to me on the couch in Sandy's living room. "Dennis seems very nice," she says.

"Thanks. I think he is."

"So is this serious?"

"For now. I mean, we're living together. But he has to go abroad for his next posting, so I don't know what's going to happen."

"Have you met his family?"

"He introduced me to his kids when I was in Washington."

"Kids! He has kids?"

"Yes, Mom. They're nice. Not very talkative, though."

"But did they like you?"

"Hard to tell. They're teenagers."

"Is it strange being with someone after Dial?"

"A little. But he's so different. And the relationship's so different."

She raises an eyebrow. "Better? Worse?"

"Just different, Mom. Apples and oranges."

"Well, you always liked both when you were little."

Oddly, I don't snap. A year, six months ago, I'd have been all over her for saying something most people would find innocuous, sweet even. To me, though, it'd have seemed—what? Banal? Presumptuous? Deserving of the electric chair? Then again, historically, if she said the sky were blue, simply on principle I'd feel compelled to argue for teal. Or just shut her out completely. I don't know if it's Dennis's calming influence, or the Zen of domestic bliss—maybe the wine?—but for once my stupid, childish need to reject her outright is held in check. Not that this is any miraculous conversion; I can't suddenly fly or sing on key. And I still begrudge her the intense dislike she radiates around Dad like a human space heater. But at least it's something.

Not long after that, I'm in Chile, reporting on political opponents whom the ruling dictator has banished to internal exile. The dissident I'm profiling, a leftist psychiatrist, was expelled from the capital to the country's southern tip, where the land mass seems to get tired of holding together and breaks into pieces. She's been relegated to a tiny, remote fishing village of tumbledown shacks and wooden boats painted rainbow hues. The despot president might have thought the psychiatrist would be ostracized in so insular a place, but she just hung out her shingle and started seeing patients—for free. The townsfolk are ecstatic; they've never had access to a therapist before. "And we get thoughts in our heads that are just as strange as the ones people in the city have!" a fisherman says proudly. So now, instead of being a pariah, the dissident is a celebrity.

The two security goons assigned to keep an eye on her obviously aren't thrilled with this development, lest it give leftists a good name. Nor are they happy I'm writing a story about it. They make vague

attempts to trail me as I'm doing interviews, but really, in so small
and parochial a place, a couple of large men with aviator sunglasses
permanently soldered to their scowling faces are as inconspicuous as,
for example, twin gnus. And no one seems much intimidated by their
presence. After my story runs, though, in what I hope is purely a
coincidence, the government moves the psychiatrist to an even more
isolated village further south, close to Antarctica.

Far more daunting than the security guys, at least to me, are the
fleas infesting the room I'm staying in above the town's pub, there
being no hotel. I awaken on the last morning with a neat line of bites
marching across my buttocks. Which, ick factor aside, are only mildly
unpleasant. But by the time I arrive back in the capital, they've swelled
to giant, itching welts the color of a well-tended poinsettia; at a late
afternoon interview with a political scientist, it's all I can to do keep
from scooting across the carpet of his office like a dog with worms.
Afterward, I race to my hotel and jump, just about fully clothed, into
a cool bath.

I'm drying off when Dennis calls. "How are you?"

"Itchy," I say, and proceed to tell him about the bites and the security goons—but, as usual in this police state, someone is listening in
on the line. He's perusing a newspaper at the same time; we can,
quite literally, hear him rustling the pages.

I say, "I wish he'd either just listen or hang up and read the sports
section. I'm offended he isn't riveted by our witty repartee."

"Maybe if I talk dirty, it'll get his full attention," Dennis says.

"It would get mine."

Dennis yells at the person in Spanish, telling him to stop making
so much noise and do his job properly. A slight pause—then the page-
turning resumes.

Above the crackling, Dennis says, "I have something important to tell you."

"Uh-oh. The last time you said that, I ended up with a roommate."

"Well, now you're going to lose him. I got my onward assignment. I'm going to be a deputy chief-of-mission. In Malawi."

"Africa! That's a bit of a commute for me, darlin'."

Does this mean I'm actually going to lose him?

Long pause. Dennis says, "Why don't you come with me?"

"Are you crazy?"

"I love you. Come with me."

How can I go with him?

I say, "I love you, too.

How can I not?

It's a question that dogs me for months and comes, coincidentally, at a time when working at the *Journal* is increasingly less fun. Not that being a reporter there was ever a barrel of monkeys; most days, the job induced mild-to-moderate angst. To say nothing of occasional outbreaks of despair. There's been a change in top management, though, and it no longer feels like the same paper—which, by itself wouldn't be enough to make a coward like me jump ship. But since Dial's death, the sense of glamour I once had about the profession, of boundless expectation, has vanished; something in me has changed. And now there's my life with Dennis to consider.

More and more, when I'm feeling unappreciated by the new bosses in New York, or miffed because the bureau chief looked at me the wrong way, my thoughts drift to Africa. Amid white rhino and elephants, with a giraffe or two thrown in for added textural interest, I picture myself in a tasteful pith helmet with delicate netting, longish skirt, riding boots of a high polish—doing what, exactly? *Missionary work a la Katherine Hepburn in* The African Queen?

I'm Jewish. Coffee farming a la Meryl Streep in Out of Africa? *I hate bugs.* It was hard enough trying to be with another journalist; reconciling my career with that of a diplomat seems impossible.

Then, just when I'm about to give up hope of ever finding a satisfactory solution, I get the kind of break I thought was behind me. Our *Christian Science Monitor* friends tell me the paper is looking for a new Southern Africa correspondent, based in Johannesburg, which is a relatively short plane ride from Lilongwe, Malawi's capital. Love *and* work! I can hardly believe my good fortune—yet again.

"Maui?" Mom says when I tell her my plans. "I didn't know we had an embassy in Hawaii."

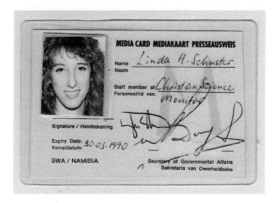

CHAPTER SEVEN

SOUTHERN AFRICA, 1986

So, Dennis buys me the *teeniest* of diamond rings. We have to pretend to be husband and wife when I'm in Malawi because His Excellency, the president for life who's been in power for decades, doesn't allow anyone to cohabit unless married. Anyone except himself, that is; he has a live-in girlfriend whose formal title is "Official Hostess." You can do such things when you're a life president. Also, it helps that anyone who could oppose you is in prison or dead, usually having met his end under mysterious circumstances.

Dennis has already been in Malawi for a couple of weeks when I arrive. Even though I don't have a diplomatic passport, or even a civilian one bearing his surname, he whisks me through the VIP lounge at the tiny airport and out to a waiting car. Vincent, his driver, does a slight bob when we're introduced. "Welcome to Malawi, Madam," he says.

"'Madam?'" I whisper to Dennis.

"Yeah, well, I'm *Bambo*," he says.

"What's that?"

"'Sir' or 'father' in Chichewa."

"Okay, Bimbo."

"*Bambo*, Schuster, *Bambo*."

I don't know if it's my jetlag, but the landscape seems to have a hazy tinge to it, like looking through a windshield after driving through a dust storm. July is winter here, the dry season. Bits of scrubby brush dot the undulating savanna; every so often, a bottom-heavy baobab tree suddenly appears, a kind of gigantic gray Coke bottle with branches. The clumps of mud-and-wattle huts we pass have curlicue ribbons of blue smoke from cooking fires floating above the thatched roofs. Just when you think the scenery can't possibly get any more prototypical of the continent, a termite mound, as tall as a man and rising from the ground like a ziggurat, comes into view: Africa as advertised. And the people! The sides of the two-lane asphalt highway are positively packed: people walking, riding decrepit bicycles, pushing carts piled with kindling. Women, many of them barefoot despite the cold, trudge along with babies tied to their backs and loads the size of an under-counter refrigerator balanced on their heads.

After all this, arriving at the gated compound of Dennis's house in Lilongwe, the capital, is like landing on another planet. His abode, courtesy of the US government, has spacious rooms with wide windows and doors that open onto patios. A guest cottage the size of my Miami home comes with its own swimming pool, barbecue, and thatched canopy to shade the chaise lounges. There are English flower gardens straight out of a Jane Austen novel—this *is* a former British colony, after all—and flame trees and jacarandas. Not to mention crops: lettuce, spinach, cabbage, tomatoes, cucumbers, radishes, onions, garlic, peas, beans, carrots, basil, mint, thyme, oregano, bananas, limes, lemons, and papaya (which Dennis, who's from New Mexico, insists is mango). Of course, *he* doesn't grow any of it. That's the job of Victor, the gardener, and his two assistants, who also do that little bobbing movement when I walk by.

Inside, Dennis introduces me to Tenson, the cook, and Kitwell, the steward, both dressed in uniforms of beige leisure suits. Baobabs, termite mounds, now stewards: it's all too much to absorb after flying for two days. *Isn't Queen Victoria dead?* I think, getting into bed and snuggling next to Dennis. *Aren't the days of the British Empire in Africa done?*

And awaken the next morning to Kitwell looming over us with steaming cups of tea. "Dennis!" I hiss, pulling the blankets up around my neck.

"Uh, Kitwell, thank you," Dennis says. "But we'll just have tea with breakfast."

When I finally stumble, now fully clothed, from the bedroom, the dining room table is set with gleaming silver and china. *In the morning!* Kitwell scurries from the kitchen to inquire what we would like, thanks us for the order, and scurries back to the kitchen. While we're eating, the bed is magically made, furniture dusted, bathroom scoured, our dirty clothes whisked away. The dining room gets the same treatment as soon as we finish, as does the rest of the house. Hotel living at its best! And you don't have to worry about the laundry losing your undies—although mine do come back ironed by Kitwell.

Afterward, Tenson meets with me in the kitchen, his kitchen, really. He, too, addresses me as "Madam." When I demur, he makes clear he'd just as soon call me bitch as Lynda, or even—taking my little charade to its fullest—Mrs. Jett. Furthermore, Tenson only wants to confer with me because Bambo is too busy with weighty embassy matters; he can barely contain his dismay when told I will also be working in South Africa. Every day we must go over the menus for lunch and dinner and the shopping that needs to be done.

Tenson is thin, thin, thin, with a closely shaved head shaped like a tree nut atop his rickety boy body. This wouldn't seem to bode well for his craft, but I will quickly learn that Tenson isn't so much a cook as a magician, a conjurer from whose hands cakes ascend heavenward and soufflés defy the bounds of gravity—despite only a fifth-grade education. "What are you making, Tenson?" I ask brightly, having gotten a tour of all the cupboards and wanting to seem interested in the pot boiling on the stove.

"My lunch, Madam," he says.

"And what is it?"

"A sweet potato, Madam," he says, lifting the lid to show the tiniest of tubers.

"That's not very much!"

Tenson gives a sardonic little laugh. "That's what we can eat, Madam," he says. I don't know, given the rather formal English of Chichewa speakers, whether he's telling me that's what he *wants* to eat—or that's what he can *afford* to eat.

In any event, a couple of days later Dennis and I are sitting in the garden having drinks. I'm wearing jeans, even though the life president has decreed women can only wear skirts that fall below their knees. I figure the Pants Police can't arrest me in a diplomat's house. "Will you look at that!" Dennis says, noticing a pair of largish birds, with green-crested heads like dunce caps and a flash of crimson showing under blue-and-green wings, perched in a tree.

He runs to grab a guidebook from the study. "Green louries!" he announces, triumphantly. "And carmine bee-eaters!" he says, pointing to a clump of hummingbird-like creatures cavorting in the birdbath, their brilliant little red bodies offset by black bandit masks across the eyes. It's like being on a birding tour in the comfort of your own backyard.

I recount to him my conversation with Tenson. "Do you know how much he earns?"

"Not off the top of my head. But I guarantee you he's better paid than 95 percent of his countrymen."

"Yeah, but does that mean he can live on it? Or raise a family?"

"Welcome to one of the poorest countries in the world," he says, taking a long sip of beer. "We have to pay local rates, even if it's a pittance. Much more than that, and the bean counters in Washington dig in their heels."

"While we live like Masters of the Universe!"

"Look, Miss Liberal Guilt, I'm not going to make them better off by living at their level. Also, I'm not in the Peace Corps."

"Then why are you here?"

"We have aid programs—"

"Yeah, that go right into the pockets of His Greediness, the Life Despot," I say, cutting him off. "I mean, this man has, what, six palaces? Six! While his people live in mud huts and can barely survive? Even one would be obscene under these circumstances."

"Lynda, I don't like the politics or economics here any better than you. But this is my job . . . " he says, his voice trailing off. I follow his gaze to a nearby flowerbed: there, trundling along, is what appears to be a massive monitor lizard. Think our cute little reptile in Miami if it took a banned substance and suddenly bulked out, a kind of Hulk of the claw-foot set—but in a more muted color scheme. Also add a bone-crushing Stegosaurus tail. "Holy crap!" Dennis says, grabbing our glasses and making a dash for the house.

I'm right behind him. "But can you at least check into a raise for the guys?" I ask, watching the lizard's progress from the patio door. "And while you're at it, maybe do something about the *National Geographic* special we've got in the garden?"

Dennis ultimately increases their salaries to a whopping fifty-five dollars a month plus overtime—a princely sum in a country where the average income is two hundred dollars a year. And I take to giving them all our leftover food. Still, Tenson has five children and Kitwell has six; even with their new pay, I have no idea how they can afford to feed them.

Tenson (after receiving his raise) says: "Madam, God sent Bambo and you to us."

I (embarrassed) say: "No, Tenson, it was the US government."

Dennis is right, as I'm coming to realize he often is about things that drive me to a frenzy: he won't improve anyone's existence by moving into a hut and eating *nsima*, maize mush. But having this privileged position allows him, at the very least, to help change a few lives directly—so different from the abstract effect of sending a story out into the world as a journalist and hoping it does some good. Anyway, how could you *not* want to do something in the face of such poverty? People here wear faded, torn dresses or trousers that look like rejects from clothing drives. Shoes are rare; disease is not. Women walk miles just to collect water. And you can forget about any kind of sanitation in the villages. The little food to be found in stores is usually imported and might just as well be emeralds or Ferraris. Most children stop their education at the end of elementary school because their parents don't have money to pay the fees. There is one upside to the privation, though: no litter. The population is too poor to throw anything away. They even wash used pieces of plastic wrap and hang them on bushes to dry. *The ultimate recycling program!*

One Saturday, Dennis and I set out to visit a Catholic mission that's two, maybe three hours to the southeast of us, near Lake Malawi. The priests run a crafts center on the grounds where the locals learn woodcarving and sell their creations to the public. We start off on a pitted, two-lane road that has little vehicular traffic, just the usual stream of people flowing along the shoulders and carrying astonishing loads. One woman we pass is somehow balancing a whole tree *on her head!* We overtake a few oxcarts and the occasional rider on a rickety bicycle, but for the most part it's people. And villagers, holding up goods for sale. Each stretch of the highway, if you can call it that, seems to specialize in a particular item: here's your district for charcoal, your district for live chickens, etc.

There's no place to stop for refreshments, though, so Tenson packed sandwiches and a thermos of tea for us. I unwrap a little bundle swathed in aluminum foil. "The cook's gone mad, dear," I announce in my best British accent.

Dennis checks the rearview mirror. "Why do you say that?"

"Because I can. I mean, who has a cook?" I hold up the foil packet. "But he actually has gone mad. I asked him to make some peanut butter and cheese sandwiches for the trip—and that's exactly what he made: peanut butter on one side, cheese on the other."

"Well, he was just following orders, Madam."

"Don't 'Madam' me, Bimbo."

While I'm trying to salvage our snack, we pass a group of boys brandishing sticks by the side of the road. "Wait," I say, whipping my head around. "Are they holding up skewered mice?"

"Mouse kebabs!" Dennis calls out when, a bit further on, we encounter more youngsters wielding stakes, each with seven or eight crispy little vermin bodies crucified on them.

"Do people here actually eat things like that?"

"They must. Why else would the kids be peddling them?"

"Yuck."

"Don't be judgmental. What would they think of gefilte fish?"

After we breeze by another group of roasted rodent salesmen, Dennis says, "Hey, I've got a great idea for a Christmas card. What if I make up a little sign that reads, 'Wishing You a Merry Crisp Mouse,' then drive out here and pay these kids to hold it and their mouse kebabs up while I take a picture? What do you think?"

"I think you're a very, very sick man," I say, kissing him on the cheek. "Cute, but sick."

We turn off the main highway onto an even more decrepit road that winds scarily down an escarpment, but with a view of the lake: a string bean body of water dividing Malawi from Mozambique. A few more miles along the lakeshore blacktop and we arrive at the mission. It's a tidy campus dotted with round brick huts called rondavels, painted in intricate designs. As soon as we emerge from the car, a voice calls out, "Muli bwanji?" I look around, startled, not seeing anyone. "Good morning!" the voice says, this time in English. I look down. There, on the path, a young man is crawling along the ground on his arms, dragging his withered, paralyzed legs through the dirt.

"Welcome!" the man says. "Is this your first time here? Would you like a tour?"

Should I squat down? Would that seem patronizing? "Thank you," I say, rooted in place. "We'd love a tour."

We slowly follow the man, who cheerfully points out the living quarters for the priests, the chapel, the workshops. Artisans chisel away at chunks of wood, some the size of small trees, in open-air pavilions. Our guide knows everyone: greeting each carver by name, reciting a bit of his background, allowing us to admire his handiwork. As he pulls himself along the path, the young man recounts the history of the mission—the oldest in Malawi—and its programs. He saves the showroom for last. Dennis dashes in and buys up just about everything in sight; I remain outside, chatting with the man. He's charming and articulate and funny—and all the while I can barely keep from weeping.

Which I do, once we're in the car. "How can he live his life like that?" I sob. "Why doesn't he have a wheelchair? Why should he have to scrabble around on the ground like, I don't know, like a *spider!*" All the way back on the lakeshore blacktop, back up the scary escarpment road, past mouse kebabs, live chickens, and charcoal, I'm fulminating about the man's situation: Unspeakable, in this day and age! No one should have to live without dignity! It's a disgrace, dragging himself through the dirt! And such a sweet man! I don't care if I have to import one from the States, he's going to have a wheelchair!

Dennis, in the face of my Lady Bountiful rant, remains quiet. The next day, he makes a few inquiries. The young man, it turns out, already owns a wheelchair; he simply didn't feel like using it on the day of our visit. The mission's bumpy paths make for rough going.

Welcome to Africa, White Woman.

Maybe this semi-hysteria is about me not working. I've obviously lived in impoverished, oppressed places before, but always as a reporter. Then I could justify my presence with the thought, however delusionary, that my journalism would somehow contribute to the population's betterment. Here, I can't even try to fool myself into believing that. As if this weren't guilt enough, then too there's the feeling of having been catapulted into a holdover from the British Raj: a life of luxury and privilege and let-'em-eat-cake. Also add in entertaining.

Because entertaining is what diplomats do. Particularly here, where there are no restaurants or theaters or clubs to speak of; the sole cinema, the Seven Arts, is known as the Seven Rats. The first time we have a formal dinner party, I emerge from the bedroom about a half hour before it starts to find Tenson, like Kitwell, attired in a white jacket and trousers—obviously their special occasion outfits. "Madam," Tenson says. "Your hair."

"What?" I ask, hastily touching my tresses that I wear longish, aiming for a careless, wind-blown look, but usually achieving just plain messy. "Is there something in it?"

"You look like a small girl."

I think he means unsophisticated.

The evening begins on the terrace with Kitwell discreetly dispensing MGTs (Malawi gin and tonics) and proffering hors d'oeuvres from a silver tray. For the meal itself, we move to the dining room table, with its little buzzer to summon Kitwell from the kitchen nestled near my chair on the floor. Of course, when I go to press it, I misjudge the location and end up playing footsie with the shocked Egyptian deputy ambassador. Dinner is served with great flourish and pomp, including two choices of wine and three desserts. Afterward, we repair to the living room. Kitwell lights a fire, pours coffee, offers brandies or port and, having ascertained from Bambo his services are no longer needed, retires from the room on whisper-tipped tennis shoes.

How am I ever going to fit in here, even if it's only to visit? I think later, when we're going to sleep. *Foot buzzers to summon stewards and after-dinner brandies by the fire? Servants bringing me tea in bed, instead of me cowering under it?*

The next morning Tenson says, "Madam, Stanley wishes to see you at the kitchen door."

Stanley is the night guard. He's in his blue uniform of short pants, knee socks, bush jacket, peaked cap. He's also holding aloft, proudly, a dead mamba—highly poisonous—that he killed with a panga (machete) while on duty. *In the backyard!* This is the moment when it becomes clear just how impossibly strange Dennis's life here is: liveried servants and lethal serpents, all in one neat parcel. "Uh, thanks, Stanley," I mumble.

It would probably feel less weird and insular if we could have Malawians over to the house. After all, isn't getting to know the peoples and culture of a foreign country half the fun of living abroad? But an air of fear permeates. Free speech is nonexistent; the government controls the country's only newspaper as well as its sole radio station. Nor is there television. Spies, however, abound, mostly in the form of the Young Pioneers: paramilitary thugs in Boy Scout–like uniforms who are neither young nor pioneers, but informers and enforcers for the dictator. And they're everywhere. As a result, the Malawians I meet are reserved to the point of aloofness—or terror—making socializing out of the question.

For women, submitting to the despot is particularly time-consuming. They're required to partake in a spontaneous display of gratitude and adulation anytime the life president pops up in their corner of the country, say, to tour the crops or celebrate Youth

Week or just hang out in a palace. It's all part of being his *mbumba*, his community of women, of which he is "guardian." To pay tribute, the *mbumba* don wraparound skirts, blouses, and headscarves all imprinted with a picture of the life president as a younger man. The background color differs from one group to the next, though, so when they're all seated by section in the local soccer stadium, the effect is that of an exceedingly well coordinated, college-style color out. The set-piece program is always the same. Each of the twenty or so groups is called down from the stands to the field; bending at the waist, the women shake to a drumbeat, singing the life president's praises and ululating. Eventually, the life president feels obligated to descend from the podium. The dancing women form a circle around him: a small, elderly man dressed in a dark, three-piece suit, shuffling his feet and waving a lion-tail fly whisk at the sea of gyrating buttocks and breasts emblazoned with his likeness. And so it goes until the next group is called.

Diplomats are required to attend these extravaganzas as well when they're held in the capital, which means, essentially, being locked in an open-air stadium for six or seven hours without shade or any kind of facilities. After he returns from one such outing, sunburned and desperate to pee, Dennis says, "I have another idea for a Christmas card."

"Yes?"

"How about a photograph of the life president in the middle of his *mbumba*, dancing with his fly whisk."

"And the greeting?"

"'Whisking You a Merry Christmas.'"

"Enough," I say.

Which is how I'm beginning to feel about being here. Luckily, my job is starting in South Africa. The night before I leave, we show a sixteen-millimeter film from the embassy in our living room. Dennis invites some of the expatriates we've befriended: his counterparts from the British and German embassies and their wives; an American public health worker and her husband; a few others. Michael, the Brit, and Peter, the German, are known for their prodigious drinking: dressed in business suits and holding hands, the two of them jumped into a swimming pool during a recent reception. Watching the incident, the wife of the British High Commissioner, Michael's boss, hissed, "That man's career is over if I have anything to do with it!" I ask Kitwell to keep an eye on how much he and Peter imbibe.

Tenson pops popcorn and makes chocolate ice cream for the evening, and things are going along swimmingly. There aren't enough couches to go around, so I settle myself on the floor. A few minutes later, I—and everyone else—see a big blobby thing, outlined in the projector's light, moving toward me. "Oh my," says Monica, Michael's wife, in what turns out to be one of the understatements of the century.

I flip on the lights. There, ambling across the carpet, is a very large, very furry tarantula. Dennis immediately jumps up, removes his sneaker, and makes as though he's going to squash it—only to realize the tarantula is wider than his shoe. It would be like trying to flatten a hairy beach ball with a ping-pong paddle. At which point, I flee to the bedroom. Shrieking. I have no idea how Dennis ultimately dispatches the beast; I'm hoping he called in the Marines. I refuse to budge from the bedroom and refuse to talk about it afterward. The next day, though, when leaving for my flight, I do note a sizeable dark stain on the carpet that Kitwell is busily trying to scrub out.

Only a two-and-a-half hour plane ride away, Johannesburg might just as well be on another continent. Huge houses behind gated walls, elegant shopping malls, well-paved highways, traffic jams: Los Angeles with the seasons reversed! Of course, under apartheid's racial segregation laws, that's only for the 15 percent or so of the citizenry who happen to have been born white.

For the rest of the population, the people of color upon whose backs the white cities were built, it's a different story. They're relegated to miserable, crowded townships, most of them miles from urban centers and jobs. The architects of apartheid ingeniously put them out of sight of white communities, so those residents wouldn't be inconvenienced with the reality of how their maids and gardeners are forced to live. The first time I drive the dozen or so miles out to Soweto, the sprawling township southwest of Johannesburg that's home to perhaps two million people, the sight is overwhelming: an endless vista of tiny matchbox houses of two or three rooms squeezed together in rigid, monochromatic rows; outdoor pit latrines and cold water taps; narrow, rutted roads, many of them unpaved; mountains of decomposing garbage. By design, there's no easy way to get from this world to that of the whites.

So for the denizens of Soweto, the day begins well before dawn, when many of them have to set out to try to catch one of the mini-van taxis—overcrowded, poorly maintained vehicles with drivers who are maniacal in their competitive zeal—that will transport them to Johannesburg. From there, it's another taxi ride or two to their jobs, where they work long, exhausting hours, often for ridiculously low wages. Reverse the protracted and dangerous slog home, eat, sleep, repeat. And that's only if they're fortunate enough to be employed.

Although I'm struggling to get up to speed on coverage, there's one glaringly obvious truth that even I can't miss: here, race is destiny. It determines where you're born, where you're educated, what you study, what profession you can aspire to, whom you marry, where you live, where you go for entertainment, what kind of medical care you receive, where you die, where you're buried. No matter the ability of your brain or stirrings of your heart, under apartheid your chances in life are bound—or not—by luck of the epidermal draw. It's an astounding and horrifying phenomenon to witness up close, made more so by the government's brutal enforcement. And there's little hope of legal remedy. A few courageous and tenacious judges aside, most adhere strictly to apartheid's draconian laws—and to the opinion expressed by a justice I interview not long after arriving: "When I look down from the bench at a black man, I don't see a human being," he says. "I see a monkey."

It's enough to make you want to weep.

Which I do, sometimes, when not shaking my head in utter disbelief. In moments like these, I almost find myself looking around for Dennis to share in the amazement. It feels strange, after living with him for well over a year now—longer than I lived with Dial—not to be together. To say nothing of a little lonely. So after weeks in a hotel, when I finally move into the house that's going to double as my office, I buy a sweet little black Labrador puppy. And then a yellow one. And another yellow. Jackie, a sociologist who befriends me, warns it's a serious sign of nesting. She should talk! Jackie has a half dozen or so yappy little dogs from the local pound, all of which, with the exception of the one she calls Baby Jesus, appear to be fully interchangeable furry rats. They have the run of her house and even sleep in her bed at night. Still, Jackie's nothing if not militant on the subject of procreation.

"Ain't happening," I assure her.

"We'll see about that," she harrumphs. "One minute it's pure-breds, and the next thing you know, you're breeding."

Actually, that last yellow puppy is for Dennis. He imported a black Lab from Zimbabwe, whom he named Lucille, and wanted a mate for her. I call him on my recently installed telephone in my house to talk about the dogs. "They're really cute," I say, watching them try to escape from a large basket. "I'm going to name the yellow one I'm keeping Sam, and the black one, Blanche."

Dennis warns me that my Aunt Blanche in Skokie is going to be offended. Then again, he's going to call his puppy Butch. *Butch?* "And while we're on the topic of dogs," he says, "Lucille tried to challenge a spitting cobra in the garden and it spat in her eye."

"Oh my gosh! How did you know?"

"Because she started screaming in pain. I've never heard a dog scream before."

"Is she okay?"

"Yeah, but only because I rushed her to a veterinarian who washed out her eye and saved her from going blind."

I'm about to tell Dennis that I'll be wearing a hazmat suit from now on when we have drinks in the garden, when we both hear the distinctive little *click-clicking* on the line: my phone's been bugged. "Well, that didn't take long," I say. "And I haven't even started writing stories that might piss off the government! But at least no one's reading *Dear Abby* while listening."

Dennis flies down to South Africa not long after that to collect Butch. We have a grand time doing all the things he can't in Malawi:

dining out, going to the movies, drinking potable water from the tap. It feels like the days when we were commuting between Miami and Washington, except that now, when he leaves, I miss him much more. Much, much more. Which is surprising, given how engrossing my reporting here is.

In fact, it's probably the best story I've ever covered, one of the great morality plays of the times. I mean, who can be in favor of apartheid? Beyond, of course, those benefitting from it and thus wanting to ensure its perpetuation. And they're not about to give in politely to demands for change. There's been a state of emergency in force for months now, slapped on by the government to crush antiapartheid riots—some quite gruesome—that had engulfed parts of the country before I arrived. Once again, I obviously don't agree with the protesters' violent tactics. But I understand the desperation that drove them to such things. In response, the government has detained thousands of activists, many of them mere children. And it outlawed television journalists from filming the brutal police crackdown, effectively preventing the images from being seen throughout the country, let alone the outside world. The rest of the media is censored, too. Even those antiapartheid groups that are adherents of peaceful protests have been banned, effectively gagging their leaders and shutting down most overt opposition activity.

So on the dissident side, my reporting isn't about mass protests and smashed windows, but stealthy resistance. Working in the townships amid this repression, though, is daunting; even the activists are scared to talk. Most interviews I do in Soweto are at night, when people return home from their jobs. On my way to interview a shop steward one evening, I'm stopped, as usual, at a checkpoint at the township's entrance, near a military base. A Casspir, an armored personnel carrier, is parked off to one side. The submachine-gun toting soldier walks slowly around my car, peering in the windows and occasionally tapping the body.

The soldier leans in my window. "Where are you going?" he asks in heavily Afrikaans-accented English.

"To visit a friend."

He pauses for a moment. "You from America?"

"Yes."

"Now why would a lady from America be going to Soweto at night?" he says, leering. The soldier on duty with him says something in Afrikaans, and the two snicker. I'm starting to perspire.

I say, "People work during the day. This is the only free time they have."

"Is it? Are you sure about that?"

"Yes." *You should know; you watch everyone who goes in and out.*

"Well then, don't keep them up too late," he says, grinning.

As I drive away, in my mirror I can see the two soldiers yukking it up. *Assholes,* I think—but I'm trembling nonetheless. And desperate to find the spot where I'm supposed to meet the steward, whom I don't know but who was described to me by another contact. The township has a Dickensian look to it at night: a pall of acrid, choking smoke from charcoal-burning stoves hangs over everything, making it even more difficult to navigate the poorly lit roads. Pedestrians materialize and dissolve with eerie suddenness. I'm positively sweating by the time I finally see a handsome, solidly built man in his thirties wearing a knitted cap.

"Hi, Lynda Schuster," I say, as he slides into the passenger seat. "I'm so sorry. The soldiers at the checkpoint were being idiots."

The steward chuckles. "That's nothing new. Were they hassling you?"

"Just making racist innuendos."

"Typical. Are you scared being here?"

"Only of the soldiers," I say, turning onto a cratered street. "With all the restrictions on the press, and what you can and can't report, they could make my life very difficult. But that's obviously nothing compared with what you have to put up with all the time."

"Yeah," the steward says, indicating where we should stop. "Rubber bullets and tear gas can really mess up your day."

His house is a tiny, cinder block structure. There's a postage stamp-sized living room with a small sofa and a couple of chairs, a kitchen the size of a telephone booth, a single bedroom. An elfin elderly woman, dressed in a bathrobe and slippers with a scarf tied around her head, occupies one of the seats. "This is my *gogo*, my grandmother," the steward says. "She only speaks Zulu." I bend down to shake her hand; she smiles, displaying a gleaming set of gums, and launches into a soliloquy that consists mostly of clicks and pops. "She's pleased to meet you," the steward says. "She apologizes for not being dressed, but she's almost a hundred years old."

I say, "Please tell her it's an honor to meet her and I love her bunny slippers."

The steward translates, then explains his wife is putting their young daughter to bed. While he makes tea in the kitchen, Gogo toothlessly babbles away. I smile and occasionally nod. Stupidly.

Talking with the steward, even in the privacy of his own home, feels perilous. The police have spies everywhere in the townships; by tomorrow morning, the Special Branch will not only know I was here, but how much time I spent and my movements after I departed. All of which is far more dangerous, really, for the steward than for me. Although there's nothing illegal in our meeting, the state of emergency's provisions practically make even *thinking*

antiapartheid thoughts a crime. The police could unceremoniously pick up the steward, haul him off for interrogations and torture, then detain him indefinitely. You can forget about anything
even vaguely resembling a writ of habeas corpus. And once the
security police have him in their clutches, there's no telling what
can happen. Over the forty years of apartheid rule, scores of activists have died in detention from official "causes" that would be
laughable if they weren't so tragic: slipping on a bar of soap in the
shower, for instance, or jumping from a tenth-story window *while
imprisoned.*

"We're the only ones left," the steward says, blowing on his tea.
"The unions and the church. We're the only ones they haven't yet
banned."

"Do you think the government will?"

"Ban the unions? I don't know. But they've gone after everyone
else."

"How do you feel about that?"

"It's a setback," he says.

That's putting it mildly. I say, "Uh, I'd think it's more than a
setback."

"It is difficult. We're going to have to adapt. But that's what
we've had to do for almost a half-century now."

"So what do you do now?" *Come on, specifics!*

The steward sips his tea. "We just keep educating our workers
about the struggle, about the history of peaceful protest."

Nice agitprop. "But in practical terms, what do you do?"

"We're working on new strategies," he says, nodding.

Which you're not going to tell me. "Okay, but what about the radical youth who are fed up with nonviolence?"

"I explain to them that as a tactic, violence is a nonstarter. It only gives the authorities an excuse to lock us all up. Or worse."

"Yeah, but they say nonviolence hasn't worked. They're impatient."

"I know," he says. "And I tell them this can't go on forever, the government trying to suppress three-quarters of the population into submission. The demographics are in our favor."

"Have you ever wanted to take up arms?"

"No."

"Really? Not even as a hotheaded youth?"

He grins. "Not even then."

"Why not?"

The steward looks at Gogo, whose head is starting to droop on her chest. "Because that would make me just like them," he says softly. "Just like our oppressors. And I don't want to be like them."

"Even after all they've done to your people?"

"Lynda, our cause is a just one. I've always believed that. We have justice on our side. You don't become bitter when you're fighting for justice. You just keep fighting."

"Forgive me for sounding cynical, but that's *so* hard for someone from the outside to comprehend," I say, shaking my head.

"But where would revenge get us? A bloodbath? That's not what our struggle is about. It's about liberation. It's about equality."

Tell that to the guys with the guns—on both sides! "Okay, so when?"

"When what?"

"When will that come?"

"Maybe not in my lifetime," he says, sitting back in his chair, arms folded. "But in my daughter's, that I'm sure of. Time is on our side."

The months pass. On weekends I fly to Malawi to see Dennis. Or he flies to Johannesburg to see me. The story in South Africa feels in-

creasingly compelling. Dennis feels increasingly like home. *Home?*
Until now, the concept has been as much a part of my life as, say,
heavy metal or bondage. And just about as likely. It's as though I
woke up one morning to find I'd suddenly acquired another language. *What's happening here?*

As much as possible, I try to drag out our time together. On one
of my visits, we spend the night at the embassy's cottage on Lake
Malawi. It's a simple, cinder block structure with a couple of bedrooms and a *khonde*, a small porch, overlooking the lake. The view
is lovely: the escarpment's dramatic plateaus, some scattered palms,
azure water. Mozambique is visible on the other side. After the
quiet and solitude of Lilongwe, it's nice to escape to the quiet and
solitude of the lake. There are no cigarette boats or jet skis here to
break the serenity with aquatic chainsaw sounds. A few pirogues
dot the lake, some with three, perhaps four fishermen standing in
them, casting nets and bringing up *chambo,* tilapia. That's what's
being prepared for dinner by the cook who, along with a small sailboat and collection of dog-eared bodice rippers, comes with the
cottage. Lucille the Labrador is a big *chambo* fan. On Dennis's last
visit to the cottage, he stopped off at a tiny processing plant to buy
some fish. The manager insisted on showing him around the facility; Lucille, meanwhile, trotted off on her own inspection tour that
consisted mostly of vacuuming up discarded tilapia heads—which
she promptly spewed all over the back of Dennis's station wagon
once they got under way.

Dennis is itching to take the sailboat out, but there's barely been
a ripple on the lake's surface all day. Finally, close to sunset, he notices a slight movement in the fronds of a palm near the cottage.
"Wind's up!" he says, running down to the water's edge to drag the
boat in. "Want to come?"

"Uh, this isn't exactly a gale," I say, eyeing the rickety wooden hull and diaper-sized sail. "I think somebody down the beach might just have sneezed."

"C'mon, it'll be fun!"

"You go, Captain Ahab. I'll just imagine it."

Despite his upbringing in landlocked New Mexico, Dennis studied for a while at the Naval Academy and knows how to sail. I watch him maneuver the tiny vessel across the water, though the twilight makes it difficult to follow his progress from the *khonde*.

Lulled by the lapping waves, my mind drifts to our trip here from the capital. On the way, we stopped off to visit Major Ted, a former British military officer. He seemed straight out of central casting: erect bearing, trim mustache, clipped speech. His modest house was bedecked with photographs of himself, mostly in uniform, as a younger man. "That's me and Mountbatten in the good old days," Major Ted said, pointing to the handsome last viceroy of India, circa the 1940s. Pausing for a moment, he added, "It's a pity we lost it."

"Lost what?" I asked.

"Why, India," he said, pronouncing it *In-juh*. "Whatever else could I have meant?"

After we'd admired the pictures and settled into chairs in the living room, he called for his "boys." That's when two young Malawians adorned in white waiters' jackets, red fezzes perched jauntily atop their heads, entered the room *on their hands and knees!* Speaking in Chichewa, Major Ted told them to bring a bottle of whiskey and three glasses. The men acknowledged the order and exited *on their hands and knees!* Okay, this sort of thing happened all the time around the life president, but Major Ted was neither Malawian nor official despot. Dennis leaned over to me. "We're guests here," he whispered. "Don't judge. And close your mouth." I snapped it shut. And kept it that way for the duration of the visit.

His calm is a great antidote to my crazy, I think now, peering into the dark to try to locate him. The moon is beginning to rise; I can barely discern, about a hundred yards from shore, the outline of the sailboat, which Dennis now seems to be paddling. The wind must have died completely. I'm about to shout some wisecrack at him when a herd of snorting hippos suddenly floats by. Hippos! They're among the deadliest animals in Africa, prone to capsizing boats when feeling frightened or threatened—not to mention biting humans in half with their enormous molars and canine tusks. And Dennis is headed directly into their evening water aerobics.

Another man I love is going to die. I race down to the shore, screaming, "Don't come back! Stay out there! *Don't! Come! Back!*"

Dennis's voice wafts across the still lake. "Why? Is our love affair over already?"

"Stop paddling! You're going straight into a bunch of hippos!"

"Hippos? Where?"

"Between you and the shore. Please stop!"

"They're vegetarians. They won't eat me, maybe just nibble around the edges."

"Dennis, please!"

The alarm in my voice must finally have registered with him; the boat stops. Dennis stays out there, bobbing, until the puffing and panting of the hippos passes and I tell him it's safe to paddle ashore. My trembling's down to a minor shiver by the time he drags the hull onto the sand. "Sorry about freaking out," I say, helping him pull down the sail. "I probably overreacted."

Dennis puts his arms around me. "Don't worry, Lynda," he

says. "Everyone knows government employees are really nasty. The hippos would have spat me out."

"I love you," I say, my mouth muffled in his chest. "You need to stay safe."

My little nervous breakdown is still on my mind the next day, like the aftermath of a migraine, when we arrive back at the house in Lilongwe. Tenson is hunched over a cooking magazine at the small table in the kitchen. He was desperate to learn new recipes, so I took out a subscription to one of those gourmet monthlies that is filled with gorgeous photographs of utterly perfect dishes—the culinary equivalent of a girlie magazine. And, like the latter, no matter how much you tell yourself the pictures are touched up, they still make you feel inadequate.

After saying hello and putting the cooler on the counter, I'm almost out the door again when Tenson stops me. I assume we're going to have one of our earnest discussions about, say, how many minutes of cooking until penne is *al dente*, but it's something far weightier: he wants Dennis to take him to his next posting. *Take him, as in making him a kind of a ward? Shades of neocolonialism!* Much as I'd like to be flattered, his request apparently isn't because of our pleasant dispositions and irresistible charm. Tenson says he has asked each of Dennis's predecessors for whom he worked to take him abroad—each of whom obviously declined, despite it being permissible under State Department rules. When I protest about him leaving his wife and children, he quickly cuts me off. "It's the only way I'll ever earn enough money to send my kids to secondary school, Madam," he says. "Besides, my wife thinks it's a good plan."

Dubious, I wander outside to find Dennis. He's standing at the edge of the pool, dipping a tennis racket into the water. "Why is your racket going for a swim and not you?" I say.

Not taking his eyes off the pool, he says, "Come look at this."

The water is covered in chunky greenish frogs, barely moving, some riding piggyback on one another. They seem dazed or drugged or just exhausted. Many are trailing long, translucent strands that shimmer in the sunlight.

"I am *never* getting in this pool again," I say, shuddering. "What happened? Moses and the Ten Plagues?"

"Breeding time," Dennis says. "A frog orgy."

"So now it's like they're all sitting around, postcoital, smoking a cigarette? What are those disgusting stringy things?"

"Must be the fertilized eggs." Using the racket, he scoops up two frogs still attached to each other and lobs them over the fence with a *thwack*, a slimy thread sailing behind.

"Oh, Kermit," I chirp. "Did the earth move for you?"

"Funny, Schuster."

"Seriously, why don't you use the pool net?"

"I can't find it."

"But aren't you hurting them?"

"Lynda, the idea is to get the little buggers as far away as possible. Or do you want a pool filled with tadpoles?"

"I don't want this pool under any circumstance. Period." I flop onto a chaise lounge. "Not to change the topic, dear, but Tenson wants you to adopt him."

"What do you mean?"

Thwack!

"He wants to go with you to your next post so he can make enough money to send his kids to high school. I told him you probably wouldn't be crazy about taking him away from his family."

"You're right," Dennis says, moving to the other side of the pool. "But it's not as farfetched as it sounds. There's a tradition here of men going off to work in the South African mines."

"Yeah, but South Africa's probably a lot closer than wherever you're going next," I say, shading my eyes against the sun. "So, uh, where *are* you going?"

"I don't know yet. Most likely somewhere on the continent, probably West Africa."

Thwack!

"And what's going to happen to us?"

Dennis stares down at his racket. "We'll be together."

Isn't that a little presumptuous? "But how?"

Thwack!

"Why don't you quit your job and follow *me* around the world?" I say, trying to sound nonchalant. "You know, become a kept man."

Dennis peers at me as if I were suggesting something truly radical like a sex-change operation, say, or even podiatry. "Sorry, I'm already spoken for. The government owns me. Besides, isn't writing a lot more portable than diplomatting?"

So should I become a kept woman? How can I even be considering such a thing?

"You know, Lynda," Dennis continues. "The only impediment to us living happily-ever-after isn't that you're short and I'm tall." *Thwack!* "Or that you're Jewish and I'm an aspiring-to-be-excommunicated Catholic." *Thwack!* "It's that you're a journalist." *Thwack!* "And I'm a bureaucrat." *Thwack!* "And we both love our work." *Thwack! Thwack!*

I can't guarantee that no animals were harmed in the making of this scene.

———

I have to hurry back to Johannesburg to do a story on local elections, so our future together is left unresolved. It seems a common motif in my love life. *Maybe something will turn up*, I think on the plane. *It always has before.*

In South Africa, the government is holding the municipal vote as part of an attempt to co-opt black communities and forestall the dismantling of apartheid. But with just about every opposition group outlawed, their leaders under arrest or banned, getting the message out to people in the townships to ignore the election is difficult. Even a whisper of boycott could land you in jail. Still, it's happening, if only furtively. I know this because the shop steward, after several interviews, decided to open up a bit. He tells me church organizations and unions are printing up anti-election pamphlets and surreptitiously distributing them at prayer meetings and on trains, and puts me in touch with a colleague who's going to show me the illegal activity.

We meet during the afternoon rush hour at the train depot in Johannesburg's industrial sector. The place is thick with workers heading back home to the townships for the night. "That's ours," the man says, indicating a train so tightly packed with riders they're spilling out the windows and clinging precariously to doors. "Second car from the end." At the last moment, just as the train is departing, he glances around nervously, grabs my arm, and hauls me into the car. I can barely breathe, squeezed in among all the bodies. My contact says something to a small man in a baggy, double-breasted suit who, yelling to be heard over the train, tells the workers in Zulu that I'm an American journalist writing a story about the boycott.

From somewhere in the crowd, a voice rings out, "Comrade, what is your name?"

Comrade? I shout, "Lynda!"

"Comrade Lynda, stand up! We can't see you!"

"I *am* standing!" I bellow.

"Comrade Lynda, you are the first white woman ever to ride this train! Are you scared?"

"No, should I be?"

"No, Comrade Lynda! That's the right answer!" he yells, and a cheer goes up.

By now, the engine has picked up speed and there's at least a hint of air in the car. The man in the double-breasted suit is distributing leaflets that say *DON'T VOTE* and belting out a song about how town councilors are just a bunch of dogs. The commuters join in. "Are you going to vote?" the man yells.

"No!" they respond.

"Are you going to resist?"

"Freedom!" they roar.

For a political exercise, it feels more like a cross between a pep rally and a fitness class. All around me, people are doing the *Toyi-Toyi*, a kind of quick jog in place, knees lifted high, punctuated with grunts and singing in time to the steps—a trademark of the protest movement. Every so often I take a knee to the kidneys because of the crowding, but the overall effect is infectious. Our car is bouncing, and from the outside it must look like a prizewinning lowrider as the train hurtles toward the township.

It's dusk when we reach the end of the line. Eager to get home, a wave of commuters, hastily stashing the illicit propaganda in pockets or under hats, sweeps me out of the coach. The double-breasted suit and my contact quickly melt into the crowd; I'm left standing on the platform. But I am not alone; about a dozen youths from the train surround me and begin a barrage of questions:

"You're American, you had a revolution; how do we have one here? What can we do to speed it up? Is there anything different we should try?" They're so young, so earnest, so impassioned, their interrogation is heartbreaking. As if holding a passport from a country that rebelled two centuries ago makes someone an expert on insurrection!

What am I doing? A policeman might happen by at any moment and see me, a foreign journalist, giving out tips on how to topple the government. Which would be a joke in itself; the candy bar one of the teens is holding probably knows more about the subject than I. What's not funny, though, is the ease with which the authorities could expel me from the country, at the very least. I mumble something to the youths about only being a reporter and that they should look to their few leaders not yet jailed, then leave. Fast.

A couple of days later, I get a call from Max, a political officer at the US embassy who's been a great source for stories. He wants to talk—but at his home, not the office. "Let's go for a walk," he says when I arrive, pointing to the ceiling and indicating the listening devices the South African government has presumably installed.

As soon as we're outside, Max says, "I'm worried you're going to have a car accident."

I laugh. "Max, I know I'm not the greatest driver, but that's what you had me schlep here for? I thought you were going to tell me something juicy."

"Obviously you don't understand what I'm saying. Let me put it this way. You're everything the government hates: you're a woman, you don't hang out with the other foreign correspondents, you spend all your time in the townships, and you're writing stories too close to the bone for them."

"So?"

"So I'm worried that one night, you're going to be in a fatal car crash. And no one will be able to tell it was deliberate. Everyone knows that people here drive like maniacs."

I stop walking. "Wait a minute. You're telling me the government wants to kill me?"

"Maybe not the government per se, but the security apparatus. The stories you've been writing about them are a threat."

"Okay, but it's a big leap from being pissed off to killing me."

"Lynda, do not underestimate the brutality of the system here. These guys will stop at nothing to stay in power."

The jacarandas are in all-out spring bloom; a dreamy, purple-blossomed cloud hovers over the city. *How can there be such evil in so beautiful a place?* I already knew the authorities didn't like me. Unlike my colleagues, who routinely receive visas for six months, a year even, I've been kept mostly on a three-month permit. It's meant to be a tight leash: upon receiving a visa, I immediately have to apply for a new one. Every few weeks, I'm called to Pretoria for a chat. A bureaucrat from the Home Affairs ministry lectures me about my stories; I feign contrition. The bureaucrat smiles; I smile. We're done with the charade. *But kill me?*

"Max, are you saying this because you have specific information or because you're just generally worried?"

He pauses for a moment. "I can't tell you that. I just want you to be careful."

"I'm not going to start censoring what I write," I say, shaking my head. "So what am I supposed to do? Stop driving? You have to drive everywhere here."

"I know, but please be careful."

At first, our conversation makes me utterly paranoid. There are thousands of vehicles on Johannesburg's roads, many of which— obviously—are following me. Dennis suggests telling my editors back in the States, but I'm worried they'll want to do something drastic like pull me out of the country. And then where would I be? Even further from the action *and* Dennis. After a while, though, I start to relax. It's like receiving one of those chain letters that threatens unspeakable horror if not immediately forwarded to sixty thousand people: by about the fifth day, with Armageddon not even vaguely on the horizon, you triumphantly crumple it up and throw it in the trash. *Maybe Max was overreacting; maybe he saw some random intelligence report and was just being melodramatic.*

A few weeks later, I'm sitting in my car after interviewing a realtor about Johannesburg's housing market, checking the address for my next meeting. Suddenly, the agent is knocking on my window. "You won't believe it," he says breathlessly. "But I think someone's following you!"

"Really?" I say, trying hard to sound nonchalant.

"Yeah, I was watching you go, and as soon as you left the building, these two large chaps came out of nowhere and got into a car up the road. One of them, the driver, keeps looking out his window."

I glance in my rearview mirror. "Are they still there?"

"Yeah, about six cars behind you."

The agent is clearly one of those turn-a-blind-eye, go-out-to-fancy-restaurants-and-have-a-good-time, parallel-universe whites. For him, this place is of no more political concern than, say, Andorra or Lichtenstein. If he noticed the Security Branch guys, they must be obvious.

"Do you want me to do anything? Maybe call the police?" he asks.

"Uh, thanks, but that would probably be redundant."

The rush-hour traffic is too heavy to discern anything in particular after I leave; everyone and no one could be trailing me. It's a wonder I don't get into an accident, though, given how obsessively I check my mirror. I finish my last interview and make it home without incident. *They're just trying to scare me,* I think, pulling into the driveway. *But they're doing a damned good job.*

Not long after that, I'm leaving Soweto after a night of interviews. It's late; the roads are deserted. As soon I get onto the empty highway back to Johannesburg, headlights pop into my rearview mirror. *It could be anyone,* I think, forcing myself to take slow, deep breaths and concentrate on the road ahead. I'm in a kind of no man's land between the township and the white city; there's nothing around for miles. I speed up. The headlights stay with me. I slow down. The headlights are still there. My hands are so sweaty, I can barely grip the steering wheel. "It could be anyone," I say aloud, then break into a rendition of "Oh! Susana," at the top of my lungs, even though I can't carry a tune and know only one verse. The noise keeps me company, though.

A couple of exits before my usual turnoff, I leave the highway. The headlights follow. "Sheer coincidence!" I say, trying to convince myself. But at least now I'm in a residential district. It's comforting to know there are people behind those high walls and locked gates—although in reality, they'd have no clue if anything happened on the street. Two blocks before my house, the headlights disappear. "Sheer coincidence!" I say. Safely in my own garage, I turn off the engine and rest my head against the steering wheel for a second or two to compose myself. *How am I supposed to function here?* I wonder. *Take the bus? Just the thing for an intrepid foreign correspondent!* I'm still trembling when I walk to the house, and Blanche, the Labrador, comes bounding up to lick me. Sam, her brother, inexplicably disappeared a couple of months ago; maybe the Security Branch went after him, too.

Inside, I bolt the door and pour myself a glass of Chardonnay the size of a Grecian urn. *Covert war is just as nerve-racking as the kind with exploding bombs and land mines,* I think, gulping down the wine. Calmer now, I call Dennis to tell him the story.

Short pause. He says, "I have the perfect solution."

"And what might that be?"

"Marry me."

"Dennis, you know I love you. But how is that the perfect solution?"

"Because I just got my onward assignment. I'm going to be the deputy ambassador in Monrovia, Liberia."

Liberia? That's millions of miles away, in West Africa!

"Telephoning there is impossible," he says. "Don't renew your contract with the *Monitor*. You can write about things in Liberia. Marry me."

"That's so romantic!"

"Lynda, I'd get down on one knee but the telephone cord won't stretch that far."

"Isn't that cowardly, though?"

He says huffily, "Well, if you put it that way—"

"No, I mean I'd be running away from South Africa. I'd be getting married to run away from the story here."

"Lynda, you'd be getting married because we love each other and want to be together."

Funny how these things go. One minute you're utterly resolute in your convictions, convictions you've held steadfastly to your whole life: immutable, unshakable, indestructible, never-give-up-an-inch, Berlin Wall–type convictions. The next thing you know, in a split-second flash of clarity, they all come clattering down. *I'd be getting married because we love each other and want to be together.* It isn't just that I've lost my nerve; I'm beginning to grasp—obvious to most sentient beings—what's important. Love, for instance. There's no way of getting it back with Dial. But having found love an astonishing second time, I'm not about to lose it again. Not to my job, not to his, not to anything within our control.

Am I becoming my mother? In an earlier incarnation, that question might have triggered a panic attack, if not full-on shingles. Not now. Not after the bombs, the bugged telephones, the headlights in the night. If the tradeoff for being happy again is to embrace something that veers perilously close to looking like Mom's life, then so be it. And that includes getting married again. After all, diplomats don't die—at least, not at the same rate as journalists. I'll be safe. He'll be safe. We'll be safe together.

Silly me.

CHAPTER EIGHT

LIBERIA, 1989

Five days before our wedding, I'm obsessing over last minute preparations when Dennis calls from the embassy. We talk about the
party, then he adds, "Oh yeah, and about a hundred rebels apparently
crossed the border from the Ivory Coast a day or two ago, killing
some customs officials." Normally something like this would, at the
very least, prick up my ears. But we've been here for a few months,
and I know enough about the geography to shrug off the incident—
the obvious tragedy of the deaths notwithstanding. We're in Monrovia, on the coast; the incursion occurred upcountry, in an impossibly
remote area. Figuring out the number of chicken breasts for the
wedding dinner seems more pressing at the moment.

In the evening, though, when Dennis returns from the embassy, he tells me a second rebel group also entered Monrovia itself. This gets my attention. The conspirators, wearing new blue sneakers to identify themselves, had arranged to meet at the downtown army barracks where disaffected officers were to give them guns and ammunition to attack the president in the Executive Mansion. A potential defector must have tipped off his superior: loyal soldiers were waiting in the market at the appointed time and arrested twenty men sporting blue shoes.

"Were they suede?" I ask.

"I don't understand," says Dennis.

"The shoes. Were they blue suede shoes?"

"Why do you want to know?"

"It's a joke, Jett. So is this serious?"

"I don't know."

"What do you mean, you don't know?"

"I don't know."

"Seems pretty amateurish to me."

"Lynda," Dennis says slowly, as though I'm a non-native English speaker, "the government isn't saying anything, so it's hard to tell what exactly is happening."

It's remarkable how the rest of the world ceases to be important when you're getting married, how willing you are to gloss over events that might otherwise trigger alarms, to accept explanations that would normally set you howling —just so you can get back to focusing on what truly matters. Like whether to wear nylons in the sweltering tropical heat. Or if the whalebone-ish thing built into the bodice of your strapless dress is really going to hold your breasts in place.

We're getting married at our residence, which was the Dutch

embassy until about a decade ago. That's when the current president—a lowly master sergeant at the time—jumped the fence of the Executive Mansion one night and, along with some army buddies, disemboweled the then-president in his bedroom and declared himself head of state. The Dutch government found the coup d'etat rather distasteful and pulled out of the country, selling its property to the US embassy. The structure served as both chancery and residence for the ambassador who lived, as it were, above the shop. It's ludicrously large for just two people: downstairs is a maze of former offices that we use for guests and storage; upstairs, the living and dining rooms have all the charm of airplane hangars. But there's a wall of windows and French doors that open onto a terrace with a stunning view of the Atlantic Ocean.

That's if you look straight ahead. To the right is a former Health Ministry office, a once beautiful building with high ceilings, arched entryways, imperious stone lions guarding the curved stairs. Squatters long ago took it over. The last time anyone counted, eighty-seven people lived there without running water or toilets, amid crumbling walls and pyramids of garbage on the front lawn that grow ever-taller from trash that's flung out the paneless windows. Occasionally someone decides to burn the piles, usually when the wind is blowing in our direction. The residents do have electricity, though, having apparently tapped into our lines. At night, when I let the dogs out, I can see lights shining throughout the building and sometimes even the bluish, cathode ray glow from a television set. *Foreign aid at its most direct!*

Tenson, who managed to convince Dennis to bring him along, doesn't have a very high opinion of the country. Although he's earning a lot more here than in Malawi, it barely compensates for the contempt he feels for Liberians. He was raised in the stern, Scottish missionary branch of the Presbyterian Church and, like many of his countrymen, is reserved almost to the point of prudishness. (The only time I heard him curse was shortly after I arrived and accidently sliced open my leg on a sheet of glass; he took one look at the yawning wound and spurting blood and exclaimed, "Oh, shit, Madam!") Liberians, by contrast, are a lively lot: loud, brash, emotive, assertive. Which explains Tenson's animus; it would be like dumping someone from rural Kansas into the middle of the Bronx.

Precisely because they're *not* Liberian, he holds our stewards, Abdoulaye and Moussa, in higher regard. Like Tenson, they both left their wretchedly poor country, Guinea, in search of better wages. The two couldn't be more dissimilar, though. Think classic buddy movies in which the big, moody, brash guy, (in this case, Abdoulaye) is forever searching for the perfect get-rich scheme, while his slender, unassuming, soft-spoken sidekick (Moussa) tries to save his pal from himself. Also, add in slight French accents and an aversion to dogs because of their Muslim faith. Our three Labradors probably disgust them, but they've never let on and always laugh politely when, in that loathsome way of childless dog owners, we share with them our pets' latest adorable stunt: chewing up a table leg, say, or peeing on the guest room carpet.

We're getting married on New Year's Eve; that way, as Dennis says, we'll have a *real* reason to celebrate the end of every year. Setting a date was the easy part. Then came the touchy little topic of a guest list. "Let's invite everyone from the embassy," I said, when we finally got around to the discussion. "It'll be fun. But no family."

Dennis looked taken aback. "No family? Your father's coming to visit with your stepmother and sister. So is Simcha. And Ali." (His teenaged daughter.)

"But they're not actually *invited* to the wedding, they'll just happen to be here when we get married."

"Yeah, and what're we going to do? Not let them come to the ceremony?"

"No, silly. But the point is, we didn't *ask* them to the wedding. They all planned to visit us at Christmas, and then we decided to get married on New Year's Eve. It's that simple."

"Lynda, I think you're getting a bit Talmudic here," Dennis said. "This is all about your mother, isn't it?"

"No, it's not!"

Dennis narrowed his eyes.

"Okay, maybe a little," I said.

He narrowed his eyes further; anymore, and he'd have to use a guide dog.

"Okay, maybe a lot," I said. "But I have a tradition of not getting married around her."

"Well, I don't feel the same way about my mom."

"But if you invite her, then I have to invite mine."

"I thought you were getting along better with her."

"I am," I said, picking at a stray thread on the armrest of my chair. "I just don't want to have to deal with the drama between her and my father."

"And how do you think she's going to feel when she finds out not only was she excluded from yet another of your weddings, but your father wasn't?"

Stupidly, the question of empathy for Mom always stumps me. There I was, the bleeding-heart former foreign correspondent who had wept over the oppressed, railed against the plight of the downtrodden, championed the underdog—but couldn't muster even a nanoparticle of compassion for her own mother. *How can I be such a hypocrite? Why can't I just let this go?*

Dennis continued, "I mean, how would you feel if your daughter did that to you?"

"Well, since I'm never having children, it's a moot point. And if one of the Labs runs off with a mutt without me, I'll be sad but respectful of its decision."

"Cute, Schuster," he said. "So now I'm a mutt?"

And that's how we came to have family, who weren't invited to the wedding but are attending anyway, staying in the house. A couple of days after the border incursion and guys with blue sneakers, we're all in the library when the two-way radio starts squawking. The walkie-talkie is a regular feature of our Liberian life, much like the intense tropical humidity that makes it feel as though you're stepping, fully clothed, into a Turkish bath when you go outdoors. Or the mold that grows on your shoes if you don't keep a light on in the closet. The radio's alert, a high-pitched, two-toned blast, never fails to make me jump. "There is machine gun fire near Rally Time Market," the embassy's Marine guard intones. "Remain in your homes. Do not go outside."

Everyone looks at me expectantly; a coup wasn't on the list of prenuptial activities. After several attempts, I reach Dennis on the telephone at the embassy. He says government soldiers are running amok in the market, probably trying to round up more blue shoe sympathizers. Knowing my knee-jerk, journalistic reaction to jump into a taxi and head straight for the action, he adds, "And Lynda, stay inside. Please."

After several hours, the advisory is lifted. But there are checkpoints now at every entrance into the city, and a curfew in effect. Soldiers block off the road in front of the Executive Mansion, cutting Monrovia in half. Only by taking a long detour can you get to the other side. The capital is effectively sealed off from the country, and the president sealed off from the capital—all without any kind of official explanation.

That is, until the eve of our wedding, when the president suddenly appears on television to make a speech about the rebel attack. He looks calm and assured: his pudgy face in outsized designer glasses and pudgy body squeezed into a spiffy, double-breasted suit—a far cry from the shy, skinny soldier who first took over the country. Ten years as a cruel and vicious dictator will do that for you. "Liberian dissidents tried to invade the country and overthrow my government," he says. "Two people were killed. But everything is under control. There is no need to panic. Everybody should go out and celebrate the New Year."

Go out and celebrate with checkpoints?

Dennis turns off the television. We're alone; everyone else has gone to bed. "I think we should postpone the wedding," I say.

"Don't be ridiculous," he says.

"You don't understand. I was the one who never wanted to risk getting married again. And now there's this, this, *thing . . .* "

Dennis puts his arms around me. "It's nothing."

"It just feels, I don't know, sort of menacing, like my old life. This isn't the way I wanted us to start off our marriage."

"I know. But the night before is a little late to cancel."

He does have a point. A Lebanese restaurant is cooking a big spread for the buffet; we've hired a band by the inspired name of the Music Messiahs to play on the terrace. And an associate justice of the Liberian Supreme Court is going to marry us. I'd invited him to lunch a few weeks earlier to discuss the ceremony and request the "obeys" be excised from my vows. An elderly man, the justice said the procedure was painless: ten minutes, and it will all be over. Dropping "obey" was another matter, however. He launched into a long discourse on the legality of modifying the accepted wording, at one point looking over the tops of his glasses and asking sternly, "And why *don't* you want to obey your husband, young lady?"

In the end, though, he relented, and we moved on to other topics. He nodded when I asked if he had children, swallowing a mouthful of rice. "Eight," he said.

"Eight! You must really love your wife!"

"Her? Oh, I only have two by her. As for the rest," he chuckled, "well, you know that a judge has to travel up-country a lot." At that, he laughed uproariously, slapping his knee and throwing his napkin onto the floor.

Precisely the sort of person you want to marry you.

Coup or no coup, clearly it *is* too late to cancel. Anyway, the next day, our wedding day, thousands of reenactors could be staging the First Battle of Bull Run below our terrace, and I wouldn't notice—that's how nervous and distracted I am. *All the things that can go wrong!* I think, watching Abdoulaye painstakingly fold linen napkins into little birds-of-paradise. It troubles me that I'm acting like the stereotypical bride, but what can you do? The last time I got married, everything happened so quickly there wasn't time to become preoccupied. All I had to worry about back then was finding an outfit to wear at the last minute. And maybe being kidnapped by the guerrillas I interviewed before the ceremony—which now, in my nuptial foolishness, feels less daunting than tripping on my high heels and falling flat on my face in front of all the guests. *How can I be such a ninny?*

Abdoulaye finishes with the napkins and disappears into the kitchen. I trail after him, but am waylaid by Simcha, who's standing outside the laundry room. "I just gave Moussa my dress to iron," she says. "He does everything so beautifully. How are you holding up?"

"Not well. I think I'd rather have to face shelling from the Druze militia."

"Please," she says, shuddering. Sim is on loan from her kibbutz to work in some official capacity in London, which made traveling to Liberia relatively easy. "Chin up, it's your big day."

"I know. It's just that I'm feeling so jittery and stupid. And a little guilty about my mom."

"Well, nothing you can do about that now."

"But it's worse because I think something's going on between my father and his wife," I say, lowering my voice. Before Sim came, Dennis and I took them, my sister, and Ali on a trip to the north. They were hoping to see the Africa of the movies—open savannah, herds of animals, a cute little village or two with people in colorful native dress—but instead were treated to mile after mile of impenetrable bush and rain forest. Every time we stopped, Dad and Gerrie each tried to corner me just to whisper nasty things about the other. "I mean, the whole point of not inviting my mother was to avoid her drama. And now they're more than making up for it."

"Oh, dear. That's a bit much to burden you with."

"Exactly why I'm just going to avoid him."

"Here's something that might cheer you. I saw Tenson pay a little boy from next door to climb up a palm tree in your garden and throw down a coconut."

"Really? He probably needed it for the cake."

"It was quite remarkable," she says, walking to the kitchen with me. "The boy just scrambled up the tree trunk barefoot, like it was nothing at all. What sort of cake?"

"Carrot with pineapple and coconut. Cream cheese frosting."

"How wonderful! How many brides can say that someone scampered up a tree in their own garden for the coconut in their wedding cake?"

"I suppose that's something to tell the children we're never going to have."

Sim shakes her head. "Never say 'never,' Lynda. You should know that by now."

Luckily, I have to leave to get my hair done after that, which gets me out of the house and out of everyone's way. It's pleasant to drive through Monrovia on a Sunday afternoon when the streets are deserted. Pleasant, that is, if you ignore the way many of its people live. The city has a spectacular setting, built on a hilly peninsula that juts into the Atlantic. The nicest neighborhoods have stately homes with wide verandas overlooking the ocean and high security walls; graceful palms line the streets. A few high rises, mostly government ministries, poke over the horizon. Most buildings, though, are two-story structures painted white or a pastel color in the tradition of Caribbean cities. And everywhere, everywhere, there are slums, hovels really, fashioned from corrugated tin, wood, bits of cardboard, old newspapers. Rivulets of raw sewage run through these areas; garbage putrefies under the tropical sun. Normally I would take time, at the very least, to contemplate this injustice, but not today. Today my wedding bell brain can't consider anything more socially conscious than observing a traffic signal.

The hairdresser, who's from Lebanon, has a small shop in a downtown arcade. Nothing fancy, just a few posters on the wall of Teutonic blondes promoting a German hair coloring company and some bottles of German nail polish on display. Most days the taps in the sinks run dry, and the shampoos and tints have to be rinsed out with water stored in large jugs. The place is crammed with women waiting to get their hair done for New Year's Eve. I have an appointment, but the hairdresser shrugs apologetically and motions to a stool in the corner. There I sit, watching him and his two brothers coax beautiful Lebanese hair into soaring styles, checking my watch and feeling the panic rise. *Relax. Take deep breaths. Keep it in perspective. It's only your coiffure.* I leap up and stick my face in the hairdresser's.

"I! Am! Getting! Married! In! One! Hour!" I bellow over his blow dryer.

At that, one of the brothers pushes me into a chair. He empties a can of mousse—it's still the eighties, even if only for a few more hours—then a can of extra-hold spray into my hair, applies a dryer with enough wattage to make the Hoover Dam tremble, and hustles me out the door. My hair now has the look and feel of a helmet: nothing that would meet today's safety standards, but might have been welcomed by a Roman gladiator. I race back home, squeeze into my dress with the worrisome décolletage and join Dennis, resplendently calm in a tuxedo, in the living room. "You're wearing *that* to your wedding?" Sim says, looking me up and down.

Then we sit around waiting for the Supreme Court justice, who shows up almost an hour late. I'm so nervous I can barely think. The guests, who've been milling about and cracking cold-feet jokes, troop onto the terrace. Dennis and I stand in front of them, holding hands; Ali, our ring-bearer, is to Dennis's right. The justice solemnly dons a black robe and cap, produces a sheaf of papers the thickness of a college course catalog, looks around at those in attendance, and clears his throat. Reading from the top sheet, he begins, "Marriage, according to universal and accepted principles of law, is a contract made in due form of law by which a man and a woman reciprocally engage with each other during their joint lives and discharge to each other the duties imposed by law on the relation of husband and wife." The justice pauses to wipe his forehead. "Marriage," he continues, "in our law, as distinguished from agreement to marry and from the act of becoming married, is the civil status of one man and one woman united in law for life for the discharge to each other and community of the duties imposed upon them."

Liberian English is often difficult for foreigners to understand, and I had asked the justice to speak slowly for our guests from abroad. Which he does, kindly, pronouncing each word with excruciating precision—while citing every civil case relating to marriage and property in the Liberian justice system, including the presiding judges and dates on which they wrote their decisions. *Is this payback for the brevity of my first wedding?* I wonder, sneaking a glimpse at my family, all of whom have that head-cocked, resigned look of people forced to endure their niece's first violin recital, say, or a poetry reading. Dennis keeps squeezing my hand, probably for encouragement and to make sure I'm still awake. Or that he is.

The ceremony drags on. I had scheduled it for sunset, based on the justice's promise of a ten minute rite. But the sun has long since doused itself in the ocean and darkness descended on our gathering. I'm doing head feints worthy of a professional running back as mosquitoes, the size of attack helicopters, buzz my hair. When we get to the part where Dennis and I exchange rings, Dennis fumbles to find the right finger in the gloom. The service finally ends with the justice, who needs a miner's headlamp at this point to read his script, marrying Dennis Jett to Harriet Shoot. (My middle name is Harriet.) Dennis takes me in his arms for a lingering kiss, and everyone applauds—most likely in relief.

"Well, that had all the majesty of a Marx Brothers film," Sim says afterward, in the receiving line.

Then the band sets up on the terrace, and we do what you're supposed to do at a wedding: eat, drink champagne, make toasts, stuff cake into one another's mouths. You could almost forget there's been a rebel incursion. I'm watching my tipsy father try to dance with Michael, the portly, ruddy-faced British diplomat who was in Malawi and is now the ambassador here, when Dennis slides in next to me on the sofa. "Are you happy?" he asks, kissing—or trying to—the top of my head.

"Let's see. Somebody spilled champagne down the front of my dress, I'm so sweaty you're going to have to peel me off this couch, and my shoes are killing me. Oh yeah, and you're apparently married to someone named Harriet Shoot. But at least nobody launched bazookas at the terrace. So am I happy?" I say, putting my hand— now adorned with a thin gold band!—in his. "Yes. Ecstatically so."

After the wedding, Sim returns to England, my family to the States, and I go back to researching a book on Liberia, which was founded by freed American slaves in the mid-1800s. The rebel incursion seems to have fizzled out. There was something on New Year's Day, an interview with a disgruntled former government official, who telephoned the BBC to say he had started a rebellion to overthrow the Liberian government. But really, how can you take someone like that seriously? What kind of revolutionary phones in an insurrection? *Maybe nothing bad is going to happen after all.*

Here's the thing about being in a developing country with a civil war brewing in the hinterland: because the fighting is occurring in places where the government—let alone its tightly controlled press— barely has a presence, it's easy to deny the gravity of the situation. Especially before the ubiquity of personal cell phones and their shaky little videos bearing witness. In the cocooned capital, you blithely get on with normal life, baking brownies and bleaching your mustache and being irritated by the toilet that won't stop gurgling—until the conflict rears up and smacks you in the face.

A few months later, I'm on a morning run with my friend Mary. She's the wife of one of the diplomats at the embassy, thin and angular, with a breathless way of speaking. For maximum aerobic effect, she hastily smokes a cigarette before starting and tucks another into the top of her sock to inhale at the end. We set out before dawn, before the heat and humidity and stench from the decomposing garbage become unbearable, and follow the shoreline toward the Executive Mansion. People stumble from their houses, sleepily making their way down to the water to relieve themselves; some squat in gutters to brush their teeth. Our run takes us by Redemption Beach, an historical landmark of sorts, where ten years ago thirteen cabinet members of the former government, dressed only in underpants, were lashed to poles to be shot by soldiers after the coup. But because they were drunk, the executioners—in full view of the international press, who were invited to watch—kept missing their marks and took several horrifying rounds to finish the job.

Mary and I jog past Faz 2 Bar and a video shop, then turn at the army barracks back toward the sea. Suddenly, I hear the unmistakable sound of a submachine gun being locked and loaded. I stop dead. A voice comes out of the half-light: "Halt! You can't go there!" Beside me, Mary slows a bit. "You can't go there!" the voice insists, louder and firmer. "That's the way to the Mansion!" Mary is now jogging in circles and working up to argue with the solider, someone she recognizes from the gaggle of congenial fellows who always greet us when we run by. I grip her arm.

"Let's go home," I say. "These guys are serious."

After all the vague reports from up-country, of being lulled into thinking the rebellion is nothing, really—the war has erupted in full view. In a series of surprise attacks, the rebels captured several important towns. They took control of the coastal road and, within days, cut off the southern shore from the rest of Liberia. They're now three hundred miles from Monrovia. Which is why our buddies guarding the Mansion are so touchy—and why the capital is swarming with equally agitated soldiers.

Three hundred miles? That's roughly the distance from Detroit to Chicago, just a long afternoon's drive! Even faster without toilet breaks! You'd think with all this going on, the government would be in some sort of emergency mode, canceling its usual activities and hunkering down for strategy sessions. Or at least say something! But its only reaction is to trim a three-day gala celebration, marking the tenth anniversary of the president's ascension to power, to just two events on one day. The first—a morning ceremony—is somewhat subdued, despite the party favors handed out by people from the Foreign Ministry: a tenth-anniversary beer mug, a key chain, and a plastic coffee cup that can be affixed to a car dashboard. The president reads a short statement, and soldiers form an honor guard for a twenty-one gun salute—of which thirteen shots are fired. Then the president drives off in his motorcade to inspect a new thoroughfare, only to return a couple of minutes later; the road is a dead end.

"A good metaphor for his presidency," Dennis says on our way into the luncheon in the fifth floor ballroom of the Executive Mansion. War or not, this is my first time here, and I'm hoping to see splendor. But the scene is more bar mitzvah banquet than presidential pomp: the waiters wearing T-shirts plastered with a picture of the honoree, multicolored strands of crepe paper hanging from the walls; people awkwardly clutching gifts. Any minute now, a DJ might take the microphone and urge everyone to start dancing the hora. Instead, an official booms out, "The president of Liberia!" We stand, a band plays a march, and the president strides into the room, a dark suit flanked by men wearing reflector sunglasses. A dozen or so soldiers clasping M-16s to their chests take up positions around the tables; photographers rush forward to snap pictures.

Now maybe the president will say something about the war, I think, my attention momentarily diverted by the vice president's sister, who's seated to my right and compulsively cleaning her flatware with a corner of the tablecloth. He only talks of his achievements, though. When he finishes to perfunctory applause, the chief of protocol grabs the microphone. "C'mon," he says. "I think the president deserves better than that." And, like a college cheerleader, he coaxes out another round of slightly more enthusiastic clapping. The president nods and sits down at the head table.

His wife is conspicuously absent. She and the president don't get on well; she has her own house in town and frequently flies off to England to shop and visit their four children who attend school there. Talk about Cinderella stories! One minute she was the wife of an army sergeant, selling dried fish and peppers in the open-air market; the next thing she knew, she was the First Lady. It was a difficult transition, but she made an effort. Monica, Michael's wife, says she once invited the spouses of the foreign ambassadors to tea. They arrived at the Executive Mansion elegantly dressed and coiffed and were ushered into the sixth floor living room, empty except for a few sofas where the First Lady and her ladies-in-waiting sat. A band of six soldiers in khakis and sunglasses played loud rock music in the hallway, making conversation impossible. The wives were offered their choice of whiskey or brandy; the First Lady and her entourage took theirs neat. One by one, the wives were introduced to their hostess. They shook her hand, were allowed to admire the view from the terrace, and were seated again.

Then the First Lady stood. "And now ladies, we're gonna shake our bodies," she announced. The bewildered wives were led into the hallway, where the band struck up a reggae tune and the First Lady and her friends began to dance. The wives, looking horrified, tried their best. After a couple of songs, they were asked to go. The First Lady never invited them back.

Her absence here only heightens the strangeness of the occasion. The president sits alone at the head table, several empty chairs separating him from his closest neighbor; a toothpick dangles from the side of his mouth, and his eyes dart as armed soldiers patrol the room. *Is he afraid someone's going to run at him with a soup spoon?* Then again, he does have a lot of enemies, especially with the fighting taking a decidedly ethnic turn. The rebels have found lots of recruits among the Gio and Mano tribes, the traditional rivals of the president's Krahn clan, eager to avenge a decade of corruption, nepotism, and human rights abuses.

Halfway through the luncheon, the guests are called to the table to offer their gifts. Then the president is served dessert. After staring at it for a moment, he abruptly rises and, borne along on a wave of security guards, departs. Lunch is over. Everyone files out of the ballroom, leaving the befuddled waiters balancing trays of unserved cake. Downstairs, we wait with Monica and Michael and the other guests on the Mansion's steps for the cars to be brought around. "In three years here," Michael says, shaking his head, "I've never once got dessert."

Dennis has to rush off to a meeting with Michael and European ambassadors afterward to chew over the situation. The closer the rebels get to Monrovia, the more brutal the president becomes. If the Liberian army can turn against its own citizens, what's to stop them from venting their frustrations on foreigners? The envoys fear their nationals could not only be caught in random acts of violence—an American, inadvertently driving through the barricades surrounding the Executive Mansion, was recently shot—but also become specific targets. No one is immune, not even diplomats. A few days earlier, the Japanese embassy's third secretary accidently cut in front of the vice president's motorcade; Liberian secret service men chased the diplomat back to the Japanese compound, pulled him out of his car, and knocked him to the ground. Fearing the military may become even less restrained as the war moves closer to Monrovia, Dennis—who is now charge d'affaires—and his counterparts issue a statement recommending that all dependents and nonessential personnel immediately leave the country.

Leave the country? Immediately? "What does this mean?" I ask, tremulously, when Dennis returns to the house.

"It means we think the army is out of control. If it can attack diplomats with impunity, then nobody is safe."

"Do I have to go?"

"That depends."

"On what?"

"On whether things get any worse. If they get worse, you may have to."

"Well, I'm not going," I say, grabbing his arm. "I'm not leaving you."

"Why worry about this now?"

"I just want to go on record that I'm not leaving."

Dennis rolls his eyes. "Lynda, we'll burn that bridge when we get to it."

The ambassadors' edict has the effect of validating everyone's worst fears. People start hoarding supplies and the shops run out of some foods. As the rebels continue their progress toward Monrovia, panic replaces the normal rhythm of life and rumor becomes the stuff that sustains it. Gone are the conversations about mail-order catalogs and low-carb diets at social events; now all anyone talks about is leaving. Even those in my Monday night women's group, an eclectic, polyglot bunch who usually discuss highbrow issues, with an occasional detour into such topics as, say, cellulite. As soon as we're all seated in her living room, Maria, a Chilean journalist and this week's hostess, says, "Well, should we stay or go?"

Karen, who has three children, interrupts. "If we leave now, we'll have to pull our kids out of school and they could lose the entire term. To say nothing of the cost of four tickets!"

Miamah, a tall, elegant woman and the sole Liberian in the group, asks where she would even go with her family if she left. Karen says, "Back home to Mom? Or to my mother-in-law's? Now there's a pleasant prospect."

Everyone laughs. Miko grabs a handful of popcorn from one of the bowls. "But for how long?" she says. Miko is from Japan and specializes in English-language training. "How would we even know how much of our belongings to take?"

Janet, a Peruvian-American development worker, turns to me. "You're married to the charge d'affaires. Should we leave?"

What can I tell them? These days, Dennis is so edgy I can barely ask if he wants sweetened or plain yogurt at breakfast, let alone anything about the fighting. And my war correspondent's experience is useless. To be on the ground during a conflict as a civilian, watching the inexorable march of violence headed my way, is very different from watching—clearheaded and rational—the same situation from afar as a journalist. On the ground, it doesn't feel inexorable. It can't. This is my home, however temporarily; these are my friends. It's unfathomable that all this could be destroyed. Magical thinking has a way of taking over in these circumstances; I understand now why people don't flee at the first whisper of war. *Something is going to happen to stop this before it reaches us: the guerrillas will give up; the government cave in; the president bow out.*

Except that it doesn't.

The rebels capture a large agricultural company a few miles from Buchanan, Liberia's second largest city, and that settles the matter, at least for "official" Americans. The city is only an hour's drive from the international airport, which is itself only an hour from Monrovia. The US embassy, fearing the commercial airlines will soon stop flying into the airport, decides to evacuate all dependents and nonessential personnel from the capital. Dennis disappears into the chancellery for days on end, figuring out who should go. Although the embassy has stopped short of ordering its people out of the country—it's a "voluntary evacuation"—Dennis is determined to get anyone with children to leave.

One evening I find him perched on the edge of our bed, reading a computer printout list of embassy families. "You're not going to make me go, are you?" I ask, yet again. It's the only conversation we seem to have these days.

"No, no," he says irritably, not looking up. "You have dogs, not kids."

A couple of nights later, the first convoy of one hundred and thirty-six Americans leaves. I tag along to keep Dennis company and to say goodbye to those departing; it's unclear when—or if—they'll be returning. Families gather at midnight under the streetlights in front of the embassy compound and board four yellow buses that will take them to the airport. An armor-plated vehicle leads the way. Our car and a truck carrying spare bus parts follow the convoy; another armored vehicle brings up the rear. Although the embassy has been assured the evacuees will be allowed safe passage through the city, everyone is worried about the soldiers, now almost always drunk, who man the checkpoints. The convoy snakes slowly through the deserted streets, hazard lights flashing. During the hour-long journey, Dennis tensely monitors the constant reports on the car radio from the forward and rear vehicles and lets out an audible sigh of relief when we make it past the last barricade, just before the airport.

There, everyone troops upstairs to await the plane in the stifling transit lounge. I pick my way among the mounds of luggage and boxes and raucous children and already-exhausted parents—mostly mothers—and find Janet sitting on a suitcase with her young daughter. They're going to stay with Janet's mother in Miami. "I guess we won't be meeting next Monday, huh?" she says sadly. Looking around the lounge, I'm stunned by the number of friends leaving and suddenly feel very lonely. In one night, virtually my entire community disappears.

The convoys continue all week. The US Peace Corps program closes, sending all 150 volunteers home. The administrators, agronomists, chemists, computer analysts, development experts, doctors, economists, lawyers, medical technicians, middle managers, nurses, professors, secretaries: they all pack hurriedly and are gone, not having a chance to say goodbye, even, to their Liberian colleagues. Every night I accompany Dennis out to the airport, mostly to spend time with him. But he's worried and preoccupied by the jittery, drugged soldiers; for companionship, I'd be better off staying home and playing with the dogs. By week's end, the official American community in Liberia is reduced from 621 to 143.

And the exodus fever spreads: the evacuations prompt hundreds of Liberians to leave, too. Those with money for an airplane ticket besiege the consular offices of the American, British, French, German, Italian, Spanish, and Swiss embassies for visas. The applicants swarm around the gates of the foreign compounds in shapeless crowds that form and re-form like anxious amoebas. If they get a visa, the travelers have a long wait at the airport, sometimes lasting days, while they try to bribe someone, anyone, for a seat on a plane. The airport is packed with people surrounded by their suitcases, bags, baskets, backpacks, boxes, cartons, crates. They are hot and dirty and tired from waiting. There are Nigerian women and children trying to get to Lagos, Ghanaians to Accra, Lebanese to Cyprus or Beirut.

Monrovia is thus reduced to a city of men.

One afternoon, I get the gardeners to drag two enormous garbage pails up to the house and into one of the bathrooms. Tenson watches from the doorway as I fill them with water.

"What are they for, Madam?"

"In case the water supply is cut."

He looks dubious. "And how long will this last, Madam?"

"Not very long. But at least it's something."

"I mean the war, Madam."

Does he regret leaving Malawi? "I have no idea. I'm hoping the president will come to his senses and a political solution can be worked out."

Tenson smirks.

"Do you want to go home?" I say. "Because now's the time, while the airport is still functioning."

Slight hesitation. "No, Madam."

"Okay, let me know if you change your mind. But you need to decide pretty quickly."

Then I'm off to scour the city for cases of long-life milk, bottled water, pasta, canned tuna: siege food. There's already no flour left in Monrovia, and when you can find rice—the main staple—it's selling for a dollar a cup, more than triple last week's price. And I need quantities large enough to feed the household staff. But the daily outing takes my mind off what I fear will be the inevitable order from Washington to leave and gives me—if I come upon a food stash—a momentary feeling of normality. A delusion, really, that's neatly shattered when I return home and find the place crawling with US military special operations people photographing rooms, measuring doors, sketching windows.

"I hope you don't mind, ma'am," says a hunk with a buzz cut and biceps the size of small cantaloupes, looking up from architectural blueprints spread across the dining room table. "But in case you get held hostage, we have to know the best way to rescue you."

Not long after, I organize a barbecue on the beach. The plan is to make myself "essential"—an actual State Department designation—so the bureaucrats in Washington will see that the embassy can't possibly function without me. Surely they can recognize how vital cocktail parties and sit-down dinners are to morale here—to say nothing of Sunday brunch with the last frozen bagels in the country and *real cream cheese!* The irony of my situation doesn't escape me. Marrying Dennis was supposed to keep me away from war, but here I am, yet again, desperate to be in the thick of it. So desperate, in fact, I'd even throw a beach party in the middle of an insurrection. Only this time, it's not for the experience of the conflict—but for love.

The embassy's greatly pared-down staff—military pilots, communications technicians, security men built like small bulldozers—turn out in force for the barbecue. They swim and sunbathe, drink beer, and play Frisbee. Then a marine guard, who has come directly from the embassy, arrives with the news that Buchanan, just eighty-five miles down the beach from us, had fallen to the rebels. Someone turns off the boom box so he can be heard. The marine says the army planned a massive attack on the rebels in the city; they had the soldiers, reinforcements even, and all the vehicles they needed. What they lacked were arms and ammunition, which remain locked up in the Executive Mansion; the president refuses to part with them. He's preparing for a last stand here in the capital.

"That man is determined to destroy this place," Dennis mutters. "Along with himself."

As if in response, three heads are found a few days later on the outskirts of Monrovia. Their torsos are in a nearby field, hands tied behind their backs. The heads are taken to a hospital morgue, where they're put on display "to enable curious friends to identify the victims." This might seem a tad macabre, to set them out for viewing on a table as though they're lost-and-found items, but hundreds of people flock to the hospital. And by day's end the victims have been identified: they were soldiers, one a Mano, the other two Gios—the very ethnic groups that have joined the rebellion. The next morning, four soldiers are found with their throats slashed. Again Gios and Manos. Then another six bodies turn up, some with their penises severed; more Gio and Mano soldiers. Now it's clear that, with the rebels bearing down on the capital, the army is turning on its own and taking the war to the barracks.

Two days later, the chief of police comes to our house. He's tense, grim, ashen-faced. The chief paces the living room, dressed in a uniform modeled on the Chicago police force summer outfits of the early 1960s. He stops to stare out at the sea. "I'm a professional and I'm a Christian and I just can't live with what's happening," he says finally. "They're locking up soldiers from those tribes in the stockades, then dragging them out to be executed. That's what they did two nights ago. They got those five boys out of the stockades, dragged them across the road, and butchered them. There've been eighteen murders—and that's just the ones we know about.

"How can I do my job? I can't protect the public. If I start investigating, I'm told to leave it alone. Anyway, we all know it's sanctioned from the top. If they wanted to stop it, they could." The chief turns to face us. "I could resign so that I could live with my conscience, but then I'd have to tell the president why I was resigning. How long then would I have to live? I'd have to get on a plane and mail him a letter. And if I don't resign, I'm a dead man when the rebels take over. How could I justify my actions, as chief of police, to them?"

What choices! He's right about one thing, though: the president's soldiers have just about gone berserk. All sense of restraint, of reason, is broken. One morning Miamah, my Liberian friend, hears a commotion outside her office and rushes outdoors to see soldiers arresting one of her employees, who just arrived in a taxi. His offense? Reading something in a newspaper that made him laugh, then shaking hands with the taxi driver. Miamah manages to extricate him, but not before getting a glimpse of a list one of the soldiers has with the names of her Gio employees. Scribbled next to each one: *saboteur.*

Soon after the first mutilated bodies appear, one hundred and fifty Gio and Mano soldiers—previously all of good standing—are arrested and held in the open-air reviewing stands above the barracks' parade ground. I feel desperate seeing them on my daily foraging missions, huddled on the bleachers in little, exhausted groups. After all the anonymous death in the country, here are living, breathing beings, almost within reach, who still have a chance. When I implore Dennis to do something, anything, he scoffs. He and the other foreign envoys already delivered a protest, the usual polite claptrap, to the president's advisors—who, of course, denied there's any singling out of particular ethnic groups. *Screw diplomacy,* I think. *Those poor soldiers need to overpower their guards and make a run for it!*

If keeping the soldiers on exhibit is meant to advertise the government's murderous intentions, it works. About a thousand Gio and Mano civilians have started crowding outside the United Nations compound, pleading for refuge. Someone must have suggested that embassies, too, are safe havens, because the terrified people descend on foreign missions as well. In the afternoons, I see packs of twenty, maybe thirty residents hurrying along the roadside. The women carry babies tied to their backs, bundles of belongings on their heads and cooking pots in their hands; small children straggle alongside, trying to keep pace. Their fathers follow behind, loaded with everything else: sleeping mats, charcoal, heavy bags of rice, blankets. They rush from embassy to embassy, begging for a place to stay before sunset. They might have taken a taxi, but the cabbies, fearing death at the hands of the rebels because of *their* ethnicity, all drove away in their vehicles a few nights ago to neighboring Guinea.

A delegation of ambassadors troops off to the Foreign Ministry, yet again, to remonstrate. They tell the official who receives them it's an outrage these people feel so frightened they're seeking shelter with foreigners; the UN envoy demands a central site in which to house and feed the refugees. The official refuses. So the Spanish ambassador takes in sixty people; the German, fifty; the French thirty-five. When Dennis and I pull into the compound of the Moroccan charge d'affaires to drop off some extra rice I found, our headlights pick out hundreds of eyes glinting in the darkness. "Good lord," Dennis gasps. "Those are people!"

The charge's chief of security says they're Gios and Manos who jumped the fence and were spending the night in the yard, women and children crammed into the garage in case it rained. The charge and his wife gave them sheets, blankets, cushions, drapes, towels, pillows, and whatever else they could find to sleep on. "Actually, this is the second night," he says. "By the time I came on duty this morning, all the things the charge had given them were folded in nice piles and they were gone. The guards said they left before sunrise, before the soldiers could see where they'd been sleeping."

As soon as we're home, out of earshot of our driver, I begin pestering Dennis. "Why aren't we taking in any people?" I ask, trailing him through the dining room into the kitchen. "This house is big enough to contain the entire Grand Duchy of Luxembourg. Maybe the Republic of San Marino, too."

Dennis is silent as he pulls a glass from the cupboard, grabs a few ice cubes out of the freezer and pours himself a tall Scotch. "First of all," he says, after taking a long swallow. "Our government doesn't allow it—"

"I'm sure the French and German governments don't either," I interrupt. "But the ambassadors are still doing it."

"I wouldn't be so sure about their asylum policies, especially given what they had to deal with after World War II." He pauses for another sip. "Look, I appreciate your humanitarian concerns. God knows I'm as upset about all this as you are. But our policy is we don't grant asylum in our embassies or residences. Period."

"It's a stupid policy. Where's your humanity?"

"Yeah, well, where's your pragmatism? If we started taking in people, we'd be overwhelmed. There are literally tens of thousands of persons at risk in the capital. If you start accepting them, where do you stop?"

"We don't have to save the whole world!" I say, almost shouting. "We just have to do what we can!"

"But Lynda, we can't feed them or protect them. The Marines only guard the embassy, not us."

In my self-righteous rant, I suddenly notice the dark circles under his eyes. "I know. But at least we'd be an extra layer between them and these psychopathic soldiers."

"Uh, not to put too fine a point on it, but I assume you've noticed that no one, as yet, has even tried to jump our fence."

"It's because of the bad karma you're putting out."

"Or because we're so close to the Mansion and the barracks. If you're Gio or Mano, this neighborhood is the last place you'd want to be."

"That makes sense. But if people do try to jump our fence, I'm not throwing them out. I have to do something. I don't have journalism anymore."

Dennis drains his glass. "Lynda, if people jump our fence, the Labradors will probably lick them to death."

Later that night, I find out that the police chief has gone. He left on a British Airways flight a few days ago, then called his deputy from London to tell him where to find his letter of resignation for the president. *Now there's no one to police the police,* I think, letting the dogs out to pee in the front yard. Gabriel, one of the guards who works until midnight, says, "Good evening, Missy." (A Liberian female honorific; Dennis is "Bossman"—one word.)

"Good evening, Gabriel."

"Missy, you know I'm Gio?"

"No, I didn't."

"I am. And I am scared, scared to travel through town after I finish work here." He leans in closer and says, almost in a whisper, "Last night, some soldiers went into my neighbor's house and took him from his bed, put him in a Jeep, and drove away."

Here's my chance! "Gabriel, if you'd like to stay here, I can give you a bed downstairs, where Tenson sleeps."

"What about my family, Missy?"

"Your family, too."

Even better than journalism, I think, herding the dogs back into the house. *This way you know you've actually helped someone.* Then I go off to inform Dennis of our very first refugees.

A few days later—just as Dennis had foreseen—we hear that the army has been on a rampage. Soldiers showed up at the UN compound at around three thirty in the morning and ordered the guards to open the gates; they claimed rebels were hiding inside. When the guards refused, the soldiers stabbed one in the back, shot a second, killed a third, then broke into the compound, firing submachine guns into the air and at the fifteen hundred terrified refugees sleeping there. People were running, falling down, trampling one another, clawing at the fence to get away from the shooting. The soldiers grabbed about thirty men and boys, threw them into Jeeps, and zoomed away.

Pieces of people turn up all morning: three fingers are found in a pool of blood on a bridge. A journalist friend, driving into town from the airport, sees four corpses dumped by the roadside, their heads resting on their crooked arms as though looking at the traffic. The rest of the world finally takes note—this is the United Nations, after all, inviolate real estate—and there's widespread condemnation.

The president makes a conciliatory visit to the site to speak with the outraged diplomats gathered there. Weirdly, he instead ends up addressing a group of shocked refugees still milling around; twenty army soldiers brandishing submachine guns, one with a rocket launcher, stand between him and his people. "I want you to know that those who do this kind of thing are doing it on their own," he says forcefully. "I'm going to deal with them drastically. If you're not happy, I'm not happy." A low rumble starts from within the crowd, but the president ignores it. "We're going to provide you with security," he continues. At that moment, a woman pushes toward him, screaming, *"Where is my husband?"* Her words have an electrifying effect on the crowd: they suddenly start booing the president—unthinkable!—hissing at him, pressing forward, everyone crushed together. He looks confused. The soldiers look agitated. The people are chanting, "Who's gonna believe you? Who's gonna believe you?" when the security men grab the president, push him into his black Mercedes limousine, and roar off.

That night, the television news presenter stares into the camera and says gravely, "The government of Liberia is conducting a massive search tonight for men dressed in army uniforms who yesterday attacked the United Nations compound. The government reiterates that it is illegal for noncombatants to dress up in army uniforms."

"And I'm Cinderella!" I howl at the television, turning it off in disgust and heading downstairs to go with Dennis to visit our Moroccan friends. No one is sleeping in their yard tonight. I mention this to the wife, who takes me aside in the dining room.

"They came back again just before dark, pleading for a place to stay," she whispers. "They were so terrified. But after last night with the UN, it's not safe for them to sleep in the yard. They begged us anyway, and finally we allowed them into a laundry room inside the embassy." French-born and usually exuberant in her abuse of the English language, she pauses to light a cigarette, her hands trembling slightly. "That way, if the soldiers come, we can show them the garage and they will see nothing."

I ask how many they're hiding, and she explains that at first she and her husband figured maybe ten people could squeeze into the room. "But then the refugees saw it and said, 'No, we can fit twelve, even sixteen people with children. We don't have to sit, we can stand.' Can you imagine? Standing all night?" She takes a deep drag and slowly exhales. "In the end, there were twenty-seven people in that room, all standing. Silent. Imagine the desperation!" She asks me not to say anything to the other guests for fear of implicating them if the soldiers show up.

The Moroccans make a brave stab at gaiety: she bustling about serving drinks and glasses of mint tea, he playing rock 'n' roll cassette tapes. It's a glum party, though. After a while, she gives up offering anything; he lets the tape run out. The Spanish ambassador looks as though he's going to cry. He's furious about the UN withdrawing its staff in response to the attack. "Who will feed all these refugees now?" he asks indignantly. "Who will protect them? Doesn't the rest of the world care? White people are killed in Europe, and the world is aghast, full of condemnation. Why not here? Isn't a black life as valuable as a white one?" After his outburst, the ambassador sits back silently on the low, North African–style couches, nursing a drink and becoming more morose as the evening progresses. A small, intense man, he's hiding sixty-five people in his embassy and doesn't have enough rice to feed them.

The evening ends with another diplomat breathlessly arriving with news that one of the thirty kidnapped men, left for dead by the soldiers after being shot, had crawled for miles on his belly to a missionary hospital. The story makes me shiver. "Unbelievable," our host says, shaking his head. "Simply unbelievable. And we're impotent to stop any of it."

He's right. The rebels are almost in Monrovia and determined to accept nothing less than the president's immediate departure. The president, meanwhile, appears totally oblivious to the destruction and dislocation, the gruesome ethnic violence, the capital teetering on the brink of Armageddon. Instead, he's acting like a politician who's simply having a bad spate of public relations. Nothing a good ribbon-cutting ceremony here and there can't fix! With that mindset, any negotiations between the rebels and the president's representatives are bound to fail. And that's exactly what happens when the United States, in an attempt to stave off catastrophe, tries to broker peace talks—yet another sad lesson in the limitations of foreign governments to stop brutal wars such as this.

It's now clear the conflict won't be decided without a massive battle for Monrovia. The capital is built on a narrow peninsula, wedged between a mangrove swamp and the sea. A couple of well-aimed rockets, a few shells, some grenades—and the place could be in ruins. Which, seen through the eyes of the international journalists who've descended on the country—some of them colleagues from Johannesburg—has the makings of an exciting story.

From this side of the looking glass, though, it feels like desolation and disaster.

So we wait. Shops—the few that still have any goods—close by noon. One of our telephone lines goes dead and can't be fixed; the technicians at the telephone company have left. Ghana Airways makes its last run into Monrovia. Air Afrique cancels all future flights. Notices start appearing in the newspapers: "This is to advise customers having vehicles under repair at Gateway Motors to take immediate delivery of such vehicles. Management will not be responsible for any vehicles that remain on its premises from today." There's a listlessness about the city. Acquaintances I run into downtown start a conversation, then wander off in mid-sentence; polite chitchat seems frivolous and not worth the effort. What's the point, really, of doing anything when holy hell is about to break loose?

I awake several mornings later not to the rebels, but to four US Navy warships, with 2,500 Marines aboard, steaming toward Liberia in case the remaining Americans have to be evacuated. Besides being stunned, I'm a little hurt that Dennis didn't tell me about this beforehand. What did he think I'd do with the information? Call the wire services? I'm his wife; we're supposed to share everything! "Don't you think this is a little extreme?" I ask while he's brushing his teeth in the bathroom, the only place—along with our bedroom—where we can talk nowadays without his exceedingly polite and omnipresent security entourage overhearing everything. "The entire Sixth Fleet!"

"Don't exaggerate," he says through a mouthful of toothpaste.

"Okay, maybe only half. But still."

"Look, the situation here is very unpredictable. We don't know how quickly the fighting will reach Monrovia, we don't know how the government will react to the foreigners still here when that happens, we don't know how much longer the airports will remain open." He pauses to spit and rinse. "We need a way to get people out quickly, if that becomes necessary. These boats will be standing by."

"Well, thanks for the official line."

"You're welcome, dear," he says, wiping his mouth and planting a kiss on my cheek, too preoccupied to notice my consternation.

After that, he has to hurry off to field phone calls from other envoys in Monrovia and officials in Washington about the make-up of a master list for full evacuation. It seems we'll take not only the two thousand Americans citizens still in Liberia, but our friends as well. Senegalese, Ghanaians, Israelis, Belgians, diplomats residing in Monrovia—hop on board! Also add in the Liberian children born in the United States, who are American citizens. Little girls dressed in pinafores and ankle socks, their hair done in neat cornrows, start appearing at the consulate with their US passports. They've come to register for the evacuation, they say, clutching long, damp lists of Liberian family members who need to accompany them. Overwhelmed by the numbers, officials in Washington decree that only one Liberian adult can escort each American child. The US consul-general has the horrible task of telling the distraught families only these youngsters will have a way out to safety; everyone else—siblings and parents included—must stay behind.

Then Michael, the British ambassador, turns up at our house with news that his government is sending two warships and three helicopters to link up with the American fleet. This thing seems to be taking on a life of its own. Dennis, Michael, and I sit in the living room, staring out at the ocean, imagining all those vessels sailing around in circles off the Liberian coast. "Helicopters," Michael says wondrously, between puffs on his pipe and swigs of Scotch. "Bloody helicopters!"

The Liberians, on the other hand, are ecstatic. All manner of rumors spread: the Marines are coming to shore up the president! They're coming to topple the president! They're coming to aid the rebels! They're coming to quash the rebellion! There's something here for everyone—except that everyone's got it wrong. The Americans are coming not to intervene, but to pluck their own people from the midst of the impending ethnic butchery and leave the country to its fate. And one more thing: later that afternoon, Dennis tells me he received a cable from Washington ordering me out of the country. Marines or no Marines, I have to leave tomorrow.

Leave? Tomorrow? "You don't understand," I say, trying to steady my voice. "I can't leave. I could get married again only because nothing like this would ever happen."

"Lynda," Dennis says gently, "it can't be helped."

"But what about all the cocktail parties? The beach bashes? The bagels and cream cheese! Listen," I say, changing tacks. "I'm the only one in the embassy who's actually been in a war. I was in Beirut, El Salvador. I know what it's like. Can't you explain that to your bosses?"

"If you don't go, they said they'll order both of us out. "

"Wait, they're threatening you with your job if I don't leave?"

Dennis shrugs. "Washington just wants to get the numbers down now while there are still planes flying, in case we really do have to evacuate by ship."

"I am not a number!" I shout. I'm working myself into a melodramatic, incoherent lather because of—what? Fear, mostly, that something will happen to him, that the most painful part of my life is about to be relived. But also the realization that in marrying a

diplomat, I'd married the State Department, too, and ceded my independence. *A fine time for this little epiphany!* "If that's the way they're going to be, I'll buy a wig and dark glasses, fly to the Ivory Coast, and hook up with the rebels as a reporter! I'll march on the Executive Mansion with them; you can wave as I go by! Then I'll check into a hotel and watch the war from there!" The Labradors, disturbed by the yelling, come bounding over to lick my arms and legs, which only adds another grievance to my hysterical litany: "The dogs! I don't want to leave the dogs!"

Dennis is silent, dumbfounded, most likely, by my outburst. "Lynda, I'm really sorry," he says, finally. "I'm as upset as you are. But there's absolutely nothing I can do about it."

He has to return to the embassy after that, leaving me to my hyperventilating panic. I wander through the house, pulling pictures off the walls and rolling up rugs, doing something, anything, to make me feel as though I'm in control. It's hard to imagine what a crowd of crazed soldiers who break into our house might want. My Italian sandals? A favorite recording of *Madam Butterfly?* Dennis's collapsible kayak that turns into a rowing machine?

It's not hard to imagine what a crowd of crazed soldiers might do to Dennis.

Neither Dennis nor I can sleep that night, especially after the telephone rings at one o'clock in the morning. There's heavy fighting at the international airport; as usual, the government soldiers fled at the first sound of gunfire. KLM is diverting its Monrovia plane to nearby Sierra Leone; British Airways canceled its flight. They were the last scheduled airlines still flying into the country, which means the airport is now effectively closed. "This is why you have to go," Dennis says, returning to bed. "Now."

"I only have to go because the State Department says so. I used to do this kind of thing for a living, remember? What about you?"

"I'll be fine." He enfolds me in his arms. "Don't worry, it'll probably all be over in ten days and you can come back."

I want to cry. "Do you promise, promise, promise to stay safe?"

"I promise, promise, promise," he says. "Besides, if anything happens, you'll still have the dogs. And their breath isn't nearly as bad as mine in the morning."

"Not funny, Jett," I say, burrowing into his chest. "True, but not funny."

In the morning, I show Tenson the present I'd hidden in the basement for Dennis: a windsurfer I bought from Miko, of my long-ago women's group, before she was evacuated. "Dennis's birthday is in three weeks," I say as we ascend the stairs to the first floor foyer. "If I haven't returned by then, will you please give it to him and bake him a chocolate cake?"

"You will be back by then, I am sure, Madam," he says.

"I hope so. Will you also please tell the gardeners and the rest of the guards they should move into the house with their families? They'll be safer here." By now we've got a regular little commune: once Gabriel, the guard, took up residence, Moussa and Abdoulaye followed soon after, along with their wives and children.

"Certainly, Madam," he says.

Why did we ever agree to bring you? This isn't your fight; this isn't even your country.

He and the dogs walk me to the car, where a driver is waiting to take me to meet Dennis at the city airport. "Go well, Madam," Tenson says, grabbing my hand and solemnly pumping it.

I falter, unable to say anything.

The airstrip is chaos: honking cars trying to unload passengers, soldiers shouting at them to move on, husbands shouting at wives, wives shouting at children, children howling. Most Liberians huddle on one side of the waiting area, Americans on the other. The Liberian half has a heavy, desperate air: these are the families of the president's soldiers, hundreds of them, all vying to get onto a green Caribou transport to take them to the presumed safety of the president's home county and out of the rebels' way. On the US side, though, it's a carnival: local boys work the crowd, selling beach towels, mangos, ice cream, sunglasses, hairbrushes, headbands, gum. One youngster wanders around trying to polish the men's shoes, but most are wearing sneakers. The Americans stand under a corrugated tin awning, out of the sun.

Finally Dennis arrives, after being called to the Foreign Ministry where he tried to explain, yet again, that the United States doesn't think there can be a military solution to the conflict. I feel strangely distant and detached, as though watching the scene unfold through the wrong end of a pair of binoculars. It's the only way I can get through this. Because if I were truly able to think about what I'm doing—leaving Dennis to likely calamity—I'd lay down on the sizzling tarmac, stiff-limbed and screaming, and refuse to move. Instead, in a dazed sort of way, I can let Dennis escort me out of the car when his driver comes to tell us the plane has landed.

Passengers rush to the aircraft, where another apartheid-like divide occurs. The flight has been chartered for foreigners, so they board first, leaving a mass of Liberian civilians—who have abruptly appeared—to wait. I stand off to the side, letting Dennis say goodbye to the evacuees. Then, with all the Americans seated, I kiss Dennis and start up the steps to the plane. Too late. A great wave of Liberians suddenly rolls forward, pushing their way up and crushing me. Those who managed to make it to the top are trying to hoist their loved ones up from the bottom, and I'm about to be shoved off—the steps have no rail—when one of the Americans reaches down from the plane's doorway and virtually lifts me over the Liberians.

The airplane is full; the flight crew has to dislodge people clinging stubbornly to the stairs. Scores of frightened Liberians stand there, shouting to be allowed on: they know this is one of the last planes out of the country. It's a wrenching thing to witness, and I'm shaking as we taxi to the end of the airstrip. The British deputy ambassador's wife, sitting in the next row, is crying. The plane turns, stops momentarily, then races down the runway, rising past the hundreds of upturned faces. We bank hard right, fly low over palm trees and sand, then out over the ocean.

And Monrovia becomes a small, still spot, glistening in the sunlight.

PART THREE

CHAPTER NINE

WASHINGTON, 1992

The first time Tenson walks into a Safeway in northwest Washington, he stops short and gives a little gasp. "Madam," he says, gazing down the aisles. "Are there ever food shortages in America?"

His amazement is understandable—thirty-two different types of breakfast cereal alone, all under one roof!—given that Tenson is the product of one of the poorest places on the planet. And it's even more staggering when he considers the number of similar establishments throughout the greater metropolitan area, let alone the rest of the Mid-Atlantic region. To say nothing of the entire country.

Having Tenson here is to see the United States through virgin eyes: all the excess and extravagance and waste that only a rich nation can afford. Like his reaction to, say, a local bicycle shop. Tenson is no stranger to bicycles. He owned one in Malawi: a worn, second-hand model that he spent hours tenderly polishing, patching and re-patching its tires, protecting it from the sudden outbursts of the rainy season. Still, ownership put him a cut above most of his countrymen, who have to travel everywhere on foot. But stepping over the threshold of the Washington store, Tenson's eyes flit across the glistening new ten-speeds, racers, and mountain bikes lined up on the floor, hanging on the walls, suspended from the ceiling. And he sighs softly, saying, "I feel as if I'm in a dream!"

He also likes the National Zoo. Not for the animals, whose confinement he finds sad, but because he can look at "all the fat people." (In his country, obesity is reserved for the wealthy few.) And the skyscrapers of nearby Baltimore: "It's as though God just put them down there." (The tallest building back home is only a half dozen stories high.) His favorite thing by far about the United States, though, is the electronic barcode scanner. The first time he sees one in action at a store checkout, Tenson stands transfixed, intently watching as the name of each scanned item appears on the screen, its price, the cumulative bill total. After a few minutes of silent observation, he turns to me. "Ah, but Madam, if this machine is so clever, does it know the day on which you are going to die?

Talk about cutting to the chase!

Truth be told, Dennis and I aren't all that far removed from Tenson's sense of awe. Ordinary life here feels positively extraordinary. We've bought a sweet old house whose plumbing hasn't been updated since Dolly Madison's time and whose rooms were designed with leprechauns in mind. It backs onto woods where the Labradors can roam freely through the underbrush, bringing back dead squirrels or other decaying creatures they proudly deposit on the porch. I'm freelancing, and Dennis is working at the National Security Council as President Bill Clinton's advisor on Africa. Every morning he runs to the office dressed in shorts and a T-shirt, a small backpack slung over his shoulders; each evening he returns similarly attired. After observing this for a few weeks, Tenson says, "Madam, what kind of job does Bambo do that he wears the short pants of a small boy?" When I explain that Dennis likes to run to work and carries a change of clothes in his backpack, Tenson, raising an eyebrow, asks, "But why run, Madam, when he can drive?"

Why? Because there aren't youngsters being bayonetted to death at the end of our block! Because there aren't stoner soldiers on the main roads, bizarrely decked out in stolen negligees and blonde wigs, cutting off heads and penises! Because there aren't stacks of corpses, swollen to grotesque shapes and covered with flies, lying in the gutters!

I say, "Because traffic here is terrible and there's no place to park."

I didn't return to the United States along with the other official Americans after being ordered out of Liberia, but paid for my own ticket and disembarked in Sierra Leone. As long as Dennis faced real danger, and my friends suffered unknown fates, I needed to remain as close to Monrovia as possible. I also needed to hear news. In the States, Africa never counts for much, even in its most tragic moments; when told by her reporter of a massive famine in Ethiopia, one foreign editor of a major American daily responded, "People starve to death all the time in Africa. Why should we care?" If I stayed on the continent, I could hear hourly bulletins on my short-wave radio: the BBC, Voice of America, American Forces Network, English services of the German, French and Dutch broadcasting companies—all beamed at Africa, all focused on the war.

At the suggestion of a friend, I checked into a coastal resort in Sierra Leone catering to French tourists, which turned out to be shockingly lovely: little thatch-roofed bungalows set on perfect white sand, framed by a turquoise sea and a backdrop of emerald mountains. *Here I am in paradise, slathering on sunscreen, while Dennis is about to be swallowed up by war,* I thought, feeling more than a little ridiculous. *But I have to park myself somewhere, so why not?* Besides, as Dennis figured, it would probably all be over in a matter of days.

So I settled into a routine of waking early and running along the beach. Afterward, I swam, then sat in the sun. I watched fabulous, orange-headed male lizards court dull, dun-colored females with exaggerated bobs and dips the females pretended not to notice. I watched unattached Frenchmen stuffed into tight little swimming briefs court unattached Frenchwomen —usually with more success than their reptilian counterparts. I watched the tourists arrive and depart with a kind of tidal regularity, along with the beach boys (as they called themselves) from the nearby fishing village, self-styled tour guides. They all had wonderfully Biblical names such as Moses and Samuel, except for one who was called Alfa Romeo, and they swarmed around the thatched umbrellas, offering to act as escorts to the waterfall, the rivers, the village.

Each afternoon, immense clouds gathered, a prelude to the impending rainy season, and I'd move indoors to my tiny bungalow to watch the increasing downpours. Sometimes, if the rain slackened toward evening, I'd dash up the beach to the main building and sit at the bar, hoping Dennis would call on the front desk telephone. It was a pleasant place to wait, a kind of open-air pavilion decorated with gingerbread trim, languid ceiling fans, wicker furniture, potted tropical plants. But Dennis didn't call; he probably couldn't get through. I'd drink a beer and talk to the bartenders to try to keep from getting depressed. The local staff hated having to speak French to the guests; English was the language of instruction in their schools, and among themselves they talked in an English-based Creole. We'd shoot the breeze, them pumping me for information about Liberia as I nursed my drink, then I'd run back to my room for the day's main event: listening to the news.

On one such occasion a few weeks into my stay, the bartender poured me a second beer. I raised my hand to protest, but he said, "On the house, Madame Lynda."

"Wow, thanks," I said, taking a long gulp.

"Why are you so sad?"

"I just heard on the BBC that Monrovia is now completely surrounded. The rebels have apparently closed the road to here. That was the last land escape route."

"That's very bad."

"It gets worse. The city hasn't had water or electricity for four days."

"But how can people survive without water?"

"I have no idea," I said, shaking my head. "Maybe they collect the rain."

We were both silent for a moment.

Finally, I said, "All the phones have been cut, too. So now there's really no point in me sitting here every night. There's no way my husband can call."

"Don't worry, Madame Lynda. I'm sure he'll be okay."

I nodded, then drained the glass. "I should've married a banker; nothing ever happens to them."

Back in my bungalow, I discovered I had forgotten to turn off the bedside lamp before going to the bar. The room was now filled with flying cockroaches attracted to the light, dive-bombing my blankets, swooping past my face, skittering across the lampshade. *This* would *happen tonight!* I thought, slipping into self-pity—while alternately slapping at the disgusting creatures with my shoe and emitting little shrieks when they landed on me. After dispatching the carcasses down the toilet, I checked under the sheets, turned off the light, and crawled into bed. *Monrovia's cut off from the rest of the world,* I thought, feeling the tears start to gather. *I have absolutely no way of knowing whether Dennis is alive or dead.* Sitting on the sidelines, I was becoming increasingly aware that for civilians like myself, war is about the loss of control. The physical and mental dislocation makes you crazy, not knowing what's happened to the loved ones you've left behind, your friends, your home, your livelihood, your very existence. And I was lucky. I had a credit card and bank account in the United States. Even if I lost everything, I had the resources to start over. Perhaps most important, with my American passport, I had a place to go. Unlike the millions of refugees who, quite often, hastily leave with nothing more than the clothes on their backs, searching for safety in a world that neither cares about their plight—nor wants them.

Still, the mere possibility of being able to talk to Dennis had given me a sense, however stupidly, of being able to sway the course of events. Deprived now of even that illusion, I felt a terrible foreboding. It had taken me a long time to learn how to live with the hurt of losing Dial. It took me even longer to decide I could risk that pain again. And now here I was, six months after my wedding, terrified I was going to become a widow for the second time. I'm not a praying kind of person, but that night, as I lay in bed awaiting an elusive sleep, I prayed. As the ocean crashed on the shore outside my room and the short-wave radio whispered its all-night messages from my little bedside table, I prayed to whomever would listen to keep Dennis safe.

And then, a week later: a miracle! I received a letter from Dennis, delivered by a foreign journalist who had managed to leave Liberia:

Dear Lynda:

The war goes on and on. It's a nightmare that just does not seem like it will end. We, of course, have it easy with generators for light, food to eat and enough water stored for drinking and cooking. I sneak in the occasional brief shower every other day or so. But the people outside of Little America spend their days in search of food and water. Mostly they just stand around, waiting for night to fall so they can lock themselves in their homes and hope the soldiers don't come. The area of conflict is now so large and the brutality such that it can't be avoided. There are displaced people anywhere they feel safe: 500 came over the wall of the American Community School; 6,000 at the Voice of America facility; 20,000 at Omega (a US-built navigational tower).

The American flag we hung on our home doesn't seem to have much effect outside the gates. Yesterday afternoon, in full view of the international press, three soldiers executed a man on the beach in front of the house. They knew he was a rebel because he was going to buy rice and had only $1.25 on him; rice is now two dollars a cup. They dumped his body across the street. It stayed there most of the afternoon, until we asked for it to be collected.

This morning, three soldiers took a fifteen-year-old boy from one of the embassy's residential compounds, brought him to Peaceland Car Wash next to our house, and bayonetted him to death. This afternoon, I decided to come home for lunch early when I heard that soldiers were beating up someone else. When I got here, they had pinned this emaciated man—stripped to his underwear—on his back and were holding his feet and arms out-stretched. I stood in the driveway watching the two soldiers do this while three other soldiers washed their car. When they fin-ished, the five soldiers threw the man in the car and drove off. I don't know whether being observed by a foreigner made them act differently. If so, it probably only bought the guy a few more min-utes of life.

I can't tell you how sick I am of being a spectator to this whole tragedy. Going through it without being able to talk to you is re-ally not fun. The uncertainty is as bad as the separation. If you can get into Freetown to the embassy, we can talk on their radio. They have a ham-type radio that has pretty good quality. We could use Hebrañol (Hebrew/Español—our private language) if you want to talk dirty. I want to do a crossword puzzle with you. How's that for romantic? Just know that I love and miss you greatly. This can't go on much longer. Then we can drink a bottle of white wine, I'll let you beat me at Scrabble, and we can forget this ever happened.

Much love.

Dennis

He's alive! Of course, the journalist had to mention, as he was leaving, that Dennis had almost been lobotomized a couple of days earlier by a bullet whizzing through his office window. That parting little tidbit left me thoroughly shaken, despondent really, as I trudged up to the main building for lunch in a downpour. Even the weather seemed to be conspiring against holding onto hope. The rainy sea-son had, by then, begun in earnest: serious, stinging stuff, in which gray sky met gray sea and the world disappeared for days on end. I was now the only guest staying at the 320-bed resort; who in his right mind would pay money to leave sunny summertime France for waterlogged West Africa? As the restaurant's sole customer, I had twenty bored waiters watching every forkful lifted to my mouth, every sip taken from my glass.

It was now clear how naïve Dennis and I had been in thinking—more like hoping—the war would be over in a matter of days. The rebels had metastasized into two groups, both converging on the capital, while the president remained holed up in the Executive Mansion—probably still eating leftover cake from his anniversary luncheon. Even if the fighting ended tomorrow, the State Department wouldn't let me return to Liberia until the political situation stabilized. And that could take months. With great foresight, I'd packed only a couple of changes of clothes, some running gear, four pairs of underpants—and the rains had made everything in my little hut moist and fuzzy: my shoes were beginning to rot; my two shirts smelled of mildew. *I'll give it another week or two,* I thought, not really knowing where I'd go or what I'd do.

In the meantime, I discovered the hotel had a small ham radio that, in theory, could be used to communicate with the embassy in Monrovia. But the near-constant torrential deluges tended to distort the signals. I spent hours in a cramped, airless room off the hotel's reception area, delicately twirling the radio dial until my wrist ached, listening to chatter just beyond intelligible that I was convinced had to be Monrovia. Or extraterrestrials, judging by the eerie screeches coming through the speaker. As my ham-radio skills were on a level with, say, my sword-swallowing abilities, I'd inevitably end up retreating in frustration to my clammy room, my ear glued to the short-wave radio, desperate for any news of the war.

All of which was shocking. Heavy fighting had engulfed the eastern and northern sectors of the capital, led by bands of rebels, teenagers mostly, wearing women's wigs, negligees, Halloween-type masks, Girl Guide outfits, bowler hats, blue blazers, and other random articles of clothing they had "liberated" along the way. Juju amulets hung on strings around the young fighters' necks and daubs of mud—strong medicine that would supposedly make them invisible to the enemy—decorated their chests. The overall effect was that of a well-armed costume party: one possessed of a sadistic, drug-fueled rage, hell-bent on killing any and everyone even vaguely associated with the president's ethnic group. Meanwhile, in the areas still controlled by the government, its soldiers continued their gruesome attacks against civilians linked to the rebels' ethnicity. Corpses were stacked like firewood in the streets and littered the city's fields and swamps. The few dogs that hadn't been eaten by the starving residents feasted on the decomposing corpses. Desperate civilians, meanwhile, were reduced to hacking down trees and gnawing on bark.

Listening to the radio broadcasts, I found it hard to fathom what had happened to Liberia. War I knew: fear, hunger, disease, death, chaos. But nothing like this. Not only was the totality of the devastation stunning, but also the speed with which everything fell apart. Okay, Monrovia wasn't exactly Stockholm when it came to infrastructure. Still, short of a nuclear holocaust, you'd like to think it would take more than a couple of months to blast a place back to the Dark Ages. Civilization suddenly seemed exceedingly fragile to me. *What did I ever find exciting about war?*

Then, amazingly, another miracle! I awoke one morning to news that the US Marines had stopped sailing around in circles off the Liberian coast and had landed; the US embassy was being closed and everyone evacuated. *Dennis will be able to get out!* But in the following news bulletin just a half hour later, the announcer corrected the information: the Americans were only drawing down their personnel, leaving in place anyone essential to keeping the embassy open. Dennis clearly wouldn't be among those departing. Talk about yo-yoing emotions: one minute I was imagining a romantic reunion in some far-off place, replete with sexy nightgown, luxurious bed, potable water—and the next thing I knew, I was slammed back to reality and the same clammy, cockroach-magnet of a room I'd been mooning in for nine weeks. Nine weeks! *I've got to get out of here*, I thought, going for a run in the hope it would lift my spirits. Predictably, I got caught in a blinding downpour and had to duck into the lobby, dripping like a drenched water rat, to wait for the rain to let up. "Oh, there you are," the receptionist said, handing me a letter. "Someone just delivered this." It was from the deputy ambassador at the US embassy in Freetown.

> *Lynda: Dennis has been evacuated from Monrovia by Marine helicopter and is now on a ship. Suggest you come immediately to Freetown with my driver.*

"He's out! He's out!" I shrieked, kissing the receptionist, a waiter, a passing bartender, then another waiter. I briefly considered doing a cartwheel across the floor, but that would have resulted in serious personal injury, to say nothing of damage to hotel property. Racing to the hut, I threw my things into a suitcase and flew back to the main building to pay my bill which, as befitting the longest-residing guest in the resort's history, was the length of a high school term paper. Then I jumped into the embassy's vehicle—an old Peace Corps truck from Liberia that had been driven to safety while the roads were still open—and we started for Freetown.

Where I waited, interminably, on a sofa outside the deputy ambassador's office. The embassy was the epicenter of the Liberian evacuation; the staff worked feverishly, sending cables to Washington, taking radio messages from Liberia, communicating with the US ships. Reuniting one slightly desperate woman with her husband was, understandably, a low priority. Still, short of sticking out my foot to trip an embassy official, I figured parking myself in a heavily trafficked area would serve as a visual reminder. Or better yet, an irritant. I had just finished reading, cover-to-cover, a magazine on West African agricultural commodities production forecasts for the seventeenth time when the deputy ambassador poked his head out his door. "Dennis is at the Freetown airport across the river," he said. "There's a ferry in thirty minutes. You'd better hurry."

He had barely finished speaking—and I was down the stairs, out the door, and diving into an embassy vehicle, whose driver navigated, kamikaze-like, through Freetown's cramped, congested streets. The ferry was about to cast off when we arrived. I climbed to the third deck of the huge, creaking vessel and sat on a wooden bench under a sky that promised a deluge. *Something's going to go wrong before we get to the other side*, I thought, with my usual Shirley Temple optimism, as the ferry chugged across the dullish water. *Lightning will strike. The boat will capsize. I will throw up.*

Of course, nothing happened. I even managed to find the embassy van waiting at the pier amid a sea of people hawking bananas, pineapples, paw-paws, cassava roots, and skewered meats. As I climbed into the passenger seat, an American television reporter stuck his head in the window. "Mrs. Jett, we talked to your husband," he said breathlessly. "He's fine. We interviewed him at the airport when he arrived by helicopter. Do you have anything to say?"

Interesting question. What, really, can *one say about the wanton, wholesale destruction of a country?* Luckily, the driver put the van in drive at that moment, apologizing for the intrusion. "The foreign journalists are everywhere, trying to interview the evacuees," he said.

"Well, you know those journalists!" I said. "Can't trust any of them."

The last part of the journey took forever. We hurtled past an endless, repeating vista of palm groves, thatch-roofed huts, white-washed mosques—until finally turning into the driveway of a small hotel near the airport. And there, as if it were the most natural thing in the world, was the information officer from the embassy in Monrovia, walking two dogs on the front lawn. And the husband of my running buddy, Mary, and a UN aid worker whom I vaguely knew, and an Irish priest who ran a vocational school—and, finally, Dennis.

Hollywood has got it all wrong. There's no gazing into your loved one's eyes upon being reunited; you can't see for the tears. And there's no murmuring of tender endearments; you're too busy choking back phlegm. (So romantic!) Instead, you just cling to one another like survivors from a shipwreck.

When I'd recovered enough to talk, I whispered, "Where do you want to go?"

"I want to be on the first plane that'll get us off this fucking continent," he said.

Which was a flight to Amsterdam. And then another to New Jersey, where we stayed with Dennis's mother, Helen, at the beach house she'd rented for the summer. Once again—just as when I had returned to the States from Beirut—I was awed, overwhelmed really, by the fact that normal life still existed in some places, that people could just get on with the daily business of picking up the dry cleaning and deciding between buttered or plain popcorn at the movies. The adjustment was probably even harder for Dennis, after all he had witnessed in Monrovia. But he wouldn't talk about it.

Though we found refuge in Washington, Dennis had to return to Liberia to serve the last year of his posting. We saw each other only twice during the twelve months, when he came to Washington on leave. Most of the time we had no means of communicating other than letters delivered by the occasional traveler to and from Monrovia. It wasn't easy for us—and not at all what I had imagined as the start of our marriage.

When Dennis finally came back to Washington for good—bringing Tenson with him—the conflict still wasn't resolved, despite the president having been captured and killed by one of the guerrilla groups. Tortured to death. This we knew because the rebel leader thoughtfully provided a video, a snuff film really, of his men carving off pieces of the president until he bled out from his wounds. By then, an estimated 250,000 people, one-eighth of the total population, were dead. Another third had fled to neighboring countries.

So much for marrying a diplomat and having a quiet, safe life together.

Which is why, for the couple of years we've been here, Washington is such a relief. And a pleasure. We have friends, a local farmer's market, a neighborhood watch group, a block parade on the Fourth of July—all things I, stupidly, would have dismissed in an earlier incarnation as veering too close to my mother's existence. But now they feel—what? Substantial? Comforting? *Homey?* Of course, it also helps that no one is shooting RPGs at us.

That is, until Dennis drops his own little bombshell one night, after suddenly producing a chilled bottle of champagne. "What's that for?" I say. "Did we win the lottery?"

"Better," he says, popping the cork and pouring into two flutes.

"Clinton called and wants to make you secretary of state?"

"Close. He nominated me to be ambassador to Mozambique."

"Mozambique?" I say, choking on the champagne. "But that's in Africa!"

"So?"

"So why would we want to go back there?"

"So I can be ambassador."

"I get that. But Africa? Are you crazy?"

Dennis very deliberately sets down his glass. "Lynda, I've worked almost twenty years to become an ambassador. Do you realize what a great honor this is? Something like only five percent of all career diplomats ever make it to the rank."

"I know, I know," I say, clinking his flute with mine. "And I really am happy for you."

"It's only for three years. Three years, and we're done. I promise. They'll never give me another ambassadorship after this."

"But couldn't it be somewhere peaceful and boring like, I don't know, Helsinki?"

"Peaceful and boring usually goes to political appointees, the big donors. We don't have the money to buy peaceful. I'm a *career* foreign service officer, remember?"

"What I remember is a little conflagration in Liberia."

We're silent as he refills the glasses. "As you may recall," I say after a few moments, "I reported on Mozambique when I was based in

Johannesburg. The country was still in the midst of a civil war that's been going on for, what, fifteen years? And the food situation was so bad I brought my own jar of peanut butter from South Africa."

"Lynda, things are better now," he says, draining his flute and putting his arms around me. "There's a tentative peace agreement. My job as ambassador will be to shepherd the warring parties through the peace process."

"And what am I going to do?"

"Whatever you want, Mrs. Ambassatrix."

"Ambassatrix? Leather and whips for me, sheep for you, Mr. Shepherd!" I say, feeling the effects of the champagne.

"Yeah, and when we come back, I can totter down the street to the pub, and the bartender will say, 'The usual, Mr. Ambassador?' That's the real reason I want the title."

By now, the bottle is empty; the fears I have about returning to Africa are temporarily subsumed in a fit of giggles. After that, we tipsily telephone Dennis's kids, his mother, and my parents to tell them the news. Then we call Simcha in Israel.

"Sim, it's Lynda!"

"Lynda? It's three o'clock in the bloody morning!"

"Oops, sorry. But it's not every day that Dennis is named ambassador. To Mozambique! In southern Africa!"

"That's fantastic. I'm so happy for him. I'm also happy the phone can ring at three o'clock in the morning and it's not bad news. Please give Dennis my heartiest mazel tov, and now I'm going back to bed."

As the weeks pass, my trepidation about Africa is replaced by a bigger concern: Ambassatrix School. That's my name for the two-week course the State Department requires of its envoys and spouses. The seminar is held in a classroom on an upper floor of

Foggy Bottom. There are twenty of us; a sign naming the country to which we are being posted marks each seat, along with a thick, three-ring binder. Mine says: *Ambassador's Spouse Notebook.*

I open it on the first morning and read, "The role of the senior spouse *exists,* despite the fact that it is not officially recognized . . . From the Spouse Survey, several statistics are of interest. Of those surveyed, 61 percent feel that the Ambassador's spouse should provide a leadership role at post. If the senior spouse decides not to provide that leadership role, s/he can be fairly certain that a large number of spouses and others within the community will be disappointed." Right off the bat, it seems, at least 61 percent of the women at Dennis's embassy are going to feel let down. And that's before I even open my mouth.

Despite the grammatical nod toward affirmative action (s/he) in the Spouse Notebook, all the ambassador-designates are men and their spouses, women. About half of the nominees are political appointees: the wealthy Friends of Bill (FOB) that Dennis had talked about, who donated semi-trailer loads of money to his presidential campaign and are being rewarded with posts in places such as Norway, Belgium, and France. (Later, when we have the nominee to Denmark, an FOB businessman from Atlanta, over to dinner, one of the other guests gets up the courage to ask how much he contributed to the Democrats. "Obviously not enough," the FOB sniffs, swirling the wine in his glass. "Or I'd be going to the Court of St. James.")

The remaining ambassador-designates are career diplomats like Dennis. For their decades of service in the trenches, they're off to Guinea, Niger, Lesotho, and other countries that only a cartographer can locate. I notice one FOB wife squinting at our sign from across the classroom, trying to pronounce the country name.

The lectures begin. The speakers, ex-ambassadors, and motiva-
tional experts take great pains to underscore the idea that we—the
ambassador-designate and his wife—are a team. Still, anytime the
topic becomes interesting (read: classified), the wives are whisked
off to another room. Yesterday there was a lecture on when to use
the official china embossed with the Great Seal of the United States.
Today, while the men get military briefings on their respective
countries, we wives are treated to a discourse on calling cards. The
lecturer, a protocol officer, quotes from a book. "'Calling cards are
engraved with black ink on excellent quality card stock, usually
white or off-white in color. Script lettering is the most popular, although some prefer the shaded antique roman and shaded roman.'"

My mind drifts; I notice a run in my stocking. If I flex my calf
muscle just so, I can make the run creep incrementally up my leg.
Flex, creep; flex, creep; flex . . .

"'The custom of bending the upper-right-hand corner toward
the name,'" the officer continues loudly, hovering somewhere near
my left ear, "'is practiced in many foreign countries to denote that
the call was made in person, or upon all members of the household.'" The officer, with a little flourish, demonstrates the technique
on the card. She hands it to me, and I examine the mutilated rect-
angle as if it were a rare biological specimen, then gingerly pass it to
the woman seated next to me.

The officer resumes her monologue. We can leave initials in the
lower left corner of the top card—in pencil if the cards are delivered in person, ink if mailed—to convey the appropriate message:
p.p. (*pour presenter*)—to introduce; p.f. (*pour feliciter*)—to congrat-
ulate (on a national day); p.r. (*pour remercier*)—to thank (for a gift or
courtesy received). A man should leave a card for another man and

one for his wife. An additional card is left for other ladies over eighteen years of age. In no case are more than three cards to be left in one place. A woman leaves a card for each lady of the house over eighteen, but never for a man. And so on.

Imagining a life filled with trying to get my calling card etiquette straight, I begin to hyperventilate. *Do not panic. Inhale slowly and deeply. Think of ambassadorial life as an exotic culture with rites and rituals that you, the Margaret Mead of decorum, have to deconstruct.*

That still leaves the problem of trying to stay awake.

Things get stranger when we move to the touchy-feely sessions meant to help the spouse figure out what she wants to do while her husband is being extraordinary and plenipotentiary—part of his title—for the United States president. The instructor distributes a sheet entitled *Personal Goals,* which is divided into three sections: *Within First Six Months, Within One Year, Within Two Years.* We're supposed to write out our objectives and discuss them with the class. I already know that I want to research a book about a black South African family I met while reporting on the country. A description of the project takes up about two lines, so to fill up the sheet I scribble in a few throwaways: work on my Portuguese (Mozambique's language), train for a marathon, maybe take up competitive dog grooming.

Each of us stands to read her goals to the class. The spouses of the career diplomats list noble objectives like caring for the embassy and expatriate communities or working with the poor. They're veterans of this lifestyle, and are rewarded with rousing rounds of applause for their thoughtful projects. Then it's my turn to recite: barely audible clapping follows, the wives peering at me with something verging on pity. *I'm the new girl in seventh grade,* I think, *the one from the unpronounceable country who wears polka dots with stripes and socks with sandals.*

Another day, there's an entire unit devoted to entertaining. Picturing myself in a strapless gown—tasteful boa flung carelessly across my bare shoulders, laughingly exchanging confidences with visiting celebrities—I eagerly turn to the section in the handbook. And read: "In determining actual costs for functions, add the total cost of all food prepared and the per capita cost for soft drinks and liquor, based on actual consumption. On the voucher, write the total cost." *This isn't about glamour; it's about accounting! How stupid can I be?* Each time we entertain, it seems, I'm going to have to log every ounce of alcohol sucked down, each canapé consumed, including all the butter, oil, onions, garlic, capers, cheese, olives, peppers, and tomatoes that went into its creation. To say nothing of seasonings.

I feel another panic attack coming on. What happens when we have those five-hundred-person mass receptions that diplomats so love? Or a five-course, sit-down dinner for thirty? Okay, this is taxpayers' money, but does the State Department's Inspector General really expect me to document every pinch of paprika?

On the Metro back to our neighborhood after class, I'm sweating. Maybe it's because of the homework I'm lugging: a catalog the thickness of a telephone directory of wholesale foodstuffs and household supplies, from which I have to supply our residence for the next three years. To kill time on the ride home, I randomly open to a page of options. Twelve or twenty-four packs of toilet paper? Scented or unscented? Quilted or plain? White or pastel colors? *Does any woman know how many cases of toilet paper she goes through in thirty-six months, guests included?* After that, it's on to flour, oil, furniture polish, window cleaner, canned tuna, mustard, ketchup, baking soda, popcorn, taco seasoning, and, while we're at it, cream of tartar—plus every other conceivable nonperishable item.

"I don't know if I can do this!" I wail, self-pityingly, the minute I walk into the house.

Dennis is sorting through books to take to Mozambique. "Do what?" he says, setting down—what else?—the volume of *Heart of Darkness* he'd been perusing.

"Calling cards. Expense reports. Three years' worth of hot sauce, for heaven sakes!"

"Don't worry about it, Lynda. You don't have to do anything you wouldn't do in Washington."

"How about none of it and we just stay here?"

"Not really an option," he says, taking my hand. "We do have to entertain, but only the absolutely essential stuff. The rest of your time will be yours."

"That's not the message of Ambassatrix School."

"Ignore them. The great thing about being an ambassador is you're the boss."

"Yeah, but I'm not the ambassador."

"But you sleep with him."

"Oh good. So now my power is as wife-of. How very 1950s!"

"Lynda, come on. It's only for three years. It'll be fun."

I reach into his pocket for a handkerchief to blow my nose; his mother taught him always to carry a hankie, one of the many reasons I love him. "And the stupid expense reports?"

"I'll get my secretary to do them."

"Well, she'd better bring one of those really sensitive scales that can weigh a proton."

For the moment, Dennis's reassurances are calming. That night in bed, though, reading ahead for our next assignment in the handbook, I learn that I'll have to "accumulate comprehensive lists of guests to invite to our residence, updating and revising them frequently," and "request information from VIPs before a visit as to whether they would prefer swimming, tennis, golf, shopping, or seeing museums."

Someone forgot to tell the State Department that Mamie Eisenhower is dead, I think, turning out the light.

After Ambassatrix School finishes, I fly to Detroit to visit my family. As always, it's the emotional equivalent of hitting heavy turbulence. Predictably, after all the drama in Liberia at my wedding, Dad has dumped Gerrie, his second wife, and moved onto a third. She's a year my junior and pregnant with Dad's sixth child. My sisters and I are a bit stunned; Uncle Eugene, Dad's brother, has taken to referring to him as "the serial marriage killer." Funny how different a parent can look when viewed through the prism of your own adulthood.

That holds true for Mom as well. Only in her case, it's definitely an improvement. Then again, in my bizarre brain, she had nowhere to go but up. Andrea, my shrink in Washington, says I vilified Mom in my youth because she was less threatening than my father—the one who, in fact, could have stood a little vilifying. Or at least a more objective assessment. Andrea's an excellent therapist, and that's about as close as she comes to psychoanalytic mumbo-jumbo; most of the time she's painfully straightforward about telling me what a jerk I can be. And she always has a large box of tissues at hand.

In any event, she must be doing something right because toward the end of my stay, I invite Mom to go shopping with me for a hat.

According to the State Department's Ambassatrix packing list, I need one for formal occasions—*in war-torn Mozambique!* Mom suggests a snooty department store in a snooty suburb of Detroit that has a large millinery section. In the car on the way there, she asks how I'm feeling about going back to Africa.

"Ambivalent," I say, staring out the window. "It seems a long way away."

"Really! I've never heard you say that before."

"Maybe I'm getting old. Or maybe Liberia cured me of wanting to be in exotic places."

"You're hardly old."

"I know." I turn to face her. "I'm really proud of Dennis. This is huge for him. It's just that I like our life in Washington. I realized the other day that by the time we leave, this will be the longest I've lived in one place as an adult."

Can I actually be opening up to my mother?

"But you're just renting out the house, aren't you?" she says, pulling into a parking garage. "You're not selling. You'll be able to come back to it."

It's at this moment in a conversation with Mom that I'd usually cut her off, refusing to share even the slightest sliver of myself. Instead, I say, "I know, but by leaving you lose the continuity, the sense of belonging to a community."

Mom stops to look at me. "I didn't know you cared about those sorts of things."

"I didn't know either," I say with a shrug.

In the store's millinery department, we wander among the displays of headgear roosting on candelabra-like stands and disembodied mannequin heads. "What kind of hat are you thinking of?" Mom asks, holding up a green fascinator that resembles an insect antenna.

Shuddering, I say, "Maybe something along the lines of a baseball cap?"

A saleswoman sidles up to us. "My son-in-law is going to be an ambassador," Mom says to her, confidingly. "Somewhere in Africa!"

Now, a normal person's interpretation of this might be that Mom's proud and wants to brag a bit. My typical reaction is that she's trying to appropriate my life. But today, as the saleswoman seats me at a vanity table with a plush, high-backed chair and tall mirror, I think, *Why not? Why not just let her revel in it?* Then check the mirror to make certain it's still me.

Meanwhile, Mom and the saleswoman set off on a tag-team relay, bringing me hats to try on—all of them thoroughly shocking. Aiming for Audrey Hepburn, I end up closer to Little Bo Peep with my purchase: a white, broad-brimmed number, replete with shiny ribbon tied in a bow at the back. Still, it makes Mom happy to be a part of this. All she's ever wanted, on my visits home, was to go out to lunch and go shopping; in her mind, that's what mothers and daughters do. *Why have I denied her something so simple all these years? It's not a lot to ask.*

But there's no time to act further on that not-so-small epiphany; I have to hurry back to Washington to help plan Dennis's swearing-in ceremony. Or, as he refers to it, his coronation. In the midst of preparations—engraved or self-printed invitations? Champagne or California bubbly?—Dennis telephones me at home one afternoon. Because he worked at the National Security Council on President Clinton's staff, the president has agreed to have his picture taken with us. At the White House. In two hours. Panicked, I throw on a dress and race over to a neighborhood hair salon, where a sweet little Salvadoran woman teases and backcombs my hair into what she calls an "oop-do." No matter that I now bear a distressing resemblance to my grandmother, circa 1959; I have to hightail it to the Metro. Driving would be easier, or at least less sweaty, but I can't chance not finding a parking place.

Dennis meets me at the entrance to the Old Executive Building; Allison, his daughter, twentyish and gorgeous, is with him. An aide takes us to a holding area in the West Wing. "You'll have to wait here for a bit," she says, nodding at the plush sofas. Staffers dart back and forth along the hallway. Stephen Stills, the musician, suddenly saunters by, accompanied by several fawning young women. I try not to gawk. Another aide appears to escort us to a corridor outside the Oval Office, where we join a queue of similarly dressed-up and nervous-looking people. The president does courtesy photographs between 4:15 and 4:30, the aide explains. The scene has the feel of a cattle call: one woman checks her makeup in a compact mirror, clicking it shut and sliding it into her purse—only to pull it out again a minute later.

When it's our turn, a door to the Oval Office opens and we step inside. Two things immediately stand out: the yellowness of the room and the tallness of the president. He looks Allison up and down, then glances at an index card. "Thanks so much for helping to formulate Africa policy, Dennis," the president says. Taking another peek at Allison, he continues, "And good luck in Mozambique." Clinton leers at Allison again and motions to us to stand together in front of the photographer. We smile; he snaps our picture. The president shakes our hands, ogles Allison one last time, and gently pushes us toward another open door for our exit.

Yuck factor aside, maybe there *are* benefits to being a wife-of.

Still, I'm not sure they're enough to compensate for calling cards and VIP visitors. Or for the trepidation I have about leaving. Squirrel-brained, I put the title and registration papers for the car we're selling in the pile of things that are being sent by air to Mozambique, and our checkbook among the goods going by sea—then catch the mistakes just before the movers come. *Why aren't I looking forward to another adventure abroad?*

When I mention this to Andrea at our farewell session, she says, "You have to decide what you want." We're in her office in the basement of her suburban Washington home. But for the row of intimidating degrees from prestigious universities hanging on the wall, it feels like we're in her rec room. Andrea, who's small and athletic-looking with light brown hair cut in a bob, sits in an easy chair opposite me. Being face-to-face like that, you'd think it would be hard to maintain an attentive visage for nearly an hour. But she always manages to appear vitally interested—even when it's, say, the thirty-eighth time I'm revisiting a topic and she could probably recite, verbatim, my litany of woe.

"Decide as in, steak or fish?" I say. "Red wine or white?"

Andrea rolls her eyes. "In life. In your life."

"I thought I'd already figured that out years ago."

"People change, Lynda. Even if it's a cliché and a truism."

"But how am I supposed to decide when all my time is going to be taken up finding out from VIPS whether they prefer smooth or ridged toilet paper?"

"That's precisely the point."

Leave it to Andrea to go all cryptic just when I need clarity. "Can we work this out in the ten minutes we have left?"

"I don't think so. But here," she says, handing me a small wrapped package. "I bought you a little going-away gift."

"Aw, that's so sweet. Is it allowed? I mean, the client-patient thing."

"Please stop asking questions and open it."

Inside are two tiny, gleaming brass balls, nestled in a velvet-lined case. "So beautiful!" I say, holding them up. "Uh, what are they?"

"Traveling candlesticks for the Sabbath," Andrea says. "So you can make a home wherever you are."

Make a home? Is this really the new and improved me?

Back at the house, I show Dennis the gift. He's too engrossed in writing an acceptance speech for his swearing-in, though, to offer more than a perfunctory grunt. I glance down at his notepad, filled with crossed-out lines and scribbles in the margins. "Could you please acknowledge my father's wives, past and present, in your remarks?" I say. "They're all coming to the coronation."

"Lynda," he says, "I only have five minutes for the speech."

The ceremony takes place in the Benjamin Franklin room on the top floor of the State Department, a sprawling, elegant space decorated with a crenelated gold-leaf ceiling, crystal chandeliers, marble pillars, Persian rugs, and period pieces such as the desk that Benjamin Franklin used as America's first envoy to France. (Hence the room's name.) The Chief of Protocol, a kind of diplomat-whisperer, glides us through the set-piece ritual with about two hundred people looking on and a photographer snapping away, nonstop. The rest of the afternoon unfolds like a wedding reception: an hour-long receiving line, drinks, mini-dramas. Aunt Blanche from Skokie flirts with a handsome young attendant, who's applying ice to her foot after she slipped on the marble floor and twisted her ankle. Mom, meanwhile, is hovering, as always, at the edge of my peripheral vision. And Dad huddles defensively in a corner with Uncle Todd, wives number two and three warily circling one another nearby. This is the juncture in any family gathering at which I usually wish I had been adopted, at an early age, by a clan of badgers. Instead, I find myself wistful, sentimental almost. *I'm going to miss these people.*

Then—stranger still—at the airport later, as I'm making my way back to the short-term parking lot after kissing my mother goodbye at the gate for her flight, I start to cry. Dennis holds my gaze an extra beat when I hop into the car. "Are those tears, Schuster?"

"No," I say, turning my head and hastily swiping at my cheeks. "There was a little rain falling when I came out the terminal."

"Rain?" He cranes to look through the windshield at the perfectly clear sky. "What rain?"

CHAPTER TEN

MOZAMBIQUE, 1994

Not long after our arrival in Maputo, Mozambique's capital, the wife of the Portuguese ambassador summons me to coffee in her home. Summons, because as a representative of the country's former colonial master, she considers herself a kind of doyenne among the ambassadorial spouses. It's my coming out, as it were, so I dress carefully for the meeting: stockings, pearls, high heels. A uniformed maid ushers me into the house. I shudder at the sight of a wide bowl on the foyer table and hurry past it to the living room, not daring to drop my calling card for fear of turning down the wrong corner. *What are those initials you're supposed to write on it?* I think, trying to recall my lessons in Ambassatrix School. *BFF? SOS?*

The Portuguese wife is a tiny woman who barely reaches my shoulder in her stiletto heels, and I'm anything but Amazonian. Her force of personality, though, makes up for a lack of stature. She evokes a kind of Yorkshire terrier in her tenacity—an intelligent, highly educated, multilingual Yorkie. I've barely finished stirring milk into my coffee cup when she launches into a rapid-fire description of her pet charity project: a sewing school she created up-country to teach dressmaking to girls. All the ambassadors' wives participate; it's what everyone does.

She stops to take a breath. *Now's your chance.* "In a country as poor and ravaged as Mozambique and with the educational system in tatters, your project is clearly a worthy one," I say hastily. "But I'm going to be researching a book in South Africa."

"Nonsense, my dear," she says with a dismissive wave of her hand. "Never forget that you're the wife of the American ambassador. Not as important as the Portuguese perhaps, but important nonetheless. You have duties, obligations. Besides, I need your help. Your predecessor was very helpful."

"My predecessor wasn't working on a book."

"My dear, neither are you. Or you shouldn't be. Not anymore. Think about it."

Her message delivered, we exchange pleasantries until I finish my coffee. Afterward, making my way up the street to our residence, I gingerly step around the dog excrement and decomposing trash piles. ("Where is your chauffeur?" the Portuguese wife demanded, horrified that *a woman in my position* would walk three blocks.) We both live on Friedrich Engels Avenue, a jacaranda-lined road overlooking Maputo Bay. Before Mozambique gained independence from Portugal in 1975, the street was called the Dukes of Connaught; the most exclusive address in the capital, its grand houses were owned mostly by rich whites from neighboring South Africa—and denied to black Mozambicans, the majority of the population. All that changed after the Marxist rebels, who fought the Portuguese for a decade, took over. Besides running the economy into the ground, they also renamed the streets. Getting directions here is the stuff of a revolutionary's wet dream: "Go up Mao Tse Tung Avenue until Vladimir Lenin, make a left on Kim Il Sung and continue until Ho Chi Min." So of course it's fitting that the American Imperialists live on a street named for the coauthor of *The Communist Manifesto.*

A little barefoot boy races by, rolling a rusted bicycle wheel rim with a stick. My mind drifts back to the Portuguese wife. *A woman in my position!* She makes me sound like a dowager countess. I really can't blame her, though. The foreign wives, too, spend years in the trenches training for their moment of grandeur: attending endless diplomatic functions; clawing their way up the embassy food chain; absorbing the nuances of protocol—anything to further their spouse's career. After all, his status is hers. (Like the military, but with better clothes.) And they deliver: the etiquette of a Miss Manners, the social agility of a Vanderbilt, all for the glory of man and mission.

That clearly isn't me, but then what is? Peering out over the bay, I notice a large bird—maybe a seagull or tern, wheeling above the white-capped water—and stop for a moment to watch its progress. The bird's screeching call, borne on the wind, sounds like an admonishment: "Whaddya want? Whaddya want? Whaddya want?"

"Darn you, Andrea," I whisper, remembering my therapist's parting question. "Even the birds are on your side."

———

My avian anxiety notwithstanding, Maputo turns out to be less daunting than anticipated. After the hangar-like house in Liberia, our residence feels almost Lilliputian—and with the charm of a VFW hall to boot: two living rooms, breakfast room, kitchen, dining room with a crystal chandelier and poufy, floor-length drapes so stiff and formal I want to ask them to dance. But the terrace off our bedroom upstairs has a spectacular view of the bay. And the garden! Out back, it's a wonderland filled with palm, flame, and mango trees; honeysuckle, frangipani, and banana bushes; a passion-fruit arbor; flocks of butterflies; two tortoises; an occasional monkey; and a foot-long snail that appears only at night. There's also a small pool in which Lucille, our Labrador, swims laps, while Blanche—who's a bit of a coward—runs around the perimeter, barking. (We left Butch in the States with Brian, Dennis's son, who'd become very attached to him. Besides, paying to fly three dogs across a couple of continents seemed, even for us, excessive.)

It almost feels like home after unpacking our books and hanging a few pictures. That is, if your idea of home is one filled with Early American furniture—the same furniture found in virtually every US embassy residence around the world—that looks about as fitting in subtropical Southern Africa as an Iditarod dog-sled team. Also, there's no running butt-naked through the rooms; once again, we have staff. Tenson is here, of course, thrilled that Malawi's proximity allows him to bring his wife and two youngest children. And two stewards: Lourino (tall, slim, handsome, humorless); and Adrivas (shorter, rounder, goofier). Leocadio the launderer, a chain-smoker who does his work in a tiny outbuilding and impregnates our clothes with the stink of his cigarettes, completes our happy little establishment.

Even the embassy isn't nearly as demanding as I'd feared. Happily, we're not going to get many visits from those troublesome congressional delegations; why take your wife—or mistress—on a junket to a malarial backwater when you can go on a fact-finding mission to, say, Paris? And I come to like many of the post's forty or so foreign service officers and their wives. They're mostly young, eager ex-Peace Corps types who think of Africa as a great adventure. A calling, even. Contrary to the warnings in the Ambassadorial Spouse Notebook, these spouses don't seem the type to be easily disappointed. Still, no matter how friendly we become, it's already clear there will always be a divide: I'm the boss's wife.

Truly remarkable and gratifying, though, is how much the country has changed. When I visited Maputo several years ago on a reporting trip, the only items for sale in the few downtown shops not boarded up were Bulgarian socks. Milk, butter, cheese, eggs, coffee, sugar, rice, oil, soap, toilet paper—all as rare as the dugong sea cows that used to ply the Indian Ocean waters around here. People were starving to death. There was no money for raw materials, fuel, spare parts; an economist I interviewed used shampoo for brake fluid.

A large share of the problem was the colonial legacy left by the Portuguese, considered second only to the Belgians in their brutality and racism on the continent. The British and French, for all the exploitation of their colonies, at least invested in some infrastructure and created a civil service. Not so the Portuguese. The white settlers who flocked here by the thousands dominated just about every inch of the economy. The country had a 10 percent literacy rate and only a half dozen black college graduates at independence in 1975, when the colonists fled. And in a final act of vengeance, the departing whites destroyed much of what they'd built. (A monument to this retribution stands on the outskirts of Maputo: a

crumbling beach hotel, hastily abandoned in mid-construction—
but not before its owners poured cement into the pipes, rendering
the building useless.) This was the pitiful inheritance onto which
the Marxist rebels grafted their own disastrous economic policies.
As if that weren't recipe enough for failure, a civil war began almost
immediately after independence: your typical Cold War proxy-con-
flict that lasted for fifteen years. An estimated one million people
died in the fighting and from starvation. Thousands more lost limbs
from landmines. The country was in ruins.

These days, Maputo's buildings are still moldering and mountains of decaying garbage dot the landscape. But now there are
supermarkets stocked with all the basic staples and open-air markets filled with fruits and vegetables. The fragile peace accord ham-
mered out before our arrival seems to be holding. Dennis's job,
along with other Western diplomats, is to coax the two formerly
warring sides into demobilizing their soldiers and taking part in
democratic elections.

In the meantime, I'm flying back and forth to South Africa to do
research, which leaves little time to consider Andrea's lingering
query: what do I want? Especially when Dennis and I have to attend
endless rounds of cocktail parties and diplomatic dinners that he
insists are essential. "Essential how?" I say, returning home from
one such trip to news of a dinner at another ambassador's house that
night. "To building the weekend home of the local booze importer?"

"Come on, Lynda, you know that alcohol is the lubricant of
diplomacy."

The dinner is a small gathering, just a handful of couples. We
start out in the living room. Andrew, the host, huddles in one corner with Dennis and Lukas, the German ambassador. Charlotte, his
wife, is in another corner, laughing with Giovanni, the head of the

UN peacekeeping operation. Eugenie, his long-time companion who is visiting from Switzerland and was once married to a White Russian prince, hangs on his arm. Giovanni is all charm and piles of slicked-back graying hair; unknown to Eugenie—and the rest of us—he's simultaneously carrying on an affair with his young Scandinavian secretary. There will be a theatrical, maudlin, and very public blow-up later on. Forget about nail-biting nuclear negotiations; here's real diplomatic drama!

Drink in hand, I stand under the only air conditioner, a tiny, ancient box that sounds as if it could use a rescue inhaler. Andrew has a phobia about malarial mosquitoes and insists on closing all doors and windows after nightfall. I certainly share his concern, especially since I've stopped taking antimalaria medication. (It was causing spectacular nightmares, the final straw being one in which Lucille, walking upright on hind legs, held out a dead sheep to me in her front paws as a kind of offering.) But with his house hermetically sealed, Andrew could at least invest in some decent air conditioning.

"What are you doing over here all alone, stranger?" says Fiona, Lukas's wife. She's Scottish, a former flight attendant, and my running buddy. We also go to an aerobics class together in a dirty downtown gym run by a former Cuban army advisor, who barks out orders to jump and leap in double time.

"Trying to get cool before we have to decamp to that sweatbox of a dining room. And think of a graceful way to slide under the table when I pass out from hyperthermia."

"True, true," Fiona says in her burr. "It's a shame he keeps everything so closed up. There's such a beautiful breeze that comes up from the ocean at night!"

"Maybe someone ought to tell Andrew about a new invention called window screens."

Fiona gives a short bark of a laugh and grabs a canapé off a tray offered by one of the stewards. *How do they survive this sauna?* I wonder. Charlotte makes them dress in starched white jackets buttoned up to the neck and heavy red fezzes. She must have a fetish for the hats; when we sit down at the dining table, I notice the carved African heads that decorate the sideboard are all wearing fezzes perched at jaunty angles. The stewards also have on thick, white gardening-type gloves that invariably cause one of the poor men to lose his grip while pouring wine and splash the guests. When it happens not long after we're seated, Charlotte jumps up, fussing over Dennis—tonight's victim—and declaiming the *utter* stupidity of Africans.

"Perhaps it's the gloves," I whisper to Andrew, sitting to his right. "Maybe he should take them off."

Andrew squints at me. "G-E-R-M-S," he spells out slowly, as though I'm learning disabled.

He turns back to Charlotte. They'd been discussing his disappointment at not getting a title he'd wanted. Besides diseases, this honor is Andrew's other obsession. "And now," Charlotte says with a sigh, "we're leaving."

"Do you know where you are going?" says Lukas.

Andrew makes a face. "I'm not quite sure. Everything they've offered so far is unacceptable. Zimbabwe, no way," he says, ticking off the possibilities. "Pakistan, a nation of rag heads. Sri Lanka, the land of wogs . . ."

Everyone titters and the conversation moves on. I look around the table in astonishment: it's as though Andrew had merely commented on, say, the rising cost of goldfish food. *These are representatives extraordinary and plenipotentiary?* From across the table, Dennis lowers his head slightly and fixes me with a stare, probably praying I'll hold my tongue.

Which, because we don't get home until late and are both tired, I manage to do until the next day. But not before we've bounced across Maputo Bay to a small island for a picnic. Taking the embassy's boat out for a whirl is one of the few things to do here on the weekend. The thirty-six-foot vessel comes with its own captain, boating's answer to the Blues Brothers in the crazed way he navigates the white-capped water. Between the craft's deafening motors, and the *thwunk! thwunk! thwunk!* of the hull hitting the swells at high speed, it's impossible to carry on any sort of conversation.

Besides, I'm too busy trying to keep from being swept overboard. It's a major concern ever since the wife of a Dutch businessman accidently flew out the back of their boat during a particularly rough crossing back to Maputo. Her husband couldn't hear her shouts for help and didn't discover she was missing until he'd pulled into the marina. By then, night had fallen; it was too dangerous to retrace the boat's route for fear of running over her in the water. The wife, who was wearing a flotation device, spent the night praying, loudly singing school songs, and generally trying not to think about sharks and the huge cargo freighters that traverse the channel, until she was found at daybreak. *That is* not *happening to me,* I think, strapping on two life vests and looking around for something to chain myself to the helm.

But the uninhabited little isle proves worth the journey. It has a series of World War I gun emplacements, the massive fixed cannons—now rusting and half-submerged—pointed out to sea to defend Maputo. Dennis clambers over the ruins like a little kid; I, meanwhile, can't walk two steps without shrieking at the ghost crabs skittering across the beach. Behind us, hillocks tufted with scrubby vegetation meander across the interior. We wade through the tidal flats and are just setting down a blanket when a flock of flamingos—pinkish running to rosy, with flashes of black peeking out from under the wings—lands on the other side of the beach.

"Will you look at that!" Dennis says.

"Do you think they're on the payroll of the tourism board?" I say. "I mean, perfect timing."

"Nah, this beach is probably just full of the little crawly things they love."

"Stop!"

We munch our sandwiches in silence, watching the strange and beautiful birds stir up the mucky shallows with their webbed feet: spindly necks bending down now and then, pink bills slurping up a tasty tidbit. "Dennis," I finally say. "How can you stand Andrew?"

"I don't like him anymore than you do. But I have to work with him."

"Okay, I understand that. But why'd he become a diplomat if he's got nothing but contempt for three-quarters of the world's population?"

"Lack of imagination? Maybe he's just in it for the title."

"And what about everyone else at the table?" I say, working myself into the usual self-righteous froth. "How come they didn't say anything? Why didn't they call him out? For that matter, why didn't you?"

Dennis reaches for a soda. "Lynda, we were Andrew's guests. Besides, diplomats would rather ignore a problem than confront it head on."

"Except you, of course."

"What do you mean by that?"

"Openly criticizing the Mozambicans," I say, referring to an ongoing brouhaha over Dennis's very pointed and public accusations that the government isn't fulfilling its obligations under the peace accord to demobilize all its soldiers.

"Lynda, they're threatening the whole peace process, trying to maintain their own private army just in case they lose the election. They'd rather take this entire country back to war than give up political power." Dennis squeezes the aluminum foil that covered his sandwich into a tight little ball. "I have to speak out. I'm finally in a position where I might be able to prevent more fighting, maybe even save peoples' lives. Unlike in Liberia."

"Liberia!" I say, whipping my head around to look at him. *That's where this is coming from!* "What more could you have done in Liberia?"

"I don't know. Maybe tried to arrange some sort of a cease-fire so people could leave the zones of fighting. But sitting there in the middle of it, I never realized how bad things could get."

"How could you? Nobody did."

Dennis stares out at the flamingos, delicately high-stepping through the sticky wet sand like finicky ballerinas. "Right. But now that I'm ambassador, I *can* do something."

"I know," I say, touching his arm. "And I'm really, really proud of you. It's just that you open your mouth—and suddenly the embassy adds all these extra security guards around the residence. It makes me very nervous."

"Don't worry, nothing's going to happen."

"Then why did the embassy do it? Is there any threat to you?"

"Not that I'm aware of. But I'm just the ambassador. Nobody tells me anything."

"Funny, Jett. They popped up after you started condemning the government."

"Don't worry," he says, gathering up the detritus from the picnic. "It's only a precaution."

"Yeah, but against what?"

Dennis pauses, eyes fixed on the flamingos; I can tell he's not going to tell me the truth.

"Maybe some of the junior officers who didn't like the evaluations I gave them?"

"Dennis, please be serious. I'd like to be able to spend fifteen minutes not having to worry about your safety. Is that too much to ask?"

"Not as much as some of the other demands you put on me, Harriet Shoot," he says, leaning over to kiss the top of my head. Then he adds, "Let's just get through the election. Everything will be fine after that."

Promises, promises.

Of course, the vote—which is supposed to last for two days—almost blows up. On the first day, Dennis and I drive around to polling stations to watch people cast their ballots. We're official international observers; I'm wearing a little laminated card on a lanyard around my neck to prove it. At an elementary school painted pink and white, the precinct captain becomes positively giddy at the sight of the US ambassador. He insists on showing us how each ballot-filled urn—a metal box, really—is to be secured with a green plastic tie, whose number will be recorded before the urn is transported to the counting station and verified before being untied. Then he shows us again.

Halfway through the third demonstration, I duck outside to look at the voting queue. It snakes around the schoolyard, then stretches down the road as far as I can see. This is the first multi-party election in the country's history; people have been standing all day under the scorching sun to cast a ballot. Parents bring their children, dressed in Sunday finery, to witness the event. Everyone is hot and tired and thirsty—but no one leaves. One elderly woman tells me she's waited all her life for this moment; what's an hour or two more? Dennis and I have seen similar scenes throughout the city. Watching, I can't help but think of all the patronizing and self-serving excuses I've heard over the years as a journalist from people in power to deny citizens this right: they, the rulers, knew better, or their countrymen weren't ready or, worse yet, didn't really care about controlling their own destiny. *Take that, you autocrats and oppressors!*

Later, a couple of American reporters, a newspaperman and a radio correspondent, come for dinner. They're friends of mine, part of the journalistic hordes that have swept into the country. We've just finished the first course—Tenson's famous pesto—and gossiping about mutual acquaintances, when Lourino suddenly appears; Dennis has a telephone call. He vanishes and returns a few minutes later with a walkie-talkie in his hand, an anguished look on his face.

"What's up?" I say.

"The head of the rebels claims there are voting irregularities and he doesn't think the election can be fair. He's pulling out. He's also telling his supporters to boycott the second day."

With that, Dennis dashes out the door, the reporters close behind. And I'm left alone at the table in the flickering candlelight, staring at the china and crystal emblazoned with the Great Seal of the United States. Tenson ducks his head into the dining room.

"No second course?" he says, looking at the vacated chairs.

"No second course."

"No dessert?"

"No dessert. Thanks, Tenson."

Is there a teensy-weensy part of me that wishes I could follow my friends? That I could go off in hot pursuit of a hot story? That I could feel the adrenaline rush from bearing witness to history as it unfolds? That I could get bitten by a million mosquitoes while waiting outside rebel headquarters for a spokesman to issue a useless statement?

You betcha!

Yet, truth be told, leaving daily journalism is similar to what smokers say about quitting: you only get a hankering when you're around it. And longform writing feels more satisfying now, the difference between, say, wolfing down fast food or patiently cooking a well-balanced meal. *Is opting to make the meal a sign of maturity?* I wonder, blowing out the candles and heading upstairs. *What about all the adults who eat Big Macs?*

Dennis still hasn't returned when I go to sleep. Along with his fellow ambassadors, he works through the night and all the next day to salvage the election. Which they do: the rebel leader rejoins the voting, and the poll is extended by an additional twenty-four hours. The ballots take forever to be collected from all parts of the country and counted by hand, though. Meanwhile, Dennis grows even more critical of the government—why are they dragging out the tally?—and I become even more jittery about the guards around our home. When the incumbent president is finally declared the winner, Dennis informs me that I'm part of the US delegation to the inaugural ceremony.

Me? The Jewish Eliza Doolittle? Part of a delegation? Does the State Department know what it's doing?

On the morning of the festivities, a day so mercilessly hot even the mosquitoes are stupefied, I wait for Edward, my hairdresser, to arrive at our house. Normally I don't pay much attention to my coiffure beyond the usual cut and occasional application of henna to change the color from drab mouse to a more robust rodent shade. But as an official representative to the inauguration, I don't want to let our country down.

Edward is a Brit who followed his lover to Mozambique—whereupon the lover promptly dumped him. Adrift in Maputo, Edward found work in a hotel salon and solace in the city's forlorn nightlife. He cuts an incongruous figure zooming around the pitted streets on his chopper, clad in tight leather trousers and jacket. Most African societies, even post-revolutionary ones such as this, are hostile to gays. Every six weeks or so I visit him at the salon: he sighs about wanting to fall in love again, I sigh about the limited possibilities of my hair, then we dish. That's how I found out the wife of the South African military attaché was telling everyone how *scandalized* she was by the gown I wore to the US Marine Ball, the annual birthday bash the Marines throw for themselves at every American embassy around the world. The ball consists mostly of marching: marching of the color guard; the guest-of-honor (Dennis, in his tuxedo); the oldest and youngest Marines present; the birthday cake, even. Before leaving Washington, I had purchased my first ever gown, which the saleswoman insisted was glamorous but whose bright red color, in truth, made me look like a fire hydrant. A fire hydrant with cleavage. I don't know how the South African wife even noticed, though; I was stuck in a bathroom stall for much of the night. To pee, I'd had to inch the tight, lower part of the gown almost over my head—then couldn't get it down once I'd finished. And there I stood, straitjacketed, like a half-unwrapped candy bar: unable to leave the stall, too embarrassed to call for help.

Desperate at least to get my coiffure right for the inauguration, I made the appointment with Edward for eight o'clock. Everything is perfectly timed. I wash and dry my hair, so he'll just have to dump some product into it and gather the mess into a recognizable shape. I dress in a suit of peach silk purchased in South Africa. I have Tenson bring a tray of coffee and banana bread to the bedroom to fortify the artiste. I am ready.

Eight o'clock comes and goes: no Edward.

The salon is closed at this early hour, and I don't have Edward's home telephone number. I jog between the bedroom to check the clock and the terrace to check the front gates; maybe the guards aren't letting him in. Only the official car, a little American flag fluttering from each front fender, is visible. Tenson buzzes on the intercom, "Bambo is waiting for you to come downstairs." I race back to the balcony and scan the horizon. Edward probably went on a bender and is lying comatose somewhere. The intercom buzzes again. "Madam," Tenson announces. "Bambo says if you don't come now, he will have to leave without you."

The hat! The white hat I bought with Mom in Detroit! Standing in front of a mirror, I twist my fine, flyaway locks into a bun, jab it with an entire box of pins, and slam on the hat. Perfect! "I love you, Mom," I whisper, Little Bo Peep gazing back at me in the mirror.

The swearing-in is held outside in Independence Plaza, whose traffic has been blocked off. Only the podium where the president will take his oath is shaded; everywhere else is exposed to the Sahara-like sun, even the seats of honor behind the dais. They're reserved for the likes of Nelson Mandela and other African leaders, who arrive in their black limousines to the cheers of hundreds of onlookers beyond the cordons. Dennis and I deposit the head of our delegation, an assistant secretary of state from Washington, with the other dignitaries and take our seats among the diplomatic corps. The wife of the Spanish ambassador is to my left, energetically ventilating her face with an elaborately painted fan. Her husband holds an umbrella over their heads.

Once it begins, the inauguration resembles a church service: stand for the arrival of the president, sit for the announcements of the master of ceremonies. Stand for the playing of the national anthem, sit for the president taking the oath of office. Stand for the singing of the national anthem, sit for the president's acceptance speech. Small puddles of perspiration are collecting under my nylons. Stupidly, I wore stockings because I didn't think the ghostly hue of my legs went well with the suit. My behind most likely is now outlined with peach-colored half-moons of sweat: two smiley faces visible to all when I stand. I lean into the Spanish wife to catch a breeze from her furiously vibrating fan. Misunderstanding my intentions, she moves closer to her husband.

At the end of the ceremony, Miriam Makeba, the eminent South African singer, ascends the platform to perform. The onlookers, who've clearly been waiting for this moment, jump the barriers and converge on the Plaza by the hundreds. Dennis and I are swept along on a wave of agitated fans and I lose him in the confusion. Bodies close in on all sides. A moment like this puts everything in proper perspective: what do feckless hairdressers and damp derrières matter, really, when you're about to suffocate? I'm gasping like a hooked catfish when Dennis reaches into the scrum and drags me to the other side of the Plaza.

Afterward, I try to regain my calm under the steamy tent where lunch will be served. More like a giant awning, the enclosure is pitched at the bottom of a small hill that slopes away from the presidential palace; its position ensures that no errant breeze can possibly enter. The air inside is like that of a Turkish bath. None of the other ambassadors' wives seems sweaty, though, or ruffled, even. *Maybe I missed Composure 101 in Ambassatrix School?* Most are trying to figure out the odd seating arrangements. There are place cards for our entire delegation at one table, and the South Africans at another—except for the ambassador, who's forced to stand under a baobab tree, looking on. The European Union representatives have a few seats, as well as the Portuguese. The Italians have none. Nor, apparently, do the other invitees bunched around the tent's perimeter, hungrily watching the proceedings.

After circling the tent several times, the wife of the Italian ambassador is furious. Her country, after all, is Mozambique's most generous foreign donor and it is incomprehensible— *incomprensibile!*—that no one, not even the government minister who flew in from Rome to represent the Prime Minister, can sit down to eat. She won't stay one minute longer. "We give so much fucking money to this fucking country," she announces, sweeping through the tent on impossibly high and beautiful heels. "You'd think we could get a fucking seat at a fucking table!"

Lunch is served after that bit of drama. As the honored guest, Nelson Mandela is the first to be escorted to the buffet table by a white-jacketed waiter. Mandela had been elected president of South Africa several months earlier in that country's first ever democratic vote. The shop steward I'd interviewed in his tiny Soweto home all those years ago got it wrong; apartheid's demise and equality for all South Africans *did* happen in his lifetime. Mandela's inauguration was a rare moment in history. When his limousine pulled up to the Union Buildings in Pretoria for his swearing-in ceremony, Mandela was met at the top of the stairs by the country's top military men.

These were virtually the same men who hunted him down decades earlier, who imprisoned him for twenty-seven years, much of it on a barren rock off the Cape coast, who forced him to spend what should have been the most productive years of his life apart from his family, friends, and community under brutal conditions, who wouldn't even allow his picture to be published in a South African newspaper when I worked there as a journalist. On that day, though, *they saluted him! Then formed a protective little circle to escort him, their commander-in-chief, to the podium!* And I wept with joy.

Now the waiter, who has an I-can't-wait-to-tell-my-kids look on his face, explains the various entrées to Mandela, then picks up a plate and attempts to serve him. Mandela gently protests, but the waiter insists; it would be an honor to dish up food for the South African president. Which he does, triumphantly bearing the plate back to Mandela's place. It's a riveting exchange: Mandela, humble yet regal, with an air of authority and gravity that somehow still manages to be approachable in his interaction with the ecstatic waiter. *Why can't every world leader have these qualities?* I spend the rest of the lunch trying to figure out ways to get closer to the great man, who is only one table over but well-shielded by bodyguards—all of whom look as though they could bench-press me with one hand, while fending off a herd of charging rhinos with the other.

But for Dennis's extra guards still hanging around our house, things return to normal after the inauguration and I can get back to work. My desk is covered in notes from my last trip to Johannesburg that need transcribing. I sit down one afternoon to try to plow through the piles, but instead find myself gazing out the window: an unattended herd of goats is sauntering up the street, pausing now and again to ingest the cardboard boxes, burlap sacks, egg cartons, and plastic containers strewn along the way that the municipality never seems able to collect. *They're doing such a good job disposing of the garbage, maybe the city should hire them.*

My mind shifts to the luncheon at the presidential palace. I'm still childishly fantasizing about my near-meeting with Mandela, about all the worshipful, but witty, things I would have said had I been able to make it past his bodyguards. Seeing him with the blissed-out waiter, though, was almost as satisfying. That's the thing about being an ambassatrix: you do nothing but plan dinner parties for weeks on end and then *bam!*—you get to witness Nelson Mandela's humanity, up close and personal. Still, getting excited about celebrity sightings is hardly a life's plan; besides, we'll be done here after two years.

What do I want?

I've been lighting Sabbath candles in Andrea's holders every Friday night, hoping for an epiphany. Tenson bakes a couple of challahs that Dennis and I take to the local synagogue, a lovely little white-washed building from the turn of the nineteenth century that was recently rescued from being used as a Red Cross warehouse. The synagogue looks as though it should have snow, not palm trees, surrounding its perimeter. And maybe a little bearded man in a cap, fiddling away on the roof. The congregants are an eclectic bunch: an Argentine who works for a Swedish aid agency but travels on a Dutch passport; a French-Moroccan doing alternative military service by teaching at the local Alliance Française; a Mozambican who, for some reason, is fluent in Hebrew and also attends a Methodist church; a South African beautician; a German gentile who feels guilty about the Holocaust. The Friday-night services—a mishmash of English, Portuguese, and Hebrew—are led by a UN lawyer-turned-amateur-rabbi. The evening is more social than spiritual, really; I never return to our house with any greater insight other than that Tenson makes a delicious challah.

Why couldn't Andrea have sent me off with just a Jell-O mold, instead of a Sphinx-like riddle? That way I could happily continue being the same conflicted person I've been for years.

Her question of what I want bedevils me as the weeks pass. Weeks filled with trips to South Africa and cocktail parties and diplomatic dinners and futile navel-gazing. I work on my book, yet even that doesn't provide a fully satisfying answer. Then, astonishingly, I awake one morning . . . *wanting to have a* child.

Me? Wanting a child?

Too much has already been written about a woman's biological clock and such, but I can now testify that, like the role of the State Department's senior spouse, it *exists.* You go to bed one night your usual self—and the next thing you know, you wake up a mass of quivering maternal instincts. Ambushed. Waylaid. Bushwhacked. *Bushwhacked by biology!*

I couldn't have been more shocked if I'd suddenly sprouted pinfeathers. I, who glibly told the television reporter at the bar in El Salvador that I'd *never* have a baby. Who deflected Dial's desire to start a family with lame career excuses in Mexico. Who laughed at the claim by my friend Jackie, the sociologist in Johannesburg, that buying a purebred dog was prelude to me wanting to breed. For decades, I've racked up a whole international dossier of motherhood denials—yet here I am, positively overcome by a yearning to procreate.

What was Simcha's reply, on my wedding day, to my snide comment about the children I'd never have? Never say "never?"

But surely this isn't the answer to Andrea's question! Something so cli-

chéd, so stereotypical, so—dare I think it?—like my mother! Truthfully, that last little bit no longer has the power to terrify me. In fact, after all that's happened, it almost feels like something to be embraced. Of much bigger concern to me now is how to tell Dennis.

Who, when I get up the courage to approach the subject, is reading back editions of South African dailies in the living room. "*Schmutz*," I say, snuggling next to him. "Can we talk?"

He looks up warily. I only use his pet name, *Schmutz*—Yiddish for "dirt," because of his pack-rat proclivities—when it's something important. "Yes?"

"How would you feel about, I don't know, having a baby?"

He looks at me an extra beat. "Strange, given that I've had a vasectomy."

"I know that, silly. How would you feel about having it reversed?"

"Lynda, are you okay?" He touches my forehead. "This isn't malaria talking, is it?"

"I'm not sick."

"Then why the questions about babies?"

Deep breath. "Because I'd like to have one."

Dennis lets the newspaper he was reading fall to the floor. "You're kidding, right?"

"No."

"You? The person who never, ever, ever was going to have a child? What happened?"

"I'm thirty-eight. An alarm in my womb went off."

Long silence. Finally, Dennis says, "Do you remember a long time ago, maybe we were living in Miami then, I told you about being out somewhere and seeing a little girl slip her hand into her father's, and I said, 'I can't believe that part of my life is over?'"

"Uh-huh. And?"

"Well, having a baby would mean that it isn't over."

"So you'd be willing to have your vasectomy reversed?"

"We can try. I had the operation twenty years ago," he says, shrugging. "And I don't know if it can be undone."

"Oh, Schmutz!" I squeal, hugging him. "We're going to have a baby!"

"Well, maybe," he mumbles from underneath my embrace.

Back when we lived in Mozambique, you could barely get a wound stitched up, let alone a vasectomy reversed. For that sort of procedure, we have to go to South Africa. The urologist in Johannesburg explains that the problem isn't hooking up the plumbing again. (His words.) Rather, it's getting the little swimmers, who've been doing backstrokes in small circles all these years, to undertake the equivalent of an Ironman. If the reversal succeeds, we'll make South African medical history.

"Just think!" Dennis says. "Historic sperm!"

After the surgery—which only takes a couple of hours and requires Dennis staying overnight in the clinic—we return to Mozambique, hopeful. Then nothing. Months go by, but I don't become pregnant. I try to remain calm. I tell myself I'm too old to be doing things like taking my temperature to track ovulation and only making love at the most optimum times. *Maybe Dennis's sperm aren't historic,* I think, *merely notable.* When I see my friend Jackie in Johannesburg, she says the whole undertaking, anyway, is nothing short of a failure of imagination. This, from the woman who has several little scruffy baby-substitutes jumping on her furniture and depositing dog hair everywhere and licking her face while we're drinking tea!

Back in Maputo, I write to Simcha:

If I'm ever going to have a child, I think I need to start thinking about adoption. I read an intensely depressing magazine article when I was in South Africa about how we of the career-minded persuasion have been deceived in postponing pregnancy; in fact, fertility rates drop dramatically after age thirty-five. Then there's Dennis's ability to do the dirty deed. So between his rickety plumbing and my freeze-dried eggs, I better start thinking about adopting or console myself with the joys of aunt-hood.

Oh well, I think, going downstairs to give Dennis the letter to send from the embassy, *we're going home soon. Maybe we can do something about it there.*

Dennis is in the little breakfast room, eating lunch. I take my place, sliding the envelope to him across the table. "Could you put that in the pouch, please?"

He glances at the address. "Sure."

Lourino brings me a bowl of soup and fills my water glass. Dennis and I eat in silence. "Anything the matter?" I ask after a couple of minutes.

"We need to talk."

"Don't tell me *you're* pregnant!"

"No."

"Then what?"

"Uh, the White House nominated me to be ambassador to Peru."

Gently, but deliberately, I put down my spoon. "And you told them no, right?"

Dennis stirs his soup. I can hear Tenson chopping something in the kitchen.

"Remember, you promised just one," I say. "One ambassadorship and we're going back to our house in Washington with the poor plumbing and nice woods so the dogs can pick up where they left off retrieving dead animals."

Dennis is quiet.

"Wait," I say. "Did you accept the nomination?"

He nods.

"How could you?" I whisper furiously, not wanting to be over-heard by the staff. "How could you, without consulting me? What about your promise?"

"Look," he says. "I really, truly never thought I'd get offered an-other embassy. And Peru isn't just some flyspeck of a post that no one back home cares about. It has a dozen agencies and hundreds of em-ployees and issues that are important in Washington. Just one more time, please?" Dramatically lowering his voice, he adds, "Lynda, this is the real thing."

That's precisely what scares me.

CHAPTER ELEVEN

PERU, 1996

Needless to say, I go to Peru: disappointed, a little angry, a lot hurt. But I understand how much the appointment means to Dennis. Most people never guess the true depth of his ambition, given his quiet, unassuming, soft-spoken demeanor. But it masks a profound, scratch-your-eyes-out desire to reach the top. So I can't really blame him, especially if I think of it in terms of my former profession. Why be satisfied with, say, the *Toledo Blade*, when you can have the *Chicago Tribune*?

First, though, we stop for a couple of months in Washington, where Dennis decides to get a sperm test. The results are disappointing: he's producing approximately four sperm, three of which are on crutches. The doctor isn't very encouraging. Given my advanced maternal age, as he so delicately puts it, and Dennis's paltry sperm count, we have about as much chance of conceiving a child as becoming curlers for the Norwegian Olympic team. In the car going back to the hotel, Dennis kisses my hand. "Don't be sad, Harriet Shoot."

"I can't help it," I say, blinking back tears. "I was just hoping to hear better news. What do we do now?"

"Keep trying?"

I blow my nose into his handkerchief. "That would be fun, but probably futile."

"It only takes one sperm."

"One among tens of millions."

"Well, I'm a fast swimmer. Why wouldn't my little squirmers be equally speedy?"

Giving another good honk, I say, "I don't think it works that way. How would you feel about adopting? In Peru, I mean."

Dennis is silent for a second. "I don't know. Adoption is such a genetic crapshoot."

"Right, as if our genes are so sterling. Let's see, in my family there's manic-depression and serial marriage killing. On your side, there's alcoholism and terminal quietness. Just the qualities we'd want to pass to offspring!"

"Yeah, but at least we'd know what we're getting."

"No, we wouldn't. What about all the recessive stuff dating back to chimpanzees?"

"Humans don't have recessive chimp traits," Dennis says, pulling into the hotel's parking garage. "At least, I don't."

"You've never seen yourself eating a banana."

After that, Dennis flies out to Albuquerque to visit his mother, leaving the question of adoption unresolved. I stay in Washington to try to reconvert my Portuguese back to Spanish and shop for a less-red ball gown. Then, oddly, I don't get my period. Scientists at the Royal Observatory in England have been known to set their clock in Greenwich by my menstrual cycle. I call my sister Beverly, now living in Seattle, to ask what I should do.

She says, "Go buy a pregnancy test."

I say, "But that doesn't make sense. The doctor just told me I can't get pregnant."

"Buy one anyway."

I'm staying at a hotel across the street from the Watergate apartment complex of Nixon-era notoriety, which has a small pharmacy. After dutifully peeing on what looks like an oral thermometer, I wander off to make a cup of tea. The instructions said the test would take five minutes to complete. Cup in hand, I head back to the bathroom, glance at the wand—and promptly spew Earl Grey across the tile floor. There they are, clear as day: two lines marching in lockstep across the test's window. Positive. I call Bev back.

"What should I do now?"

"Maybe it was a mistake. Buy another one."

This time I sit on the edge of the bathtub, watching the lines inch across the window. After five minutes, the result is inconclusive, as though the test can't make up its mind. I dial Bev again.

"Now what should I do?"

"Buy another one."

With this purchase, I deplete the pharmacy's stock of pregnancy tests. The average age of the Watergate's residents is around seventy-two, which explains the paucity of products to determine conception and the abundance of adult diapers and denture adhesives. The clerk at the cash register holds his stare an extra second as he hands over the third pregnancy test I've bought in the last half hour. *Three boxes of stool softener in thirty minutes, and I'll bet you wouldn't even raise an eyebrow.*

This time, the answer's a resounding negative. One "yes," one "no," one "maybe." I telephone Seattle.

Bev says, "Call your obstetrician."

When I reach him, my obstetrician is very nice and sympathetic but unable to make a definitive pronouncement without me visiting his office and having some blood drawn. Which I do. A few hours later, he telephones with the results: I'm pregnant.

Of course! I think, recalling how the previous week, while shopping, I'd suddenly become so horrifically nauseated and weak I was forced to sit down in the cosmetics department, surrounded by eye-lifting cream and firming moisturizer. I must have looked pretty ashen, because the woman behind the counter asked if I was okay. Then she asked if I'd like to try their new line of powdered blush, "Embarrassed." I managed to take a taxi back to the hotel and let myself into our room, whereupon I fell to the ground and crawled to the mini-fridge, whispering, "Orange juice." At the time I chalked it up to not having eaten, compounded by the effects of trying on semiformal attire.

Ecstatic, I telephone Dennis, who's over the moon. As are Mom and Sim. My sister Ida, on the other hand, breaks into hysterical laughter. "You? A mother? That's hilarious!"

Back in Washington, Dennis proudly shows everyone—friend, colleague, postman, sanitation worker—the little ultrasound picture of our embryo he now keeps in his wallet. "Don't you think it looks like me?" he asks, pointing to the blurred, lima bean shape. Meanwhile, all I seem to be able to do, as we race around buying last minute things for Peru, is be sick. At Dennis's swearing-in, I manage to hold the Bible while he takes his oath on a podium that feels as though it has put out to sea. "Lynda and I welcome you," Dennis intones, looking around at the two hundred or so guests gathered once again in the State Department's Benjamin Franklin room. "If she throws up, it's not a commentary on my prose, but because we've just found out she's pregnant."

Despite Dennis's warning about Peru being the real thing, I'm still hoping it will be a low-maintenance post like Mozambique—only in Spanish. That little fantasy is immediately dispelled when we land in Lima to a crowd of reporters and paparazzi. Given our history of intervention and meddling on the continent, the United States is viewed, for better or worse, as a virtual ex-colonial master. The American ambassador holds an exalted status here, which is reflected in his lifestyle. I gasp when we arrive at our residence: a 22,000-square-foot, Spanish-style, cream-colored mansion. *Twenty-two thousand square feet!* A space that size has its own microclimate.

The main sala, reception room, with its glistening grand piano, soaring ceilings, and acres of heavily brocaded furniture, could hangar a wide-bodied jet. The table in the *comedor grande*, the big dining room, seats thirty-two people. It used to accommodate thirty-six, but the wife of the previous ambassador thought it too impersonal and had it hacked down to a cozier dimension. For a more intimate affair like, say, breakfast, there's the *comedor chico*, the little dining room, into which you can squeeze only a scant twenty people. Entire marble quarries were depleted to provide the flooring. Our private quarters—living room, dining room, bedroom, dressing room, gym, two bathrooms —fit snugly into one corner of the second story. Which is reached by our personal elevator. And contains two other wings with six more bedrooms.

An enterprise this sprawling obviously requires a small army to keep it going. And there they are, all lined up in their uniforms to greet us in the foyer: three upstairs maids, three stewards, two cooks, two laundresses, one house manager. *Downton Abbey*, the Incan edition! Also add in five groundskeepers who look after the swimming pool, tennis court, and three acres of gardens.

You'd think you might be tripping over a staff this large, but after settling in I go for days without seeing anyone. We communicate with one another mostly by telephone: there are twenty-three of them in the residence, each with its own extension number I can never get quite right. Stranded in our private quarters, a taxi ride from the kitchen, I reach for the phone to call Tenson—who's here with his wife, Patience, and their youngest child—and find myself asking for seltzer with a wedge of lime from a guard at the front gate.

Then, when you least expect it, a steward or laundress suddenly appears. Two weeks after our arrival, I'm sauntering down a hallway when Blanca, an upstairs maid, leaps out of a laundry closet. "Buenos días, Señora Embajadora," she says, giving my raggedy T-shirt and sweatpants the evil eye. "Is *that* how you're going to breakfast?" As I hastily retreat to my bedroom, my mind turns back to Ambassatrix School; clearly the warning about women being disappointed applies equally to staff. *Maybe I should have paid more attention to the other lessons, too.*

I recall the session where we had to fill out the *Personal Goals* sheet and how my objectives of researching a book and learning Portuguese, when read aloud, elicited the kind of enthusiasm from the other spouses usually reserved for a sinus headache. The woman who came after me, though, was a little star. In her midthirties and perfectly attired in a crisp seersucker number, she'd been totally at ease with everything the instructors threw at us. She'd even brought in samples of the calling cards she'd ordered for us to admire. On that morning, Mrs. Seersucker stood and, taking a deep breath, said, "My plan is to combine my two great passions: rape counseling and aquatics."

Combining rape counseling and aquatics? A clinic for violated mermaids? Turning to one another to murmur their admiration, our classmates burst into wild applause.

Mrs. Seersucker in mind, I never again emerge from our quarters without first dressing as though I'm going to walk the red carpet: pearls, stockings, high heels, perfume—you name it. If I owned a mink stole, I'd throw it on for good measure. And that's just to collect the mail.

As for expectations of my role as ambassatrix, Maputo was second-string, the B-team, the Minor Leagues compared to Lima. The American expatriate community in Peru totals more than twenty thousand people; like a latter-day Joan of Arc on a white charger, I am supposed to *lead* the women. Or so says Isabel, our house manager. She ticks off some of my official duties: president of the Women's Literary Association; president of the American Women in Peru; board member of the Union Church. "I'm Jewish," I protest meekly. No matter. I'm also chair of Noche de Arte , an annual art show hosted by the US embassy. Two of its representatives await me in our library. Both are Americans married to Peruvians, with several children each. After assuring me my pregnancy will be fine, they regale me with stories of all the horrible things that can go wrong. Then they get down to business. Noche de Arte is *the* charity event of the year! Hundreds of artists and their works will be represented at our residence, the money raised going to various good causes. Of course, the women will need space somewhere on the first floor for an office—preferably something airy as they'll be here eight hours a day, supervising all the carpenters and workmen—and lunch—nothing special, a light soup and sandwich will suffice—and . . .

"Eight hours a day?" I interrupt.

"Yes," they chime in unison.

"Carpenters and workmen?"

"Oh yes," says the taller one. "We have to build displays and all sorts of things."

"How long will that take?"

"Six, eight weeks," she says, with a vague wave of her hand.

No privacy for walking arm-in-arm with Dennis to the small dining room for breakfast? For getting emotional in the library over adorable baby catalogs? For racing across acres of slick marble floors to the bathroom to puke?

I tell them we'll be in touch, then wander over to Isabel's office for our biweekly meeting. Isabel is in her late forties, smart and stylish, with boundless energy and a great sense of propriety. She has piles of invitations to various functions to parse and guest lists to scrutinize. Do I want next week's reception to be held on the Spanish patio, so named for its lovely blue azulejos (tiles) and spouting fountain? In the garden? Or perhaps in the sala with the oil painting of a dyspeptic George Washington staring down on everyone? An upcoming dinner party requires a seating chart, always a chore given the niceties of protocol and politics. "Oh, but Señora Embajadora," Isabel shrieks. "You cannot *possibly* put a member of the opposition next to you on your right!" Menus have to be drawn up, and plates, goblets, flowers, table linens selected. Which wines? Spirits? Sodas? Not to mention water: still, sparkling, or both?

This discussion takes place over a brain-splitting commotion. The garden has been commandeered by a swarm of men erecting an enormous toldo (tent): an elaborate, two-story replication of the White House in honor of our election day later in the week, when President Clinton will try for a second term. Isabel takes me outside for an inspection. If you squint, the toldo does bear a kind of resemblance to the real thing. A large television monitor, linked to the United States, will display the latest tally of the incoming vote in real time. Isabel shows me two rows of smaller tents flanking the structure, where various US companies are going to promote their wares. "How many people are coming?" I ask nervously.

"About a thousand." Seeing my look of dismay, she adds, "Don't worry, I'll introduce you to all of them."

Making small talk with multitudes, even in your own backyard, is daunting enough. But now that I'm suffering from severe ear congestion, a not-uncommon consequence of pregnancy, all those hundreds of strangers I'll be meeting and greeting will sound as though they're speaking through a snorkel. In Spanish, no less. *I've fallen down the rabbit hole of diplomatic life,* I think as I walk back to the house, hearing-impaired and feeling sorry for myself. *What about the South Africa book I'm supposed to be writing? At this rate, by the time I finish, the baby will be in middle school and doing the eye-roll thing at Dennis and me.*

But by far the biggest difference between Lima and Maputo—wouldn't you know it?—is terrorism. I knew such violence had been a serious problem in Peru in the late 1980s and early 1990s, when explosions, kidnappings, and murders by leftist guerrillas practically paralyzed the country. Before we left Washington, the State Department treated us to a security briefing that included a video of our soon-to-be residence, captured on surveillance cameras, being bombed by extremists a few years earlier—for the fourth time! Blurry, black-and-white footage lurched and dissolved behind blinding, oxygen-sucking smoke: two guards dead, master bedroom blown out, security wall erased. "But nothing to worry about now!" the briefing officer said gaily. "Of course, you'll still have to have bodyguards."

"Are you crazy?" I practically shouted at Dennis afterward. "We're not going there!"

"Don't worry, it'll be fine. Everything's quiet now."

"Dennis, I got nauseated watching that video. And it wasn't morning sickness. People died in that bombing."

"I know. But really, everything's okay now."

"Listen, I already lost one husband in Latin America. I am not going to lose another. Tell your bosses your wife is a nutcase and let's go kick the renters out of our house."

"Lynda," he says, putting his hands on my shoulders and looking me squarely in the face. "Nothing is going to happen. The guerrillas have been decimated."

"And that's why the State Department is supplying us with our own little militia? Dennis, we're having a baby. I am *not* going to be able to relax for the entire three years we're there."

Which proves to be an understatement, to say the least. Especially given that every evening at sunset, a truck pulls up to the back of the residence and disgorges thirty armed soldiers who take up positions in concrete bunkers outside the perimeter of the grounds. And anytime we go out for, say, ice cream or a last min-

ute box of facial hair bleach, we travel with ten bodyguards packing a small arsenal in a three-car, bulletproof convoy.

For my monthly visit to the obstetrician, the lead car has a siren
blaring and one of the bodyguards yelling through a loudspeaker at
surrounding vehicles to make way. People respond by giving him
the finger. We careen at Le Mans speeds around Lima's perpetually
jammed streets, the follow car loaded with enough Uzi shotguns
and teargas grenades to start a regional conflict—practically riding our bumper. I tap the driver on the shoulder.

"Why do we have to go so fast?" I say.

"A fast-moving target is harder to hit, Señora Embajadora."

"But don't we have a better chance of having an accident and
exploding than getting attacked by terrorists?"

He shrugs. "Our job is to protect you, Señora Embajadora."

Dennis is sitting next to me and flipping through a file of classified cables from Washington, his arm crooked to shield the pages
from my vision. "You're not supposed to talk with the driver or in
any way distract him," he says.

Distract him with safe driving? I turn my attention to the scene
outside the window. Generally speaking, Peru is a startlingly beautiful country: snowcapped Andean peaks, luxuriant Amazonian
jungle, verdant hills. Not around here, though. In a final act of revenge, so the story goes, the last Incan emperor—before being
garroted—convinced the Spanish conquistadores to build their
capital on the swath of sand where Lima stands today. The joke was
on them, those small-pox-contaminating, syphilis-infecting, furry-
faced conquerors. Nothing grows on this desert plain. It hasn't
rained in Lima for decades, really; the city is a moonscape of squat
gray buildings and gasping gray vegetation. And traffic.

My mind drifts to my impending doctor's appointment, which

includes a tour of the clinic where I'll give birth. I'm doing this against the wishes of the embassy's nurse practitioner, Carol, who broached the subject a few days earlier. "Ottawa or Ouagadougou, we want you to go home to have your baby," she said when I told her I was thinking of staying in Lima. "You're the wife of the ambassador. You set the example for the women in the embassy."

I can picture it now: all those gestating Americans, T-shirts taut across their bulging bellies, clinging to bedposts and refusing to fly back to the United States to give birth. But isn't it a woman's right to choose where she wants to pant and shout obscenities for eighteen hours while sucking on ice chips? Besides, I know for a fact that Carol had all three of her children in Africa, and her family seems perfectly fine—except, perhaps, her husband with his penchant for shooting pigeons in our garden with his BB gun. But where her children were born obviously has nothing to do with that.

Although this is just a routine obstetrical examination, I'm dressed as though lunching with society ladies. How can I not, when our mere arrival at the doctor's office prompts the two receptionists to run down the walkway to greet us, gushing over Dennis as if he's a minor rock star? I am dressed well, but lightly. Very lightly. That's because unlike their sisters to the north, who are encouraged to grow to the size of a vending machine, Latin women gain only a whisper of weight during pregnancy. In anticipation of standing on a scale, I did a mad workout earlier on the treadmill, drank only a little water, and refused breakfast. If I feel faint, I can always cling to Dennis's arm; anything to uphold the image of North American womanhood! Also, I have to remember to remove my watch, which could add *ounces*.

The US-trained doctor, a kind and capable man, barely glances at the clock on the wall when I pull out my list of twenty-two questions, culled from a bestselling American book on pregnancy. None of his Peruvian patients takes up his time with such stuff, but he's neither patronizing nor hurried in his answers. And he cheerfully indulges my demand for every test the book recommends—most of which he also doesn't normally do, either.

Afterward, Dennis and I walk to the adjacent clinic for the tour, the ten bodyguards scrutinizing shrubbery along the way for errant terrorists. The clinic's director shows us the presidential suite where, he says, the ambassador and his wife will be most comfortable. *Why should the ambassador's comfort be of concern when his wife is the one having the baby?* I wonder. Dennis's chief bodyguard—inscrutable as ever behind his wraparound sunglasses and dead-fish demeanor—trails behind, busily sniffing his watchband. It seems an odd response to inspecting delivery rooms; perhaps he has a phobia about hospitals and the sneaky little whiffs of metal help to soothe him. Later I learn that he's actually murmuring into a two-way radio with another bodyguard, casing out the building and deciding where to place sharpshooters.

I also came prepared with a list of questions for the director, including one about keeping our newborn in my room.

He says, "Our policy is that all babies must stay in the nursery."

I say, "But I want to be able to nurse on demand, and that will be difficult if the baby's not in the room."

He says, "You want to *nurse*? But that's so, so, so . . . "

Cholo? I think, the Peruvian equivalent of the "n" word that the mostly white patrician class uses when speaking of the majority indigenous population. *You reckon that nursing is too native? Just wait until I pull out the blowgun with the poisoned darts!* I'd gotten a similar reaction from the wife of the foreign minister, who's also pregnant, when we chatted at a cocktail party. *"It will ruin your bosom!"* she hissed. Clearly this is something considered beneath my station, but given the horror it induces, you'd think I'm planning on eating, not breastfeeding, my child.

Dennis, who is very good in awkward situations, says, "If the baby stays in the nursery, it will have to have a couple of armed bodyguards at all times."

For a second or two, the director considers the tableau: the hulking men dressed in surgical gowns, scrub caps and booties; the submachine guns clanking against bassinets; the walkie-talkie chatter competing with newborn wails. He says, "Perhaps we can make an exception in your case."

But for the gigantic needle plunged into my belly, it's a relief to go to Miami for an amniocentesis just before Christmas. No body-guards, no paparazzi, no armored convoys so loud and obtrusive they might as well have a "shoot here" sign hung across the passenger door. At the doctor's office, we're just another slightly aged couple, nervous about our offspring's genetic health. And itching to know its gender. Which a high-definition ultrasound, that shows the baby floating freestyle in the womb, reveals: female!

Afterward, we have a few hours to kill before going to the airport. Dennis and I wander the neighborhood near my old house, just happy to be able to walk around without men in dark suits and aviator sunglasses encircling us. "We're having a girl," I squeal. "I can't believe it! A daughter!"

"That's what you wanted, right?" Dennis says.

"Yes! But are you disappointed?" I say, turning to face him.

"Why would you say that?"

"Because you nicknamed her 'Oscar.'"

"I did that because I knew how much you were hoping for a girl and wanted to get you used to the idea of a boy, just in case."

"So all that chanting, 'Go, Oscar, go,' when I'm doing my Jesse Owens imitation to get to the bathroom in time to puke, that was for show?"

"Yep."

"And that ugly keychain you brought me from up-country, the one with the big 'O' on it?"

"Also for show."

"So I can throw it out now?"

"Yep."

"And you're happy it's a girl?"

"Thrilled!"

Our flight back to Peru is hideously delayed, and we don't arrive in Lima until nearly dawn, exhausted. Luckily, there's not much going on except for a cocktail party later in the day at the Japanese ambassador's residence, in honor of the Emperor's birthday. I beg off; pregnancy, for all its discomforts, is the best get-out-of-jail-free card ever created. Dennis is equally tired, but has to make an appearance. He stays just long enough to pay his respects to the ambassador and is home in time for dinner.

We've barely started on the fish stew, though, when Alvaro, the chief steward, appears. The deputy ambassador is on the telephone; he says it's urgent. Dennis disappears inside the kitchen to take the call. Minutes pass. I'm trying to be polite and wait for him to return before eating, but the food is getting cold. Dennis hurries back into the dining room. "There's been gunfire and explosions at the Japanese residence," he says. "I've got to call Washington." With that, he sprints off upstairs.

Inhale slowly. Now exhale.

Tenson tentatively opens the swinging door from the kitchen. "Is everything all right, Madam?" he asks.

"I don't know."

"What should I do with the dinner?"

"Could you please put it on a tray and have Alvaro bring it to our quarters?"

"Is this serious, Madam?"

"I'm going to find out right now."

Upstairs, sitting opposite Dennis in the living room, I listen to him talk to someone at the State Department, then his security officer, trying to piece together what happened. Half an hour after Dennis left, fourteen guerrillas, armed with submachine guns, rocket-propelled grenades, revolvers, and hand grenades, apparently blew a hole in the wall surrounding the Japanese ambassador's home and took the hundreds of guests hostage. Dennis fields calls from the Pentagon, White House, US Southern Command; everyone's trying to figure out what to do.

As the evening progresses, the guerrillas release about two hundred of the captives, mostly women. But they're still holding, among scores of others, Peru's foreign minister, the ambassadors from Bolivia, Brazil, Cuba, and Spain—and nine of Dennis's officers. The guerrillas say they'll kill them all unless the Peruvian government frees 434 of their comrades from prison. The Pentagon dispatches a rapid-response team to set up a special hotline to Washington, and there's talk of bringing in a Delta Force unit to rescue our hostages. When Dennis mentions the latter possibility to an official in the Peruvian government, he's politely rebuffed; the president, the official says, will handle the crisis himself. The fate of our captives is entirely in his hands.

Hours later, when I finally crawl into bed, Dennis is still on the phone. I can't sleep, picturing his officers being held at gunpoint, the terrified faces of their wives and kids. And Dennis! *One half hour. Thirty measly minutes. That's all that kept him from becoming the guerrillas' prize pig, trotted out for all the world to see, an AK-47 held to his head.* Before I know it, I'm weeping. I can't help it. It feels never ending, this little dance with death. First Dial died, there were my brushes with snipers in Lebanon and the security police in South Africa, Dennis almost died in Liberia, now this. *And with a baby on the way!*

The next morning, I'm awakened by a call from my sister Ida, weeping. "I am so, so sorry something like this is happening to you again," she sobs. "Poor Dennis!"

"Thanks," I say. "It is kind of mind-boggling."

"I just couldn't believe it when I heard on the radio that the American ambassador was taken hostage at the reception."

"Ida, Dennis left thirty minutes before the guerrillas launched their raid. He's *fine*."

"Are you sure?"

"Yes, I'm sure. I guarantee you he hasn't been taken hostage, unless there are guerrillas in the shower. Because that's where he is now."

Dennis holds a daily briefing at the embassy for the captives' wives, which I attend. One of them is pregnant and due to deliver around the same time as I. There isn't much to tell. The terrorists are allowing only a Red Cross representative to bring food and water to the hostages and take out communiqués issued by their leader. The representative's reports of conditions inside the house grow grimmer by the day. In an attempt to ferret out the guerrillas, the government turns off the water and electricity to the Japanese residence. Toilets cease to function. With several hundred unwashed bodies crammed into a relatively small space, the air in the house, already muggy from the summer temperatures, becomes oppressively hot and fetid. There's not enough room for everyone to lie down and sleep. People are falling ill. I want to hug the women and reassure them their husbands will be fine, but perhaps more than anyone else in the room, I know how tragically these things can turn out.

In the face of the increasingly dire news, though, the wives are positively heroic. They determinedly keep themselves occupied by sticking to their daily routines and tending to their kids. Also by trying to manage the mountains of quiches, casseroles, breads, brownies, and chocolate chip cookies that people in the embassy foist upon them. If we can't give them their husbands, we can at least give them carbohydrates.

By the fifth day, Dennis looks gray from stress and lack of sleep. He's terrified the guerillas will lose patience with the president and begin executing their captives. We're in the upstairs living room, watching local Peruvian news broadcast from outside the Japanese residence. Nothing has changed; it's the same reporting we've been hearing since the hostages were taken. Suddenly there's a little fluttering in my abdomen. *Nervousness? Gas? Or did I just feel* life?

I'm about to say something when the telephone rings; it's for Dennis. He listens for a moment, thanks the caller, then puts down the receiver. "You won't believe this," he says with a huge grin.

"What?"

"The guerrillas are releasing another two hundred hostages, and our guys are included!"

At that, Dennis grabs my arm, propelling me down the stairs

and out the door to the car. *So much for fetal news!* I think, as we race to the hospital where the men will be released. Ten or fifteen years ago, this would have seemed the height of glamour for me: zigzagging through traffic at high speed in a foreign city, sirens blaring, to receive hostages from a dramatic terrorist attack. But fifteen or ten years ago, I wanted a baby as much as I wanted, say, chlamydia. A truly deviant thought crosses my mind: *Why can't I just have a normal life? A life where, the first time I feel our daughter do a frog kick, we can fully focus on that instead of people held at gunpoint?* Still, after the buses supplied by the Red Cross arrive at the hospital, it's deeply gratifying to witness the former captives file out, one by one: haggard and exhausted—but safe. When the head of the embassy's narcotics section emerges, I smother him in a hug. "I don't think you want to do that," he says. "I'm pretty disgusting."

There's rejoicing at the embassy, but the guerillas still hold seventy-two hostages, including the foreign minister. The negotiations for their release drag on for weeks. The foreign minister's father, a lovely old man, frequently comes to our house for dinner. The scion of a distinguished oligarchic family, he seems frailer each time he dines with us; the terror he feels for his son's safety is palpable. And yet. The oligarchs, descendants of the Spanish conquistadores, have ruled Peru for four hundreds years, systematically suppressing the majority indigenous population and denying them education and access to the country's wealth. The racism here is shockingly overt, a staple of casual cocktail conversation among the glitterati that often leaves me gape-mouthed. As in El Salvador, I obviously don't agree with the guerrillas' tactics, but understand the desperation that drives them. Although I find my bleeding-heart tendencies staunched to some extent when it's *my* husband being targeted.

Ironically, the underclasses had great hopes for the president—

who's of Japanese descent—when he came to office with promises to create a more equitable society. But the irresistible narcotic of power took hold, and now he's busily undermining Peru's democratic institutions to tighten his grip on the country. Being seen as an uncompromising leader who can defeat terrorists only burnishes his strongman image.

The weeks of negotiations turn into months. Meanwhile, the baby is growing bigger by the day; the way things are going, she'll be out before the captives. Growing within me, too, is the fear that the hostage crisis will end badly. Strange tunneling noises are heard under the Japanese residence; the government takes to blaring music over loudspeakers aimed at the house to mask the sound. Everyone is on edge. Something clearly is about to happen.

I ask Dennis about it one morning while he's shaving. "I know as much as you," he says, peering—a little too intently—in the mirror at a spot on his chin.

"Oh, come on, Schmutz, you can do better than that. What are your spooks saying?"

"Nothing."

"I don't believe it."

"Lynda," he says, going to work on his neck, "there's nothing to tell."

"Give me a break. What, do you think I'm going to call friends at the *Journal* and tip them off?"

"No," he says from under a towel, wiping off the last of the shaving foam. "But there's really nothing to tell." With that, he wanders off to pick out underwear from his dresser.

His coyness is making me crazy. He knows that I know that he knows—but he still won't say anything. In another life, I'd have thrown him to the ground, stuck my spiked heel in his back, and not allowed him up until he squealed. In my journalism life, that is. Or the fantasized version of it. Nowadays, I'm reconciled—well, almost—to the fact that I'm not a reporter anymore, but I do miss a juicy story. It would be nice, at least, to be privy to the details. Nothing like living vicariously!

Late in the afternoon a few days later, Isabel calls from her office downstairs to tell me to turn on the television. Peruvian commandos are storming the Japanese compound, spilling out of excavated subterranean tunnels. In a carefully choreographed operation, they kill the guerrillas and rescue all but one of the hostages. The television reporters who've kept up a round-the-clock vigil outside the residence capture much of it in real time. The president races to the scene; after the operation has ended, he struts around the ruined interior like a little bantam rooster, gloating over the bodies of the dead terrorists.

And I—the erstwhile, globetrotting foreign correspondent, who incidentally sleeps with one of the few people with knowledge of when and how it would all go down—was as clueless as the rest of the viewing audience until it happened.

All that violence seems a fitting—for me, at least—backdrop against which to give birth. A few weeks before my due date, I awake late one night to a feeling of liquid flowing down my legs. My first thought is that my water has broken. My second is that I haven't washed any of the little onesies, still enclosed in plastic wrap, and the baby will have to start her life swathed in newspaper. I switch on the bedside lamp.

Blood is everywhere: on the blankets, sheets, pillows, my nightgown; the severed horse-head scene in *The Godfather* is a genteel nosebleed by comparison. It pours out of me onto the floor when I stand and slip-slide my way to the bathroom. I keep flushing the toilet as the water turns bright red, yelling, "I'm going to die! The baby's going to die!"

From the bedroom comes a steely voice: "No one is going to die."

Yet another example of Dennis's calm, why I married him. He's precisely the person you want in your lifeboat after the *Titanic* has disappeared into the murky depths and the inky night blots out the world. While everyone else is shrieking and crying and tearing at their hair, Dennis is coolly jerry-rigging a sail, devising a sextant by which to navigate, and handing around hardtack he has miraculously discovered.

He telephones the night duty driver and bodyguards—asleep in the guardhouse—then calls my obstetrician and Carol, the embassy nurse. Wrapping a towel around my bottom, Dennis just about carries me down the long stairway. The driver takes one look at the bloodied towel—and revs up the car's engine to Mach 1 speed. Never have I been so grateful for reckless abandon. "Kick," I whisper to the baby, who has spent months furiously doing the Macarena in utero, but suddenly now is still. "Kick, please."

Carol and the obstetrician are waiting for us at the clinic. The doctor paces at the end of the bed as the nurses prep me for surgery. *Lose the American ambassador's baby*, I think, *and there goes business!* Everything becomes confused after that. I hear Carol tell me to try to stop shaking and hold my body still; the anesthesiologist is having a hard time getting a needle into me. *Where is Dennis?* My legs feel hot, hot, hot. Someone puts a mask over my nose and mouth. I'm about to protest that I can't breathe when a purple blur of a screaming baby flies overhead . . .

The next thing I see is Dennis sitting in a chair, head drooped on his chest, delicately snoring. The clock on the wall behind him reads 5:48; presumably that's a.m., given the polluted gray-green light of a Lima dawn seeping through the window. Dennis stirs and opens his eyes.

"I know exactly how you're going to look when you die," he says.

"Aw, that's so sweet."

"No, really. You're so pale from losing so much blood, you're practically see-through."

"Is the baby okay?"

He smiles. "Lynda, she's fine. She's beautiful."

And she is, when I finally get to meet her in the presidential suite after spending hours in the recovery room. A nurse puts her in my arms: a small, pinkish bundle with a crown of silky light hair, a delicious scent of warm toast—and my grandmother's almond-shaped eyes. "Bubbe, you've come back!" I coo to her. Then I start to cry. Dennis takes the baby from me, one arm cuddling her on his chest, the other patting me on the back. I don't know if the weepiness is because of feeling awful from the surgery and blood loss, or because of the miracle of our daughter, whom we name Noa. Besides just liking the name, we chose it for its meaning in Hebrew: "movement or motion," a tribute to the baby's gestational gymnastics. Poor Noa spends the first few hours of her life being passed between her maudlin mother and fawning father, with an occasional stop at the breast.

After a while, Dennis, reluctantly, has to go to the embassy and leaves me in the care of the nurse. She immediately begins pawing through my suitcase, muttering about how she has to get me ready. *Ready for what?* I wonder groggily.

Why, my makeover, of course! What every woman needs after nearly bleeding out!

The nurse wants to brush and style my hair, touch up my face with eye shadow, mascara, and lipstick, paint my nails, and put me in a frilly dressing gown to receive the waves of well-wishers undoubtedly about to descend on the clinic. I can't really fault her; those are the expectations of an ambassador's wife. All she finds in my bag, though, is a sensible cotton nightie, a stout pair of underpants, and some fuzzy socks.

Anyway, with bodily fluids dripping from just about every orifice, I feel more like a sieve than someone who's supposed to be holding court. The hours pass. Every time the baby cries, I have to ring for the nurse to scoop her out of the little crib—I can barely move, post-Caesarian—and hand her to me, with a tutorial on the mysteries of breast feeding. I know I should be reveling in this, but I feel too crappy. I just want the nurse to help me start walking. I want to drink gallons of water to flush out whatever has caused my legs to swell, so that I now resemble a Lego mini-figure. Most of all, I *want food.*

Postpartum, my body given over to the beginnings of lactation, I have newfound respect for Jersey cows: milk production is exhausting work. It also leaves me with an appetite the size of a Volkswagen sedan. But the nurse only doles out lukewarm, sweetened chamomile tea. Eating is dangerous so soon after surgery, she says. I plead, cajole, whine for something more substantial, something along the lines of, say, a six-course banquet—but to no avail. Tepid tea is it for the next twenty-four hours.

Decorum be damned, I have to find food.

After the nurse leaves, I heave myself out of bed—which, with my recently cut stomach muscles under the incision, only takes thirty minutes—totter to the door and crack it ajar. A door across the hallway immediately swings open: there are the bodyguards, smiling and waving, crammed into the Executive Plus Suite. I close my door.

New plan. I check on Noa: she's sleeping. Slumping to the floor, I crawl to the closet, grab my cellphone from the suitcase, and drag myself into the bathroom. Seated on the cold tile, I dial our residence.

"Isabel!" I whisper into the telephone. "Isabel! Can you hear me?"

"¿Quién es?" Isabel exclaims indignantly. "Who is this? Speak up! Who is this?"

"Isabel, it's me, Lynda. Can you hear me?"

"Señora Embajadora? Why are you speaking so softly? Are you okay?"

"They're starving me, Isabel. They're only giving me tea. I'm desperate. You have to bring me something to eat."

"I don't understand. Can you speak louder?"

Suddenly there's pounding on the bathroom door. "Señora Embajadora, ¿está bien?" the nurse shouts. "Are you all right? You can't get out of bed by yourself! You need to ring for me to go pee-pee! ¿Señora Embajadora?"

I whisper into the telephone, "Isabel, I have to go. Please bring me food. Tenson's muffins. A side of beef. Anything. But don't let them see it. Smuggle it in your purse."

CHAPTER TWELVE

PERU, 1998

It's a truism and a cliché that life changes irrevocably when you have a child. People warned me about the sleepless nights, exhaustion, milk- and spit-up stains decorating my shirts. But no one warned me about falling in love. Wildly. Crazily. Passionately. Now, though, it seems inevitable: how else could we have survived as a species if mothers didn't become hormonally captive love-slaves to their children? How else to explain educated women with advanced degrees, women who had blazed trails, braved bombs, dodged bullets— swooning over adorable little baby toes and kissing them one-by-one? *Mom was really onto something: four children!*

One afternoon, I happen to mention to Isabel that it would be nice to get together occasionally with other mothers. Isabel, who's a one-woman information bureau, takes it upon herself to put out the word—and voilà! I suddenly have a mommy group. *A mommy group?* A few wives of embassy spooks, a sprinkling of Latinas married to Americans, a couple of Peruvians, one South African. Some have careers, some don't; it doesn't matter. They come to Noa's blue-carpeted playroom with the stuffed animals lining the window seats and *kapulanas*, Mozambican sarongs, spread across the floor. Not to mention toys. For two hours, I can forget about bodyguards and three-car, bulletproof convoys and just be another clueless novice among similarly bewildered women, all desperately trying to figure out, with little or no training, the most important job we'll ever do. Amid our yammering, with occasional interruptions to save the babies from themselves, I begin to feel—dare I say it?—*a sense of community!* And oddly, it's wonderful.

Months pass, months filled with teething, rice cereal, weaning, crawling, walking, and even a few words—the usual infant stuff that, for a first-timer like myself, is nothing short of astounding. Who knew human development could bring such joy? (Of course, having staff to cook and clean and do loads of laundry obviously helps. To say nothing of the absence of a real day job.) To celebrate Noa's entry into toddlerdom, Mom flies down for a visit. I, surprisingly enough, am excited to see her. We take in all the touristy sights, the usual excavated pyramids and archeological museums filled with mummified Incan remains. One private collection of pre-Columbian artifacts has an entire section devoted to erotic sculptures. "Well," says Mom, peering at a display of assorted little naked figurines doing assorted things to one another. "Now that's interesting."

But she mostly wants to spend time with Noa. As a grandmother, Mom is transformed, chasing Noa around the playroom all afternoon or taking her for walks in the garden to hunt for hummingbirds. *Maybe she was always like this*, I think, watching them blow dandelion fluff on the back lawn, *and I was just too pig-headed to appreciate it. Or maybe having had Noa, I see her differently. Maybe she sees me differently, too.*

"Come on guys, it's getting dark," I say, scooping up Noa. "Let's go inside." We still have time before dinner, so I plunk Noa into a laundry basket, thread a piece of rope through the side, and take off at a trot, pulling her through the downstairs rooms like a yoked ox—her favorite game. Given the vast expanse of our house, this is the equivalent of a Cross Fit workout. But it makes Noa shriek with delight. I'm already out of breath when we come upon the stewards setting the long table in the *comedor grande*. The room, lit by the enormous bronze chandelier, is a shimmering Ambassatrix School fantasy: crisp white linen napkins folded like bishops' hats, gold-rimmed china bearing the Great Seal, spotless silver regimentally arrayed. Alvaro, the chief steward, supervises the work. He's a diminutive man with the profile of an Incan god and a great proprietary sense about the residence. At their first meeting, Alvaro informed Dennis that he was his *eleventh* ambassador. The message was clear: your kind come and go, Big Man, but I'm here to stay. He does have a softer, more artistic side, though. Once a week, Isabel has several bushels of flowers delivered that Alvaro keeps in a cramped antechamber off the kitchen. The floral arrangements he creates and distributes throughout the house are stunning.

This evening, Alvaro is going from place setting to place setting, bending over and looking down a stick like it's a billiard cue. "What's he doing?" Mom whispers.

"I think he's measuring how far each charger plate is from the wine glasses and making sure they're all the same distance.

"Did you tell him to do that?"

"Are you kidding?" I snort. "I can barely remember whether the fish fork comes before or after the one for salad."

The dinner is stag: just Dennis and a few dozen of his closest international and local businessmen buddies. Tenson is sending food for Noa, Mom, and me to our upstairs apartment. We take the elevator, so Noa can push the buttons. After we've eaten, I fill the tub in Noa's bathroom—but not before killing a small spider that's quietly minding its own business in the corner. "Not near my child, you won't!" I murmur.

Mom sits on a little vanity chair and I perch atop the toilet seat; Noa, barely visible amid all her toys, splashes in the water. "Mom, do you remember my friend Mary?" I say, picking up a grinning plastic dolphin that rode a breaker over the bathtub rim onto the floor. "She lived across the street from us in Washington, kind of kitty-corner from our house?"

"I think so. Why?"

"I don't know, I just keep thinking about a conversation we had once. She has three boys, and I asked her what was so great about having children."

Mom sniggers.

"Why are you laughing?"

"Because," she says with a little shrug, "that sounds so much like you."

"Okay, so I was a jerk. I admit it. But I really was mystified. I mean, here was this perfectly intelligent, very talented woman whom I'd see at Christmastime, driving around in her minivan at all hours in pursuit of the toys her boys wanted, with this look on her face like she was off to do battle."

"She probably was, against all the other mothers searching for the same toy."

"I just couldn't understand it," I say, bending over to wipe up bathwater on the tiles.

"So what did she say in answer to your question? About what was so great."

"That you get to see the world through their eyes."

"What did you think of that?"

"Honestly? I thought it was sort of stupid. I mean, it's completely incomprehensible until you've had a kid of your own."

Mom smiles.

"Okay," I say. "You've a right to look smug. But now I'd much rather take Noa to the petting zoo and watch her squeal at the capybaras than go to a cocktail party."

"What's a capybara?"

"The largest rodent in the world. Like a guinea pig on performance-enhancing drugs. And the last time we went, a yucky llama spat chewed-up grass in your face, didn't he, sweetie?" I say, kissing Noa's damp hair.

"So you like being a mother?"

"Like it? I never thought anything could make me so happy. I just wish she could stay like this forever. Adolescence is going to be awful."

"It's hard, but you still love them."

"Even me, when I was so terrible to you growing up?"

"Even you," she says, coming over to the toilet seat to hug me.

I hug her back, holding on—the first time ever—for an extra beat or two.

"Okay," I say, swallowing hard. "Let's get this baby washed and rinsed!"

Mom sits with Noa on her lap in the white rocking chair and reads her a story while I tidy the bathroom. After Noa wheedles another two books, it's time to start the long, arduous task of putting her to bed; we don't call her "No Sleep Noa" for nothing. She and I stand in the doorway of the entrance to our quarters, waving goodnight to Mom. I watch her walk slowly down the long corridor and turn the corner to the guest wing with a stab of sadness.

After Mom leaves for the States, our social schedule revs up. One night, we host a buffet dinner for an official trade delegation from Wisconsin, led by the governor: eighty people wandering around the salas and *comedor grande,* many wearing Cheesehead hats. A few days later, it's a cocktail party with two hundred guests for a congressional delegation come from Washington to learn, first-hand, about narcotics trafficking—but whose investigation, it seems, requires a lot of shopping for silver jewelry.

The next morning, I sit down at my desk determined to do some writing. The telephone rings; it's Isabel. The embassy's naval attaché is here to speak with me.

Downstairs, I find the attaché perched stiffly, resplendent in full naval regalia, on a sofa in the Washington sala, beneath the irritable gaze of our first president. He stands, shakes my hand, then waits until I'm seated to lower himself, ramrod-straight, onto the cushions. The attaché clears his throat. He's planning a reception for the officers from a US flotilla that will arrive in Lima next week. A large band, comprised of sailors from the ship, will entertain the guests—a proud naval tradition. "I want to hold the reception on the Spanish patio," he says.

The patio, in all its blue-tiled beauty, happens to be directly under Noa's bedroom. I can just picture it: a dozen or so sailors in dress uniform, instruments plugged into giant amplifiers, lead singer crooning a Spanish version of "Feelings" into an equally amplified microphone, all blaring into her room. *Nope.* I explain this to the attaché; if the band is going to play, he'll have to use the garden on the other side of the house.

He says, "I want it on the Spanish patio with the band."

Am I speaking Albanian? "Captain," I enunciate. "I'm sorry, but that simply won't be possible. As I said, you can have it on the Spanish patio without the band, or in the garden with the band."

He says, "I want it *on* the Spanish patio *with* the band."

Of course he does. Who wouldn't want Masterpiece splendor to show off to your friends and colleagues, if only for a night? And at no extra cost! The problem here is one of perception: everyone in the embassy and American community sees our house—with some justification—as his own personal event space, while I'm desperately trying, per my therapist Andrea's pre-Mozambique suggestion, to make it a home. To say nothing of a life for myself. I tell the miffed attaché I'll get back to him after speaking with the ambassador.

It doesn't help that nowadays Dennis is utterly preoccupied with work. I'm proud that he's calling attention to the president's alarmingly autocratic tendencies and trying to shore up Peru's fledgling civil society—but he sometimes seems remote, if not a little self-absorbed. It's understandable, though. Short of being the dictator of a small, corrupt county, few jobs can compare with that of a US ambassador in Latin America. Dennis is at the top of his game, a virtual demigod; he can't sneeze without it being reported on the front pages of the newspapers. The paparazzi and journalists follow him everywhere, sticking microphones up his nose to record his every pronouncement. People rise from their seats when he enters a room and address him as "Your Excellency." Heady stuff, indeed. But where does it leave us?

That evening, I light Sabbath candles in Andrea's holders; Tenson bakes a challah; I'm hoping for a cozy, familial Friday-night meal in the *comedor chico*. Noa sits in her highchair, methodically dividing up the food on her tray between herself and Blanche, the Labrador, on the floor below. I recount the meeting with the naval attaché to Dennis, who's paging through a folder of briefing papers next to his plate.

"Will you talk to him and explain the situation with Noa's bedroom?" I say.

"Talk to whom?"

"The naval attaché."

"About what?"

"Dennis! The reception I was telling you about."

"Oh. Yeah."

I'm silent for a moment.

"Schmutz," I say. "I'm concerned about our relationship."

Dennis looks up, peering through his glasses. "What?"

"I said I'm concerned about our relationship."

"Why? Our relationship's just fine." He glances down at the papers.

"Will you please stop reading long enough to listen to me?"

He quickly looks up. "I'm not reading."

"Yes, you are. It feels like we're drifting apart."

"We're not drifting apart."

"Well, it feels that way to me. Everything about your job seems to supersede us. I feel like there's barely an 'us' anymore."

"Of course there's an 'us,'" he says, eyes shifting back to the papers. "Having a baby is always an adjustment."

"Who's talking about the baby?" I say, reaching across and shutting the folder. "I think we need to do things like make mealtimes, and especially the Sabbath, inviolate and . . ."

At that moment, Alvaro pokes his head through the door: the deputy ambassador is on the telephone. Without so much as an excuse-me, Dennis jumps up and dashes off to the kitchen to take the call—leaving me in mid sentence, mouth ajar and flapping in the breeze.

I turn to Noa. "Well, that went smashingly," I say.

"Do!" she says, pointing to the dog.

One morning not long after that, Isabel tells me she saw graffiti spray painted in Spanish, across an overpass on the main highway going into downtown: USA, SEND YOUR TRAITOR DOG AMBASSADOR HOME. I do my best to wait to ask about it until Dennis comes home from work.

"Oh, it's nothing," he says vaguely, loosening his tie.

"Come on. What are your spooks saying?"

"Nothing."

"Jett, don't play games with me."

"Okay. But don't freak out."

"That inspires confidence."

Dennis takes a deep breath. "It was apparently done on orders of the military High Command."

I put down the book I was reading. "Let me get this straight," I say slowly. "The joint chiefs of the Peruvian armed forces ordered some poor grunts out in the middle of the night to spray paint this not-very-polite message for all the capital to see."

"Yeah, I guess you could put it like that. And in some other places, too."

"Oh, even better. But why?"

"The CIA station chief thinks it's because of a speech I made last week."

"What did you do? Insult the generals' manhood?"

"No, I just suggested that the hundreds of millions of dollars they spent on fighter jets might be better used to build schools in underdeveloped parts of the country."

"Bravo! But that's much worse than their manhood. That's their toys."

Dennis eases on a pair of jeans. "Where's Noa?"

"With Patience. Don't change the subject."

"I'm not changing the subject. I'm changing my clothes. There's nothing more to tell."

"What do you mean?" I follow him into his bathroom. "Dennis, this isn't some random anti-gringo crackpot. These are the very people we count on for protection and now they're turning against us."

"Lynda, the generals are just having a little hissy fit."

"How do you know that?" I say, by now almost shouting. It's his safety we're talking about. And Noa's. Not to mention mine! "How can you be sure?"

"It's nothing. Really. They're just trying to scare us."

"Well, they've succeeded," I say, stomping off to find Patience.

That night I have a hard time falling asleep, chewing over the day's events. As soon as Dennis starts to snore, I slip out of bed, tiptoeing to check on Noa. She's next door in what's supposed to be my dressing room: a long, skinny Hall of Mirrors, seemingly designed for a narcissist with a penchant for galley kitchens. It's still better, though, than having her stuck away in one of the other bedrooms, halfway to Ecuador. I adjust her little red-and-white balloon blanket and, for good measure, test that the windows are locked.

Quietly closing the doors to the apartment, I pad down the hallway to the playroom. It's where I go when insomnia hits. Shoving aside a couple of teddy bears, I curl up on the window seat, hugging a stuffed zebra. The bunker just outside our rear perimeter wall is visible under the glow of a streetlight. I can make out a few helmeted soldiers inside the shelter wearing flak jackets, submachine guns slung over their shoulders. *Now that Dennis has pissed off your bosses*, I think, *what are your orders, gentlemen?*

The very question, in all its lethal possibilities, makes me shiver. My mind shifts to Dennis's bodyguards. *What about them? Who has their loyalty?* They seem nice, if enigmatic, behind their Ray-Bans. The chief bodyguard is the most unreadable. He speaks to me only in monosyllables and never smiles. But maybe those are the qualities you want in someone packing a nine-millimeter pistol.

Would he take a bullet for Dennis? Would any of them?

And suddenly it hits me: I don't even want to have to consider these questions any more.

There was supposed to be a quid pro quo when I left journalism and married Dennis: I don the pillbox hat and white gloves; we have a safe life together. It obviously hasn't worked out like that. On the contrary. I'm tired of constantly being scared for Dennis's safety, for my own. And now there's Noa. I spend my days fighting to keep her photograph out of the newspapers, to keep her anonymous, terrified of her being kidnapped for ransom—a favorite Latin American fund-raising technique of leftists, common criminals, police, you name it.

Girl rejects mother's life, gods of war send down thunderbolts.

Or maybe all this violence has simply been a matter of chance. But how many perfectly nice countries bursting into flames does it take before you begin to suspect some sort of cosmic payback? It doesn't matter, really, because I am done tempting any more Fates. Life, obviously, is full of risks, and I'm willing to take the normal ones like, say, driving the Washington Beltway or eating fast food. But I'm finished residing in places where our house turns into an armed camp each night, where gun-toting guards protect Noa at the playground, where I break into a cold sweat every time Dennis is a few minutes late returning home. Live through enough mayhem, and even a superficial person such as myself will eventually see the emptiness of such an existence. All those things about Mom's life I so arrogantly dismissed—family, friends, community, suburbia even—now feel achingly desirable.

I finally know what I want, Andrea. I want to celebrate decades of anniversaries with Dennis. I want us to watch Noa grow up. I want us to grow old together. Glamour and adventure be damned, *I want to go home!*

Because that's who I am now: a somewhat middle-aged Dorothy, clicking those ruby-reds together just as fast as my little heels can move.

PITTSBURGH, 2014

Ever since the rockets began falling from Gaza into Israel, I've become even more of a crazed news fanatic, downloading alerts from *The New York Times, The Washington Post*, wire services, Tel Aviv dailies, middle school newspapers—you name it. I even have an app on my phone that tells me, in real time, which part of Israel the missiles are hitting. It features an insistent, hair-raising alarm that I can turn on if I truly want to drive myself insane. And since the Palestinians who are launching the rockets seem to be doing it as their day job, what with the time difference between there and here, the alarm keeps blaring in the middle of our night.

"Turn it off," Dennis grumbles through his sleep. "Noa is fine."

How can he know? We're six thousand miles away! (Settled, finally, in Pittsburgh.)

When Noa informed me that she wanted to go to Israel with her high school youth group this summer, the prospect was as reassuring as sending her into a room crawling with tarantulas. Tourism in a part of the world where the Syrian government is slaughtering its citizens in a civil war? Where Iraq is fracturing along sectarian lines? Where Iran is doing its nuclear kabuki dance? She's seventeen, just about the same age as I when I ran away to the Middle East. And suddenly there it is, all over again: the hot-breathed urgency for youthful experience, the gaze past the door to departure.

But seen now through the prism of motherhood, a foray such as hers—such as mine—seemed perilous and foolhardy, if not downright scary. Funny how these things go. Were Mom still alive, she would be grinning from ear to ear. "What goes around comes around!" she'd say merrily, always one to appreciate irony. At times like these, I no longer worry about becoming my mother; I downright embrace it. And wish Mom were still around to commiserate.

Obviously, I let Noa go. I had to. Besides, she'd be on a program so tightly supervised there was even a designated time slot for blowing her nose. And Israel had been relatively quiet for a while. About five minutes after she and her group arrived there, though, the Palestinians in Gaza started shooting the rockets over the border in the south. Then the Israeli air force began hitting back with air strikes. No matter this is a largely intractable conflict that has dragged on for decades, bedeviling even the most skilled statesmen and politicians. I'm convinced the place has exploded again because Noa is my progeny: visiting the iniquity of the fathers—or mothers—upon the children—or child—and all that. Magical thinking, yes, but I can't help it. Although the terror I feel is clearly nothing compared with what the Israelis and Palestinians are experiencing.

Israel has an anti-rocket interceptor system that works pretty well. But the directors of Noa's program aren't taking any chances, moving the kids around the country like little chess pieces to try to get them out of rocket range. Now they're in a youth hostel in the far north, smack up against the Lebanese border. Then—wouldn't you know it?—the terrorists living on the other side of the northern frontier decide to get in on the act and launch missiles at precisely the town where Noa and her buddies are staying. Panicked, I text her. *How did Mom survive me being in a war in the age of snail mail?* I wonder. *How did she not lose her mind?*

Noa responds immediately:

There was just a code red (siren) *here. We ran to the kitchen where we still are*

Why the kitchen?

No windows

Are your counselors with you?

Yeah. Do you know if the rocket got intercepted?

Can't tell from here. How are you doing?

Okay. I'm shaking

Do you want to come home?

NO!

And then, about a minute later:

You of all people should understand

She's right. I do understand. I understand she's not fleeing from me, but racing toward her future. As she should. The trajectory is unclear, but whatever its twists and turns, most likely she will circle back. Someday. With any luck. In the meantime, she has packed in her suitcase the little brass candleholders I've kept through the years. So she can always make a home wherever life takes her.

ILLUSTRATIONS

All photos courtesy of the author

ACKNOWLEDGMENTS

Getting this story down took years, and I am forever grateful to the friends who offered support, solace, and general cheerleading along the way: Marlene Behrmann Cohen, Jane Bernstein, Marge Bloom, Jaclyn Cock, Kim Conroy, Beth Corning, Isabel Costa, Ilana Diamond, Clara Germani, Marsha Ginsburg, Deborah Helitzer, Aida Hozic, Beth Kissileff, Andrea Leiman, Roger Lowenstein, Steven Mufson, Roni Rosenfeld, Nadine Schatz, Richard Scher, Agnes Tabah, Kenneth Wald, Robin West, Mary Zitello. A special shout-out to Sharon Dilworth, scribbler extraordinaire, for all the suggestions and walks and wonderful writerly talks.

I am deeply thankful as well to my family: to Jordan Harnish, Christopher Torgerson, Allison Saunier, and Brian Jett, for putting up with me as your step-monster for all these years; to my adopted mother, Simcha Arnold, for madcap sojourns, endless conversations, and bottomless pots of tea; to my siblings Sandra Schuster, Ida Benson, Tamara Grundland, Simon Schuster; to Gerrie Dijkers and Gerriann Tobkin; to the memory of my parents, Anne K. Schuster and Monis Schuster.

Fortune smiled upon me in the form of Valerie Merians, the

remarkable co-publisher of Melville House, and Taylor Sperry, my talented editor who, along with everyone else at MHP, not only believed in this book but made it immeasurably better. Many thanks, too, to Stephany Evans, my intrepid agent. Additionally, I am indebted to two people who gave unstintingly of their time to read the entire manuscript and suggest changes that were invaluable: Marc Nieson, a writer of uncommon grace; and my sister Beverly Mann, the possessor of a keen eye and true heart.

My profoundest gratitude goes, as always, to my husband, Dennis Jett, for his patience, unfailing assistance, wise counsel, willingness to read and read again. And to my daughter, Noa, whose miraculous self is a beacon of light and love, hope, and inspiration. For these and other reasons too numerous to recount, this book is dedicated to her.

A NOTE ABOUT THE AUTHOR

Lynda Schuster is a former foreign correspondent for the *The Wall Street Journal* and *The Christian Science Monitor*, who has reported from Central and South America, Mexico, the Middle East, and Africa. Her writing has appeared in *Granta*, *Utne Reader*, *The Atlantic Monthly*, and *The New York Times Magazine*, among others. She lives in Pittsburgh with her husband and daughter.